ELIHU'S KEY

Book One

"It is often the last key on the ring that opens the door."

An old English proverb

"All you need to know about the human spirit but were never told."

Mal Garvin

This book is an attempt to unlock a timeless source of wisdom. In the book of Job one of the oldest pieces of literature known to humankind, we come across a remarkable phenomenon that has recently been named spiritual intelligence.

"Kitty and I read the book of Job aloud this evening. I love it. I cannot see anything substantial that has been learnt since."

Malcolm Muggeridge (1903 – 1990). Diary entry from 1937 by essayist, journalist, sceptic, novelist and critic while correspondent in Stalin's Russia. Years later to everyone's surprise, he became a Christian apologist

CONTENTS

PREFACE

Does the human spirit weigh 21 grams?

There is a force at work in all our lives - the subtle but barely visible influence of the human spirit illuminating and active in every human soul. Strangely, it is often more active among those who believe themselves to be neither religious nor spiritual though it is largely missing from the consciousness of modern materialistic persons.

My goal is to reveal its subtle and all pervasive influence and to share the secret of how one becomes more consciously engaged with its life-affirming illumination.

How do we recognize it?

We can see it at work in small children whose eyes light up with joy when someone they love walks into the room or when they name something accurately. We can also see its magic at work in elderly people including dementia sufferers whose fading thought processes respond to familiar music, many singing along freely with songs from their past or playing instruments they hadn't touched for decades. It is increasingly clear that the spirit's capacity to respond transcends the cognitive processes of the brain.

The brain is not the mind

The uplifting influence of the spirit is at work before we have words and long after old age has rendered our speech increasingly confused. Some of us can already recognise a deep and pleasant aliveness when something moves us. Many have experienced the mysterious internal uplift in response to a beautiful sunset, a child's spontaneous responsiveness or an act of unusual kindness or sacrificial courage. Our hearts may be touched to the core during an authentic act of worship or prayer.

We may also experience negative emotions when our sense of self is at risk. Joy quickly evaporates in the face of fear threat and hopelessness. Our defensive machinery automatically triggers when our psychological safety is at risk and we often lose our peace as we brace against these disturbing and irrational forces.

In our saner moments, we know that from somewhere deep within the best part of who we are can know hope and joy. The special capacity of us human beings to be profoundly touched by love, beauty and truth is a mark of our unique human hunger for the sublime and the transcendent.

The presence of the human spirit

In this book I aim to show how our awareness of the underlying presence of the human spirit can and will grow in much the same way as many things that are so familiar we barely notice them, for instance a recently acquired car. Having barely been aware of a particular model before buying it, in what seems to be a strange kind of revelation we now see them everywhere. We are surprised not only by how many there are but also by the sense of connection we have with their owners. Similarly, parents of a new child feel the name they have chosen is unique and are then surprised to find children with the same name wherever they go!

What matters to us?

Over 40 years on a syndicated radio segment covering all the major media markets in Australia, I had the privilege of taking the pulse of a nation every day. Initially I was focused on producing radio that would fit the popular commercial radio format. Later though I looked for a consistent pattern in what the audience cared about.

There were times when what I believed to be a profound insight would get a bored yawn in response while on other occasions a simple throwaway line would get a deluge of mail. That is when I decided to ask what the universal yearnings of my audience were. I was committed to entertain the listeners - essential if I was to stay on air but my goal was not only to engage and interest them but also to communicate at a more profound level.

Could I in a short highly produced radio segment engage them, put a smile on their face and sometimes even move them to tears of joy? Was I expecting too much? My burning question? Was a nationally syndicated radio segment capable of being both personal and universal?

Eventually I was on more than 100 stations. What was the secret of making my communication so personal that listeners felt I had been reading their mail? What could I say that would be as relevant to those in Hobart in the south as to those in Darwin in the extreme north, Sydney in the east or Perth in the far west, the world's most isolated capital city?

My discovery

The search for answers to my questions had me on a quest in every aspect of my life from classroom engagement in high schools to work with schizophrenics, right through to human resource training and consultancies with large public companies.

A fascinating global tour to study the distinctives of various Western cultures significantly focused my questions. What is deeply personal, what is local and cultural and what can travel because it is profoundly universal and transcendent?

I had to leave home to see it with new eyes

At a Broadcasters' Conference in Brownsville Texas, I had fascinating conversations with seasoned broadcasters from all over the U.S.A. and received invitations to visit.

In Washington DC I saw the great monuments and asked why they mattered. In Nashville, I sat in a recording session and visited the Grand Ole Opry where I interviewed a number of country music stars.

I had a most illuminating time with Johnny Cash's late father who helped me understand the southern psyche and what moved them to tears. Then I was off to converse with program directors of radio stations across rural America and in big industrial cities like Detroit and Chicago.

Many fascinated by my quest generously shared with me the insights and instincts they had relied on to get to the top. They explained to me the focus groups and research techniques they used to arrive at their understanding of their audience. The focus of most was to pitch their unique selling proposition to prospective advertisers.

All this was very impressive but it was some time before understanding started to crystallise; strangely enough, it happened while I was in the UK.

We all laugh but we don't laugh at the same things

Thanks to a BBC executive, I went behind the scenes to look at the making of a British TV sitcom. There it dawned on me that while all humans love a giggle clearly the Brits laugh at different times from the Americans. I was of course, comparing them both with my fellow Aussies. We all like to think we are normal but sometimes we have to leave home to catch a glimpse of the culture we've come from. It was a profound experience.

All individuals, groups and races are similar yet different

I walked the back streets of London and went north to Leeds to watch Aussies play the English in a game of rugby where I heard working class lads scream, *"Kill the convicts"*. Despite my country's British roots, I knew I was not English. This became even clearer as I went further north to the old town of York still surrounded by Hadrian's Wall built by the Romans in 122 AD. There I bought sweets from a shop originally built by the nephew of William the Conqueror, yet before leaving Australia I had never seen any buildings more than 190 years old!

The unique part of us

No matter when or where we live there is a unique part of us that I now know to be the human spirit. It often rises spontaneously and can surprise us by rising from deep within and breaking through our defences. It triggers responses that make us want to laugh, to cry and go *"Wow!"*.

Our unique personality

Exactly where and when we feel permission to cry, laugh aloud and go *"wow"*, is shaped by our unique personality. The sense of self that filters the reality we tell ourselves about is usually unknown to us and has been shaped by our personal and cultural history. It is likely to be very different for a young person growing up in Tasmania – the small island at the bottom of Australia – and for the young person growing up in the centre of New York, or a young Greek in historic Athens.

This unique process shapes our character making us profoundly different: there remains though an undergirding shared humanity, and at the centre of that shared humanness is the profound animating dynamic of our soul, the human spirit.

Exploring these themes

This shared spirit is nourished by a hopeful and positive narrative and the kind of leadership that can tell a unifying story illuminating the path to a realistic and preferred future. In the two World Wars and countless other wars we see the power to create a narrative with the capacity to unite, empower and positively transform people and whole societies, or on the other hand to create a negative narrative that hates and destroys global harmony and co-operation.

These deeply felt narratives – stories of the heart - have the capacity to inspire if grasped and respected. Stories at the heart of a culture can call human beings out of their innate self-interest, lift hearts, unite communities and nations and promote global peace. Too often, though, we see the tragic results when that same human spirit is either lost to view or abused.

Both sides of the equation: the mystery in view

The goal of this book is to explore both sides of the equation to lift the veil on what is often a huge and bewildering mystery. The Bible tells us of the two great mysteries, the mystery of iniquity and the mystery of godliness. Both will bewilder most of us no matter how brilliant we are because they cannot be grasped by reason.

We come across them daily: The problem of evil - that man knows what good is but is still inclined to choose otherwise; then there is the strange phenomenon we currently call our *"better angels"*, that profound sense of what good is that surprises us and beckons us to another way. We can all be surprised by the religious responses that surface in us from time to time, throwing light on our decisions and influencing our commitments - if we take them seriously that is.

It may not be kosher to talk about these subjects but they creep up on us and confront us daily. There is always much more going on than reason alone is able to grasp or explain. In the words of Blaise Pascal 17th century mathematician, physicist and religious philosopher, *"There is more to knowing than knowing can ever know."*

An existential itch

There is always another reality knocking gently at the door of our consciousness. We may be haunted by it though not yet able to grasp and apprehend it. It is like an exquisite existential itch beyond our capacity to scratch and we avoid allowing ourselves to become aware of it because we fear its capacity to claim us.

There is a sense in which an indefinable voice beckoning us to know beyond reason can no longer be denied. Yet as 20th century French philosopher Henri Bergson said, *"The forceps of the mind does violence to the things it tries to grasp."* Why? Because the mind itself and our conventional way of knowing are clouded by archaic emotion and often distorted by ego needs. We need another mode of engagement with this multi-dimensional realm of reality.

A sense of hope and a future

The focus of this book - the human spirit - not only gives a sense of hope and a future but if developed can give courage patience and humility and help us work through complex issues to an undistorted reality. It enables us not only to be moved by a beautiful sunset, to laugh spontaneously with a friend or respond empathically to their pain, but also enables us to grasp the eternal, to be sensitive, to be excited by a dawning truth and at the same time discern a distortion or spot a phony.

Over my years of talk-radio, it became clear that while part of us wants to be entertained there is also a part in each of us that is suspicious of empty sentimentality and wants to encounter deep meaning. This is where the best of who we are lives. It is the part that often responds to things that bring joy and delights in encountering the beautiful and ineffable in everyday life.

The two most important days of our life

The radio audience gave me the growing understanding that in every human heart there is a sensitivity to the ineffable - to something bigger than time and space. Tied to that sense of the transcendent deep within all those who have even the most basic awareness of people, there is the sense that we are on earth to do more than make a dollar. A part of us knows we will never quite be at peace until we have found the reason we are here - the task, or assignment that is ours to fulfil. In the words of Mark Twain, *"The two most important days of your life are the day you were born, and the day you find out why."*

We all need help to find our place in the eternal scheme of things. We have a dilemma though. Most of us find it almost impossible to distinguish the gentle promptings of the spirit that reveal to us our vocation, from the more desperate attempts of the soul or ego to think well of itself.

What is our spirit, and does it weigh 21 grams?

The movie *21 Grams* starring Sean Penn and Naomi Watts begins by declaring, *"They say we all lose 21 grams at the exact moment of our death."* The inference is that this is the weight of our human spirit. While I have no idea of the exact weight of the human spirit when we die something leaves us that has been a profound and animating aspect of our personal existence.

This award-winning movie is a complex mosaic of people struggling to make sense of life. There is a criminal trying to go straight by finding faith, a man waiting desperately for a heart transplant and a woman wrestling with a drug problem. They are all brought together by an accident that looks meaningless. One wonders how meaning can come from all this.

At the movie's end the statement is there again, *"At the moment of our death we lose 21 grams."* It begs the question, what has gone and what in fact is the secret of our mysterious life? What is this animating dynamic that distinguishes us from the animals? What is it in our personal and collective consciousness that is able to ask, *"What is our life, and what can be its meaning?"*

What is it that leaves with our last breath?

In the ancient book of Job, a clear-eyed young man named Elihu embodied the spiritual sensitivities of my radio audience in their universal and profoundly human quest for meaning and community. It was Elihu who gave me the key to understand the role of the human spirit in our existence; to understand not only the highest yearnings of our spirit, but also the ugly source of human destructiveness.

It was Elihu who opened my eyes to what has gone missing from our now diminished daily life - our education, our marriages, our economy, our therapy, our modern media and our politics. Those whose lives have enriched human existence know the secret but we self-absorbed materialistic creatures have completely failed to recognise, let alone nourish, the treasure that is our human spirit. This in spite of clear and powerful evidence that its yearnings for expression and validation are everywhere to be seen in the cultural history of humankind. Let's find out if this young man Elihu can help all of us see the unseen and relocate the source of our highest and most beautiful yearnings.

Can Elihu help us so that awareness of our spirit becomes clear and sharp to our consciousness and present enough to enable us to redress the imbalance? Can he also help reveal what have until now been awkward mysteries?

Chapter 1

GOING BACK TO SEE FORWARD

"This is the first age that has paid much attention to the future, which is rather ironic since it's now clear we may not have one."

Arthur C. Clarke CBE FRAS (1917 – 2008) British science fiction writer, science writer and futurist, inventor, undersea explorer and television series host.

For the first time in history the human imagination has been bypassed by reality. In the past some imaginative writers seemed to have remarkable prescience, like Danish philosopher Soren Kierkegaard (1813-1855) who envisioned a box with wires which disconnected people would stare at in their lounge rooms. Of course this was well before the advent of radio or the telephone let alone television, and he certainly did not envision a room full of disconnected people silently staring at their smart phones. It seems the 21st century marvels of communication are in fact the great inhibitors of deep communication.

The broken promise of science and technology

There was a time when science fiction writers forecast images of the future. Jules Verne in the 19th century gave us submarines, while H.G Wells (1866 – 1946) forecast a bomb of infinite power using the term atomic bomb. From their limited knowledge of science they projected imaginary worlds for us to inhabit. Intoxicating as the brave new world seemed as we moved into the 20th century the sheen has gone off the grand vision. It is disturbingly clear that a little knowledge in the hands of the morally blind can be catastrophic.

The mythic genie is out of the magic lamp

Amazing as science and technology have been, a generation of millennials have learned to mistrust it. 20th century science introduced us to nuclear submarines with arsenals of nuclear missiles capable of delivering death on an unimaginable scale. And the so-called industrial revolution has produced decades of pollution and greenhouse gases with the potential to wipe out life on earth as we know it.

Science rather than compassion in service of the bottom-line is toxic

Science unbridled by the higher aspirations of the human spirit can both dehumanise us and take us to the edge of disaster. Right here is our dilemma! Science and technology continue to explode in ways we are often not allowed to know about. We, along with global governments, struggle to comprehend what they are creating let alone shape laws with some kind of intelligent engagement concerning their impact on our long-term future.

We are heading into a world where the powerful shadow of science grows exponentially but rather than be channelled by higher values, it is mostly fuelled by the desire for profit and power. If it is true that modern imagination has been by-passed by reality, reality itself has by-passed the capacity of governments to regulate it.

So much is beyond not only our capacity to regulate, but also to understand

From the study of the smallest sub-atomic particle to the discovery of worlds beyond our galaxy, our field of vision has exploded. But what are we able to see?

The entire store of human knowledge is doubling every five years, so it's now rare for prognostications of the likes of H.G Wells, Asimov and Jules Verne, to surface. In their day they would take the limited scientific understandings of the time and use them as a blank canvas for their creative imagination. In the 21st century science fiction writers simply cannot keep up with the latest breakthroughs written up in scientific journals.

From the far reaches of space to breakthroughs in neuroscience and the human genome right through to the sub-atomic world of quantum mechanics and dark matter, even the brightest among us can feel stressed by the daily need to review our internal map of reality.

Quantum physics is now telling us that at a sub-atomic level each of us is being bombarded with four billion bits of new information every second, and we are totally unaware of all but the tiniest part of it.

We can now prove the presence of a whole other reality and while having a growing sense of its profound nature and significance, we barely catch a glimpse of how it will impact us and those we care about. No wonder we have a sense we are being left behind!

Our current way of thinking about this dawning reality not only dis-advantages us as we attempt to grasp it, but also makes us blind to the meaning of almost all of it. We are largely oblivious to the future that's knocking at our door.

Historic change is underway and we are largely blind to it

While we sense something profound is underway the thought that it's largely beyond our grasp leaves most of us with a feeling of futility and powerlessness. The tectonic plates of history are moving under our feet and we often feel like a deer caught in the headlights. We wake up most mornings braced against what we fear the day might bring.

Turning on the morning news we wonder what dramatic events might have unfolded while we slept. What terrorist horror or dehumanising act of destruction has ripped apart the peace of some unsuspecting township or city? What plane- load of innocent people has dropped from the sky tearing grieving families apart? What government has been overthrown? What abuse will have befallen vulnerable women and children? And what microscopic virus can turn up and rearrange whole social systems and economies?

Daily we are forced to contemplate the unthinkable

Earthquakes, tsunamis, cyclones, wildfires and devastating floods, show to all who are willing to seethat climate change is shifting the geography of nations.

Global economies are braced against the next threatened shakings likely to be brought about by the blind and relentless greed of financial institutions and their CEOs, whose executives still pay themselves unconscionable salaries and perks. They seem to have learned nothing from the last global financial crisis in which we saw huge banks and nations become bankrupt.

The outlook is bleak unless we can find a real and motivating source of hope

Clearly motivated by mindless greed, financial institutions blithely expect tax payers to bail them out again because their size and significance in the economy makes them too big to fail. These institutions also seem to be outside the capacity of governments, regulators and lawmakers to house- train.

The conspiracy to throw off perceived shackles of restraint

Meanwhile ego-driven hunger for power by a few, transforms the politics of nations. While many wondered if Brexit would be the straw that would break the camel's back, other nations are tottering and ready to participate in the unravelling of the European Common Market. What or who, comes next? There's a grab for more territory in the Ukraine and the South China Sea, and attempted military coups in Turkey, Egypt, South Sudan and Thailand – to name but a few!

Prior to the last global economic crisis leading economics professors and princes of business had pushed to remove some of the few remaining restraints by regulators.

The great collapse took everyone by surprise, particularly the economists, but confirmed the guess we all had that economists are there to make astrologers look credible! While academics played fast and loose with our economy, poor people in America were losing their homes. The two-thirds world was bemused. All they want is a fair share of the good life as seen on Western TV shows.

Currently, there are more than 1.1 billion people without electricity which means owning and charging a cell phone is difficult, yet there are more cell phones than people in the world. Meanwhile the gap between rich and poor is getting wider by the day. Every cow in the European Union is subsidised to the tune of $2.50 a day from collective taxes, which happens to be the exact sum that more than 75% of Africans have to live on daily.

We spend more on dairy cows than on feeding the people of the third world

Who would blame the poor for wanting a better life for their children? However the looming environmental catastrophe facing the globe is largely a by-product of the very material benefits they aspire to. One quarter of all the world's armed conflicts of recent years has involved a competitive struggle for natural resources.

Evidence indicates that time is running out for our planet

At the very time we are in need of gifted statesmen and women, recent polls show we have lost faith in politicians. We don't believe in their capacity to make a difference; most seem to be more focused on the next election than the next generation.

On every hand a crisis is looming and our political leaders seem to lack the spiritual intelligence, along with the wit, wisdom and will to do anything remotely significant about it. Where will we find the spiritual wisdom and moral leadership to enable us to avoid this looming catastrophe? How can we bend science and technology so as to take hold of the potential heaven on earth that in our best moments we all yearn for? We know the future we want to believe in is waiting and is possible for all, but where do we get this spiritual intelligence from?

Perhaps we need to go back to see forward

The Chinese philosopher Confucius said in 500 B.C. *"Study the past if you would divine the future,"* and in 1775 Patrick Henry said, *"I know no way of judging the future but by the past."* As we examine the uniquely human dimension of the past in the penetrating light of mankind's social history we see that despite all the mind-boggling technical changes and scientific discoveries, there are some things about our personal existence that have never changed.

Carved into stone on the archive building in Washington DC is a shortened version of Antonio's comments in Shakespeare's Tempest: *"What is past is prologue."* So there in Washington it is carved in stone: *"Past is prologue."* The archives carry the records of hundreds of thousands of lives – people who live now only as words on paper.

Only we of all God's creatures can ask the question, why?

In 1937 Malcolm Muggeridge was working as a journalist and correspondent charting the course of the so-called revolution born of scientific socialism in Stalin's Russia. A diary entry of that year observes: *"Kitty and I read the book of Job aloud this evening. I loved it. I cannot see anything substantial that has been learnt about life since it was written."* This is fascinating given the fact that the book of Job is probably one of the oldest pieces of human literature. Though the events in Genesis come before Job, Moses compiled his inspired account much later. The book of Job that records Elihu's comments, dates before the texts of the three Abrahamic religions - Judaism, Christianity and Islam.

Could one of the oldest pieces of human literature hold the key for today?

Why have so many people studied Job? Carl Jung (1875 – 1961) was a Swiss psychiatrist and psychoanalyst who founded analytical psychology. His work has been influential not only in psychiatry but also in anthropology, archaeology, literature and philosophy. He felt he was the instrument of a higher power who took him by the scruff of the neck and led him to delve deeply into the book of Job to probe the meaning of personal existence. He said "I had to wrench myself free from God, so to speak, in order to find that unity in myself, which God seeks through man."

Jung was preceded by men like Gregory the Great, Albert Magnus, Thomas Aquinas, and John Calvin, a man whose thinking and theology made enormous impact on the Protestant West. Calvin produced one of the greatest expositions of the book of Job, giving 159 sermons on its message and importance.

What is it about the book of Job that engages serious thinkers?

It seems to scratch where most self-aware people are itching, particularly people who are trying to understand themselves but who would not normally spend a lot of time thinking about God.

Carl Jung and Job himself, discovered that people sometimes have to lose sight of the God they imagine they know, to make the profound discovery of both themselves and the God who is there waiting to be known.

Some have done the book of Job a great disservice by trying to analyse it intellectually. Samuel Wesley, John Wesley's father, devoted ten years of his life to writing a learned but dry and turgid commentary on the book. After his father's death John officially presented it to Queen Caroline who proclaimed that it was *"very prettily bound"* but put it aside unopened. Bishop Warburton likened its pedantic style to *"Job having his brains sucked out by owls."*

William Safire, the Pulitzer prize-winning journalist who spent a lifetime wrestling with the account of Job's arguments with the Divine Being, eventually wrote a famous book about it. He was quite taken with the thought that God enjoyed arguing with Job.

Why the interest?

More recently international broadcaster and chancellor of Dallas Theological Seminary Charles Swindoll published an exhaustive 350-page book on Job. But why bother?

Why are thinking people so engaged by this ancient piece of literature? While much of the Old Testament records the story of the birth, rise and fall of the Hebrew people, the New Testament focuses on the beginning of the Christian movement and its expansion. In contrast, the book of Job and the other four Wisdom Books - Psalms, Proverbs, Ecclesiastes and the Song of Songs - wrestle with personal and existential questions that only people with a high level of consciousness are likely to ask. All five books express different aspects of significant parts of personal existence.

Finding meaning

The book of Job wrestles with the challenge of finding meaning in suffering. The Psalms see King David journaling to get his head and heart clear so as to encounter the Divine Being through celebration, song, and that profoundly human activity called worship. Proverbs is about wisdom for daily living - the process of looking over your shoulder and asking, is this wise? Ecclesiastes focuses on how to find fulfilment when you've tried everything and still feel empty. Finally the Song of Songs was written by Solomon, the man with 700 wives and 300 concubines, who was still looking for real love or, as he put it, *"Love that is as strong as death."* All of these books wrestle with personal issues that are as old as mankind.

Questions we all wrestle with

The themes found in the book of Job bring clarity to significant universal questions: Why do good people suffer? Where does God, if he's there at all, stand in the battle between good and evil? Does the eternal dimension ever enter time and if so how can we experience it?

My inspiration to write about the book of Job came from a discovery in a very challenging phase of my life. A good friend recommended I read the book and I found I not only identified deeply with Job, but also came across somebody who was just like the special young man Elihu. Subsequently I've come to appreciate people who have the *"Elihu"* spirit and I'm discovering them everywhere!

This book is dedicated to those who have the Elihu spirit and to those who want it

Elihu, who turns up toward the end of the book of Job will, I believe, give us the key to keeping our spiritual bearings in this dramatically changing world. The more I studied him the more I came to the firm conviction that his orientation and way of thinking hold the key to that elusive tomorrow we all yearn for but find so difficult to define and articulate.

Elihu moves from the shadows to the spotlight

Elihu is apparently so insignificant he doesn't even get a mention from Job's so-called comforters. He is on the sidelines and maintains his frustrated silence throughout the dialogue between Job and his three friends. He comes quietly on to the scene and only speaks up when his frustration reaches the point where he can remain silent no longer.

I have since come to believe there are a significant number of Elihus out there who are bewildered by the blindness of unexamined conventional wisdom.

What does Elihu say? What is so revolutionary about his orientation?

Elihu is a young man who has not lost the clear-eyed moral vision or passion of youth. What he says is contained in 6 chapters - Job 32 to 37 - yet he hardly gets a mention in the many books written about Job by men of great wisdom and intellect. This, though the length of Elihu's dialogue in the Biblical text is longer than the whole of 12 other Old Testament books and of 17 of the 27 New Testament books and letters. It is not only what Elihu says but the way he thinks that gives us the key to a new consciousness and a new way forward. He reminds us that we need to look inward if we are ever going to see outward clearly and with wisdom.

Separating the worthless from the precious

In the words of the prophet Jeremiah we need to "separate the worthless from the precious" if we are to have the clarity to see forward. Jeremiah promises that if we do this we will find our own voice and become a spokesperson for what is precious.

Time to discover your authentic voice, the inner voice of your truth!

What has started? Possibly an era in which the spirit of Elihu is much more present and common. Could it be that now, when the world seems to be tottering, we'll find something precious has been there all along? What anchoring points do we have that will enable us to be true to ourselves and yet have the wit to transcend our lower nature and rise to the possibility of what we might be?

It is my hope and prayer that this book "Elihu's Key" will cause all of our spirits to become more available to our awareness, and that illuminated by the young man's thinking we will see older men released to recapture their dreams, and those we call millennials (reaching adulthood around 2000) will not only avoid catastrophe, but be inspired to write their own future and in doing so lay the ground-work for their children's children.

I believe it is possible that not only the young man who inspired *Elihu's Key*, but the whole emerging generation will, along with him, want to re-discover the vibrant voice of their own authentic spirit.

My hope in writing this book is that we will find the wisdom to enable us to recognise and communicate the uncompromising truth that ultimately enhances our capacity to love, enabling us to make our unique contribution to the coming of a whole new era of shalom.

Chapter 2

TRAILING CLOUDS OF GLORY

"Whither is fled the visionary gleam?
Where is it now, the glory and the dream?

Our birth is but a sleep and a forgetting:
The Soul that rises with us, our life's Star,
Hath had elsewhere its setting,
And cometh from afar:
Not in entire forgetfulness,
And not in utter nakedness,
But trailing clouds of glory do we come
From God, who is our home:
Heaven lies about us in our infancy!
Shades of the prison-house begin to close
Upon the growing Boy,
But he beholds the light, and whence it flows,
He sees it in his joy;
The Youth, who daily farther from the east
Must travel, still is Nature's priest,
And by the vision splendid
Is on his way attended;
At length the Man perceives it die away,
And fade into the light of common day."

William Wordsworth (1770 – 1850) ODE - Intimations of Immortality from
Recollections of Early Childhood

"The Youth... still is Nature's priest"

We meet young Elihu silent and a little on the outer in the cluster around Job. He is the youngest in this small group of men huddled in conversation around their friend. (Job 32}

Job, the focus of the group, is in deep distress having lost his position, his wealth and his family and now even his body is tormented by angry boils. Sensitive young Elihu listens with deep empathy to Job who'd been a hero to him. It's disturbing to see this man he had so revered in this degraded situation.

Elihu embodies the *"youth who still is Nature's priest"* alluded to in Wordsworth's poem and is moved with compassion for Job yet remains sensitive to justice, mercy and truth. He can't believe the lack of respect and insight these older men exhibit as they gather around Job, particularly since these three comforters have supposedly come with the sole purpose of supporting and encouraging their friend.

Comforters become torturers

Elihu's blood is boiling as he hears both Job and his comforters speak in ways that make things worse, widening the emotional gap between them. They insist on blaming Job for his catastrophic situation asking, *"What did you do wrong to cause this?"* Elihu manages to control his frustration forcing himself to remain silent until they have all finished talking (Job 32:4). These so-called counsellors are causing him emotional torture because he can see they are closed and coming from the stultifying conventional morality of their own time.

This mind-set is what in this book, I call traditional or Level 2 thinking (See Appendix - Levels of Consciousness.) Elihu on the other hand exhibits all the qualities of a Level 4 thinker or what American sociologist Paul Ray calls the spiritually sensitive trans-modern thinker.

The moderns, post-moderns and the moral fog

Those we call the moderns are now not so modern. They came with the mindset of the Enlightenment, pleased to be free of the old superstitions of medieval religion. Descartes, with his dictum *"I think therefore I am"*, as well as the remarkable genius Newton and others of their era, found that despite being Christian believers it was easier to pursue understanding through another prism.

The Spanish inquisition used authoritarian religion to bend thinking away from inquiry and science which was a tragedy. Our role-model Elihu would have been at risk in their time, as he would from the intellectually convinced people we now call moderns. The moderns were inclined to trust the function of their brain's left hemisphere using only rationality and reason to examine and understand the material world. This they did to great effect and were able to solve many problems.

They often called their insights laws. Atoms were the smallest indivisible elements of matter and the law of gravity was absolute. Yet we now have 26 theories of gravity and the whole sub-atomic world of quantum physics, long since proven to be true, is hardly conventional in its expression.

Science and education as dogmatic as religion has been

Pseudo-science could cloak itself in what initially looked like sophisticated language. Sir Karl Popper CH FBA FRS was an Austrian-British philosopher and professor generally regarded as one of the greatest philosophers of science of the 20th century. He put the blowtorch to the likes of Freud, Marx and Lenin who despite seeing themselves as sophisticated were committed to certain ideologies like scientific socialism. They tended to cherry-pick the facts to reinforce their preferred position and were often quite destructive to those who questioned their paradigm.

We now know that all ideologies eventually become fascist.

Those we now call post-modernists have given up the idea that education and the human mind can create the utopia promised by the ideologues of the last century. Fascism, socialism, communism and other ideologies promised to create heaven on earth but because of their inflexibility and intolerance slid into various forms of oppression with not so subtle rewards and punishments. Control was the order of the day therefore they only achieved the creation of a dehumanised hell on earth. As a by-product they succeeded in crushing the human spirit's inclination to rise to grand dreams.

Then, largely rising from the group known as the millennials came the trans-moderns.

Trans-moderns and the necessary rediscovery of the heart

Stuck between the moderns and post-moderns, the trans-moderns are those learning to listen with their heart again. Many are still a bit stuck mistrusting the old way of doing business but tentatively looking for another story.

They are looking for a story that will silence their inner cynicism and rouse the part of them that hungers for transcendence - the part motivated by the spirit. They secretly yearn to be liberated from deadening materialism and the limitations of their own protective self-interest.

Management guru and author Charles Handy believes trans-moderns account for a quarter of all of those living in Western democracies. He says, *"We won't understand them until we realize what drives them."* What is it? They want to do more than simply survive, and in Handy's words, *"They are hungry for a self of which they can be proud."*

Why they are "hungry for a self of which they can be proud"

In his book *"Generation X"* Canadian novelist and artist Douglas Copeland attempts to capture the spirit of this generation. The subtitle of his book is appropriately, *"Tales for An Accelerated Culture."* It is a collection of stories, graphic statistics and mock sociological definitions. The characters in the stories have an inability to feel anything deeply and are searching for a spiritually anchored self. The environment they try to define themselves in, is the shopping mall and the media. Theirs is a *"Mac-happy"* culture that shapes their less than fulfilled *"Mac"* lives.

Escaping a "Mac-happy" self-absorbed life

On their best days most trans-moderns know this and are not happy about it. More than 75% of America's college students rate themselves less empathic than did their compatriots 30 years earlier with an especially steep drop in the last 10 years. Over the same period self-reported narcissism has reached new heights yet interestingly, has brought with its superficial fun the thick clouds of depressive illness.

Show me a self-absorbed person and I will show you a miserable one

Empathy is the cornerstone of our unique humanity with our inclination to care about and share other people's feeling worlds. It is the secret of building appropriate attachment and community. Yale University's developmental psychologists found that even six-month-old infants show clear indication of empathic behaviour. It is part of the essential human spirit we are born with.

We have two profoundly spiritual yearnings – one for purpose and the other for community. Both stem from the human spirit and are necessary for our sense of personal well-being. Significantly, both are destroyed by self-absorption.

The reconnection with the heart that liberated the trans-moderns

In Australia, we saw the paradox of the trans-moderns worked out before our eyes in a television series called *"Go back to Where You Came From."* A group of Australians was taken on a journey to encounter the lives refugees were trying to escape from. They visited asylum centres in Australia and refugee camps in Indonesia, Africa, Iraq and Jordan. On setting out most of them were totally un-empathic to the plight of refugees and firmly against the arrival of boat people, one even talking about taking a shotgun to them.

A revelation: TV Series Go Back to Where You Came From

The outcome was a fascinating shift of consciousness. One young woman from the western suburbs of Sydney was particularly unsympathetic and a self-proclaimed racist. On meeting an African Christian father struggling to care for his family in a crowded refugee camp in Central Africa she was moved to tears. This cheerful hospitable man had been tortured by the pulling out of his front teeth and worse. The warmth of his welcome and the generosity with which he shared the little food he had was deeply moving. The hearts and minds of the two most intransigent women on the project were touched - even transformed - by this man and his family.

At the conclusion of the documentary a particularly inflexible ex-military Australian said it had been *"a deeply moving spiritual experience"* and began attending church.

Trans-moderns have latent empathy and spirituality but need leadership and education

The program series showed that the trans-moderns had in fact, latent but hidden empathy. It also demonstrated that if a responsive educational process is introduced there can be a remarkable shift in consciousness. If apparently uncaring and self-interested individuals are put in touch with their spirit a remarkable conversion can take place.

After the shift of consciousness the participants were so much more attractive as people. Their hearts were now nearer their mind and they were warm, empathic and reflective. The exercise showed these trans-moderns can rise above their lazy thinking and self-absorbed orientation. Sadly though, their undiscerning and self-focused orientation is frequently manipulated by equally lazy and visionless politicians to gain votes, thereby increasing despair.

The contemporary search for spiritual substance is intensifying

Like Elihu, trans-moderns are searching for spiritual substance and are hungry for discerning leadership that will lift the spirit and engender hope. Is it any wonder they are sceptical about political movements with all the unedifying bickering, infighting and backstabbing that is seen so often in the 24 hour news cycle.

They are particularly cynical about smooth party machine men who seem to stitch up deals in back rooms beyond the gaze of honest scrutiny. They feel disenfranchised by wealthy behind-the-scene lobbyists and powerbrokers who seem to drive the real agenda of these political movements?

67,000 lobbyists attached to Congress

In America alone there are 67,000 people employed in the lobbying industry - 125 for each elected member of Congress. No wonder one of the biggest challenges for the so-called home of democracy is to get bored young constituents out to vote.

Trans-moderns have become disenchanted yet back in 2007 they were momentarily inspired by Barack Obama in America and Kevin Rudd in Australia, both at the beginning of their first terms. It seems loyalty was sustained until the cold hand of power politics intruded into the narrative.

Who are these next generation players who are ready to act if they can't find leadership they can trust?

While initially appearing apathetic to some, inspired leadership has risen from within. They have education and like Elihu a latent sensitivity to justice, mercy and compassion.

Their commitment when focused is quick to surface and move to action

Who are these young Elihus? Just a few among the many are Joshua Wong the young Christian man leading the demonstrations in Hong Kong, Greta Thunberg the teenage catalyst for climate change, Emma Gonzalez who was roused to fight for gun control after seeing the slaughter of her school mates at Marjory Stoneman Douglas High School, and Wael Ghonim, a major catalyst of the Arab Spring. We are discovering in the words of Elihu *"It is not only the old that are wise, not only the aged who understand what is right."* In fact we are using the word *"unprecedented"* at a truly unprecedented level which means that older ways of thinking and managing in this 2020 pandemic may not provide us with the answers and solutions we need.

Something is happening amongst baby boomers!

Research tells us that over 40% of baby boomers are beginning to align with this generation of trans-moderns. Many of the baby boomers broke out of the mould of traditional thinking in the sixties and a growing number of generation X Y and Z (includes boomers' children through to today's teenagers) are reaching for spiritual bearings that can be trusted. They want bearings that respect the past yet have a keen focus on the future they and their children will have to inhabit.

Trans-moderns are looking for guide-posts to the future

They have an urgent need to believe in something that gives life meaning and when roused, care deeply about the future and will quickly build a community of people who are going there. They want to believe they can help build a just, merciful and sustainable economy, but too often fall back into apathy and despair when they see where the world seems to be heading.

The background to the oldest book in the Bible and our journey

The spiritual incisiveness of Elihu in the book of Job could well be a beckoning light on the hill, calling both boomers and trans-moderns to become their highest selves giving them a shared prophetic voice, one that brings a sharp light to the moral fog. Could this ancient wisdom book bring the spiritual insight that will give bearings to a generation on the edge of a world yet to be fully imagined?

Job, one of the oldest known pieces of literature in existence, is believed to have been written before The Torah, the first five books of the Bible. While the events in Genesis took place earlier it is believed to be Moses who later wrote them down on clay cuneiform tablets. The book of Job was probably written about the time Joseph was managing the affairs of Egypt which would place it long before the nation of Israel even existed.

Way back before the Ten Commandments this remarkable young man Elihu had what we now see as a Level 4 consciousness. What is a Level 4 thinker? (Refer appendix) Journey with me and I will let Elihu show you.

The two basic life attitudes, fear and hope and where they come from

A case could be put that the world is divided between those who fear the worst and those who hope for the best, those orientated to control and those orientated to trust. The division is between those whose mind is shaped by emotional deficits that come from the past and those whose mind is energized by life-affirming aspirations.

Therapist and philosopher Robert Sardello in his book *"Love and Soul"*, writes that man's spirit is the source of hopeful and imaginative possibilities and is a necessary and natural part of healthy human nature. He explains *"First we are able to see from our spirit that the orientation of our spirit is prospective before it is retrospective."* In other words when we are most sane our spirit is positively imagining a hopeful future.

Sardello would be almost totally aligned with Elihu

Sardello believes this hopeful imagination springs from the same source as real love. The word philosophy comes from two Greek words, sofia which means wisdom and phileo which is one of the Greek words for love. It is the love of wisdom that leads us to understanding - not simply the love of knowledge. Sardello believes our hope of getting the understanding that will lead to a sustainable future will not come from an educated human mind alone, but from illumination of the human spirit. As Elihu has asserted, *"It is the breath of God in a man, the spirit in a man that gives understanding."* (Job 32:8)

Hope rises from an uncontaminated spirit

Only the spirit can see and create the life-sustaining future that has yet to be imagined. Sardello says *"It is time to realize that what rises up from our spirit's faith imagination is not simply a fantasy but the utterly substantial reality of the possible future."*

He goes on to say, *"As long as there is a sense in our soul of a spiritual dynamic there will be a sense of a real and hopeful future."*

The spirit gives our personality a telos - a sense that we have a destiny to complete

The task of effective leadership and education is to nourish the spirit which is the source of an inspired sense of the future. Disturbingly, Sardello says, *"When the soul has no sense of future, it will have something far worse, a feeling about the future that is no more than a fearful projection of a frightening past. So instead of the truly new and hopeful unknown drawing us toward it, the soul of the whole of humanity will have been diminished, because one part will be in the dark vacuum."*

When this happens, with its resulting dehumanization, Sardello believes the end of life as we know it could well be coming into view. Anyone who reads the daily newspapers or watches the nightly news on TV knows that not only could he be right, but that he is picking up the mood precisely. With dystopian themes in youth movies like *"The Hunger Games"*, it almost looks as though all this is becoming a depressing self-fulfilling prophesy.

Hope or despair: the current great human divide

Some people are blessed with aspirations informed by a life affirming spiritual dynamic like Elihu's, while others are driven by the shadows of powerlessness and despair shaped by archaic deficits and bruises. Most are caught somewhere on the continuum between hope and despair, while others swing between both poles.

It was Alfred North Whitehead (1861 – 1947) mathematician and philosopher who said, *"Youth is life is yet untouched by tragedy."* Times have changed though and too many of today's youth have been touched by tragedy and are in a state of despair. As never before we need Elihu's key if the next generation is to unlock the door to a realistic, preferred and sustainable human future.

Elihu's spiritual distinctive

Elihu was a young man who knew the distinctive features of his own mind. He was held to ransom neither by the potential inhibitions of traditional or Level 2 thinking, nor the ego-driven self-consciousness that is shaped by what we now know is the left hemisphere of the brain.

In Job 32:8 and 9 we hear Elihu say *"It is not only the old who are wise, not only the aged who understand!"* In fact he reminds us, *"It is the spirit in a man, the breath of the Almighty that gives understanding."*

As ancient as Elihu's comments are, it is clear that he comes from a different level of consciousness from that of Job's other friends. We now recognize his thinking as spiritual intelligence or, as some call it, Level 4 thinking or integral consciousness.

The limitations of human understanding and awareness

Science has unveiled to us not only the remarkable human mind but also its profound limitations. We have seen that the human brain as over against the mind, is capable of absorbing four billion bits of information every second, yet the most aware of us are only able to be alert to a measly 2,000 of them.

Our five senses absorb remarkable volumes of information yet we fail to grasp the meaning of by far the greater part of it. We are at last catching on to the fact that the more we think we know, the more cognitive we are in our processing, the more blind we are to the extensive and hopeful reality just beyond the reach of our consciousness.

As never before, we need new ways of illuminated knowing if we are to rise to the challenges of our time

INTELLIGENT AND EDUCATED BUT BLIND

"Where am I? Who am I? How did I come to be here? What is this thing called the world? How did I come into the world? Why was I not consulted? And if I am compelled to take part in it, where is the director? I want to see him?"

Soren Kierkegaard (1813-1855) Philosopher, theologian and cultural critic.

My purpose in life?

Danish philosopher Soren Kierkegaard has been called the father of existentialism. He wrestled with the big existential questions: What is my purpose in life? What am I for? What happens when I die? How come men know to do good, but still do evil?

What can we learn from Elihu about these questions? First, that the same questions have been around for thousands of years and are unique to thinking human beings. The background to the story of Job is framed by a cosmic battle raging between good and evil that is invisible to most mortals. (Job 1:6-22)

Elihu enters the scene and holds his peace until his patience runs out

Our man Elihu is not heard from until towards the end of the book of Job when the drama is fully under way. He finally speaks up after observing a drawn out game of verbal tennis between the tortured Job and his three self-righteous, so-called friends who have supposedly come to bring him comfort. These friends have a total lack of empathy and insight and sensing the injustice of it all Elihu can contain himself no longer. He clearly remembers Job from the past and can see how far he has fallen. (Job 29)

Who's to blame? We are all so quick to allocate blame. The modern version of the old saying is, it matters not if you win or lose but where you place the blame! But what if no-one is to blame?

The big question: How come bad things happen to good people?

It is this age-old existential question Job is wrestling with. Elihu has always trusted Job as a visionary community leader but is frustrated with him because he seems to have nothing to say to these spiritual dinosaurs.

Job seems to have lost the spiritual compass that could have strengthened him against deep despair born of fading hope and rising unbelief. Elihu can see Job is sounding more and more like a victim which is a far cry from the dignity of his previous position. (Job 29)

Is all difficulty and pain punishment for wrongdoing?

Elihu is also frustrated with the three friends. They say they have come to comfort and encourage Job but they have come with the concluded position that his problems happened because he and his family have been sinful in some way. These so-called friends condemn Job without hearing him deeply or attempting to answer his profound and honest existential questions. Young Elihu is angry when he sees they have no spiritual insight, but instead condemn Job for his condition.

Lack of heart engagement can push people to the edge of giving up

Job says, *"Since I am already found guilty why should I even go on struggling?"* In other words, *"Here I am boys, threatened with oblivion, hanging by my finger tips to the edge of an emotional cliff and you're choosing to do a tap dance on my fingers!"* He has lost everything (Job 1: 6-22) and his wife is no comfort. The best she can come up with is, *"Curse God and die."* (Job 2:9,10)

All Job's friends can do is drum up a running commentary on the failure of his morals. As though gazing at a sick goldfish floating upside down in a bowl they make knowing statements about his situation. There is no heart engagement, no empathy for Job and his situation. Job can see it is too disturbing to their ego to leave the comfort of their equilibrium and identify with him in his suffering.

Too often friends back off when our life challenges confront them

In Chapter 6:21 Job says, *"When you see me, you see something dreadful and you are afraid."* In verse 26 he goes on to say, *"Do you mean to correct what I say and treat the words of a despairing man as wind?"* The so-called comforters stay safe in their comfortable, self-righteous and unexamined conclusions, while Job reflects that, *"Men at ease have contempt for those suffering misfortune."* (Job 12:5)

Elihu could see the so-called comforters have simply repeated their tired old clichés to one another keeping their emotional distance from the chaos of Job's pain. Their subconscious neurotic need for equilibrium has them explain away Job's tragedy with two dimensional moral clichés. It is the same moral formula devoid of respect and grace that has had thousands give up on their spiritual journey in despair. The worst kind of religion speaks confidently on God's behalf about the misfortunes of others without having the mercy to step into their shoes and bring grace.

Before we appear to demonise traditional thinking however, we need to see it against the backdrop of developing civilisation and culture. Later we will examine the notion of spiritual development but whether we are emotionally immature chaotic children or dysregulated adults we all have to learn how to be civilised, how to respect the individuality of others.

Respect for individuality is the secret of caring for those in distress

There is a force woven into the very fabric of who we are that if respected and not violated will eventually lead us to completion of our humanity. People who are chaotic and dis-regulated need the framework of a values-based social system that accepts them and calls them gently into the first phase of self-control. We call people in this phase of their journey Level 1 thinkers.

Often in the initial stages of difficulty it is the committed Level 2 people who offer most help. Many in the West find it disturbing to see so many adolescents attracted to the moral framework of Islam, yet we need to learn that the spirit within can only live with just so much chaos before it goes mad. Those on the spiritual journey without even knowing why can feel attracted to the community of Level 2 thinkers. This is because of the life structure they can provide.

Who are these Level 2 thinkers? Is it a case of arrested development?

These are the traditional people of any faith or profession who are comfortable with the predictability of the world as they experience it. Many of them are beautiful people who have a narrative that moved them from chaos to order: It can feel as though they have moved from darkness to light and it's a narrative that should be respected. Many drug addicts and dis-regulated people have found it was Level 2 thinkers who gave them the structure and belief systems that helped give order to their lives.

Often though, these Level 2 people become too comfortable in their world view and get to enjoy the pseudo-certainty it provides. They will not be inclined to move on in their spiritual life and are likely to become stuck in a kind of self-satisfied comfort unable to grow enough to want to leave their emotional oasis.

You can have spiritual adventure or safety but you can't have both at the same time

To grow spiritually we need to refine our faith by facing the questions our doubts confront us with. Job's friends were Level 2 thinkers. The questions raised in the book of Job about his suffering would have been disturbing for them to confront. They were not inclined to get inside Job's experience and empathise in order to share his tragedy with him. They were fearful of going beyond the safety of the familiar where the ego can tell itself it is still in charge.

Those with real and mature spirituality are ready for the adventure of the pilgrimage of life and instead of clinging to psychological safety they push on to confront the truth that leads to the Promised Land. Level 2 people prefer their old and well-worn beliefs repeated back to them like an emotional security blanket rather than try to cope with the stress and frustration that happens when the ego is challenged by the discomfort of the real world.

Like the Pharisees of the New Testament, Level 2 thinkers become reactionary if their beliefs are challenged

These beautiful people often become quite hostile when the belief systems that support their sense of security are threatened. They are prone to be sentimental and nostalgic about what they see as the golden past. They want to relive the feelings they had when they were younger and on the spiritual journey. Back then it felt as though they were moving from chaos to order - from darkness to light. At that time their faith was alive and they actually experienced miracles. They had an unexamined confidence that made them feel emotionally alive, however they often mistook this for being spiritually alive.

Feeling emotionally alive is not the same as being spiritually alive

These people tend to cling together and look for leaders who will perpetuate the black and white certainties that maintain their security. In Christianity many are wealthy businessmen who will fund evangelists and radio and TV ministries that support their own way of thinking. They will call this outreach, but too often it will be good people giving good money to have their own paradigm reinforced.

Level 2 thinkers tend to become fundamentalist

Most become stuck in a historical mindset that is unable to distinguish between ideology and spiritually anchored belief and those who don't grow beyond Level 2 thinking tend to become fundamentalists. Many of the sectarian battles in the past were about separating the supposedly right religious ideas from heresy. People were easily confused feeling the need to fight for tribal consensus around the ideas they believed to be truth.

Dotting the I's and crossing the T's did not produce harmony

Religious leaders have often gathered in conferences where they attempted to reach certain forms of intellectual and doctrinal unity. In my experience however, when large issues are at stake, it is rather a common love for the values they share that has the majority of Christians reaching out to each other for fellowship. While theologians may focus on intense discussions about subtle points of doctrine, the mass of people of faith often find encouragement and relief in well designed and sensitively programmed ecumenical events where sharing their faith's heart is what welds them together.

This for me is not simply a theory but a profound realisation

When it was discovered that prayer was to go missing at the opening of Australia's new Parliament House in 1988 I was presented with a rich opportunity to test this theory. Church leaders wrote to Prime Minister Bob Hawke in protest: It was as if the wind had blown their voice away.

After building a consensus with a very small representative group we networked with church and community leaders finding a language that unified and would speak to the shared heart of the mass of people we hoped to reach out to.

The result? Fifty thousand Australians who had never gathered together before turned up spontaneously to pray. Initially many had grimaces on their faces wondering if they were going to suffer any kind of embarrassment. However inspired facilitation released their shared spirit. Many found it hard to articulate just how amazing the shared joy and harmony they experienced was. They had created history.

They were from every denomination and style of spiritual expression

The initial task had been to find a common heart language for this event - one that focused the valid spiritual concerns that could motivate the crowd while avoiding the minefield of prejudice and suspicion that often attends trans-denominational events.

I had the exacting task of finding a common set of symbols and language that all participants could have deep agreement with. Many agree that the most profound aspect of this and many subsequent events that came under the banner of what was called the Aussie Awakening, was not the huge crowds that turned up but the remarkable sense of united purpose and cohesion. There was a palpable sense of relief when thousands of Australian Christians discovered that the shared heart of their faith was far more important than those smaller points of doctrine that might separate them.

We are not well equipped to cope with people who disagree with us

Many good people have been stymied on coming up against professional contrarians - whether it be loud atheists, assertive gays, conservationists, feminists, or narrowly committed Muslims and the like, all with concluded opinions. These people are often very at home in a narrative that tends to blame what they call the Christian West for their own feelings of alienation.

Kindly and well-educated souls who are moving in the direction of becoming Level 3 thinkers will be inclined to listen sympathetically to their argument. Agreeing with them or not, they will give them a hearing. Those who regard themselves as progressive will at the very least, be quite interested. (see Appendix)

Wanting to be broadminded but walking into a trap

Those who assume a persona with a certain level of sophistication will be happy to point out our culture's inconsistencies, blind spots and failures. They will harmonise with the accusers who will be well versed in the art of the iconoclast (one who attacks or criticises cherished beliefs or institutions).

Later in this book I refer to those V.J. Lenin called useful idiots – sympathisers who could be used. These were people from the West who thought it was sophisticated to sympathize with a system of which they had little real understanding. Many of them were like adolescents who define themselves against the prevailing beliefs of their families. It is Level 3 thinkers who buy into the narrative that it is the system that's to blame. The *ain't it awful* position becomes an excuse for failing to reflect deeply. On the other hand, Level 2 thinkers hate ambiguity and will be inclined to protect the status quo, becoming quite defensive and reactionary.

The task for the mature person is not to simplistically blame either orientation. It is to recognise the important processes that are under way in the thinking of individuals and cultures whose very mindsets are on a journey to maturity. If we are able to disengage and honestly reflect, we will eventually find our spirit is not really comfortable with either polarised position. This will be particularly true if the machinery of the ego is inclined, as in some personalities, to have a defensive tone which is likely to produce conflict with others.

When we're at our best we are stimulated by difference

We in western liberal democracies have been on a long journey to break free of oppressive structures and ideologies and at our best, have come to believe in the value of persons. It feels normal for us to care for a person at risk or to consider another person's position without over-identifying with them. Deliberate cruelty to any living thing is beyond the comprehension of mature people.

We cannot identify with anyone who would want to cause injury. Our spirit is injured at the thought so we are rightly appalled that a family would let a nine year old daughter be given to an older man for a good sized dowry or a ten year old daughter be used as payment of a debt. It horrifies us that for any sum of money a parent would let a terrorist use a remote device to blow up a son or daughter so as to wound and kill innocent civilians in a crowded market.

Respect for individuality is a remarkable value

A person's value and the need to be respected that most contrarians appeal to, is not innate in human society. It comes from a long history of people who suffered and sacrificed for that value. A long line of saintly heroes paid the price of caring, who themselves were inspired by the one who said, *"Love one another as I have loved you."* From Wenceslas to Wilberforce, from St Basil to Mother Theresa, we can trace them. This respect for individuality does not stem from the normal social pressure of reward and punishment that induces a person to conform so as to feel the need to be the same as us.

Humankind is inclined to victimise those who are different

Level 4 thinkers are touched by the spirit. In fact most *at rest* people and Level 3 thinkers are fascinated and stimulated by what is different, by what is exotic. Mind you, this fascinated and open orientation will be put under pressure the moment the other person is consistently rude, disrespectful or arrogant - by those who think they are better than us, and by those who become a threat to what we value. The sense of inter-member identification will build safety and trust until it is disturbed.

Western democracy could never have developed without the profound but little understood Trinitarian world-view. It is an orientation that enables males and females to be drawn to what is different in each other's spirit, enabling for instance, fathers of small daughters to be enchanted by them. The spiritual attraction to that which complements - to what is different - is the very thing that draws, creating a fascinating promise and sense of oneness. It is a oneness that is disposed to treasure the uniqueness of the other.

When spiritually integrated and secure we are drawn to difference

Many become fixated Level 2 thinkers because in spite of what they say they believe, the likely operating factor is that they have a weak ego. Unbeknown to them, they need external structures to give them confidence and validate their existence. The key unresolved issues of submission and authority will tend to be their emotional drivers.

In some churches and groups there are many rules, mostly invisible and unwritten norms which have developed over time. There are likely to be subtle rewards and punishments for those who are blind to these norms which are often the expression of a growing consensus among the dominant opinion formers of the group. They go far beyond things like the unstated rule that women will not speak in church or that everyone be committed vegetarians.

A measure of what is called the area of free activity

This will be experienced as a freedom from the need to second guess others in the group. If the high status people are Level 4 thinkers, spontaneity will be encouraged; if not, a certain awkwardness will be in the atmosphere. All this is usually unstated and invisible yet issues to do with trust and control will be in the air. Those with a modicum of social and emotional intelligence will soon pick up the vibes.

Hidden in the unstated norms will be key issues that influence the group's health and cohesion - things like participation patterns, social etiquette, and how far one can go without being thought rude and offensive. This is important if the group is to free all its members to contribute.

Capacity of Level 2 thinkers for social intelligence

The capacity of the Level 2 thinkers for social intelligence is usually low. They are rarely able to empathise with an opinion different from their own and are not inclined to reflect on the source of their own motivation. They seem inflexibly stuck in their brain's left hemisphere and come mostly from their head rather than their heart. They tend to hear everything through the filters of their safe, uncritically accepted ideology. Of course they are not only religious people. You will find fundamentalists amongst scientists, politicians, even atheists, feminists, conservationists and gay activists etc.

All ideologies tend to become fascist

Have you noticed that all ideologies eventually become fascist? The founder of the Australian Liberal party Prime Minister Bob Menzies used to say, *"The benefit of being ideological is that you don't have to think."* People who espouse an ideology tend to see everything through its filters. Some beautiful and intelligent women did some great thinking in pursuit of the development of women's opportunities and freedom. Some though, became stuck in the ideology and saw all men as part of some dark patriarchal conspiracy. In doing so they lost contact with the very spirit that initially prompted them - a sensitivity to injustice and a vision of a better world which would potentially enable many men to be recruited to their cause.

An opportunity lost and an unnecessary chasm created

A rule of thumb in working for change is that you rarely catch fish by throwing rocks at them. Some feminists became known for their strident views and many who probably carried archaic hurt became stuck in their bitterness, unable to move. Hence the one liner doing the rounds: Question: *"How many feminists does it take to change a light bulb?"* Answer: *"It's not funny!"* They became so easy to caricature as feminazis because they lost their capacity to see the world free of emotional dramas.

It is not true that somebody is always the victim, somebody is always the perpetrator and the caring person's task is to rescue the victim by destroying the perpetrator. If we don't stop and reflect this will be our subconscious inclination. In psychology it's called the Karpman Drama Triangle (Developed by Steven Karpman, it is used worldwide in psychiatry counselling, psychology, and business development workshops).

There is always more to any situation than first reactions can discern

This same drama process can happen in any movement in which people feel deeply about a cause. Yes, including conservationists, vegetarians, atheists, evolutionists, creationists, and diverse religious movements. All real values have a heart commitment - people care deeply about them; it is what makes them values. Real values though are not simply emotional reactions. They represent a deliberate process of conscious evaluation from a number of alternative points of view. The outcome will produce a reasonable integration that while deep, allows conversation without defensiveness.

Dramas on the other hand, are usually an emotional reaction springing from an inherited or one's own unfinished business. Because dramas are created by an uncritical reaction they tend to become fascist in tone. One wit has said, *"A fascist thinks he sees the mote in his neighbour's eye then hits him over the head with the beam in his own."*

Spontaneity, intimacy and awareness, typify the spiritually developed

In contrast to all of this we hear Elihu say, *"It is the spirit in a man, the breath of God, that gives him understanding."*(Job 32:8). Here we have the missing key, Elihu's key!

Where does our most inspired and highest thinking come from?

Not from our ego or our head, shaped by our brain's left hemisphere. This aspect of what we call our mind can't help but be contaminated by our social history with its concluded opinions and prejudices. No! Our highest thinking comes from somewhere else; from the source of our inspired intuition, our spirit.

How come simple issues become so intractable?

It is what the spiritually developed have known for centuries. Unless we learn as individuals and as a society to stop the whirring of our left hemisphere as it compulsively serves our ego's attempt to look good and be right, we will usually get it wrong.

Clarity is almost always fogged up by our underlying attempt to measure up to our cultural stereotypes as we work hard at the business of thinking well of ourselves. One wonders how many mindless wars have seen young men sent off to the battle front to their deaths because older men of the political class felt slighted.

Unless we learn the science and the art of tuning into the human spirit we will be doomed to be driven mindlessly by subconscious forces that create blind and thoughtless dramas. While we are unable to come to terms with the real source of our most intractable problems we will not find our way through to their satisfying resolution.

Chapter 4

SPIRITUAL LIFE AND SANITY IN THE MODERN WORLD

> *"Mental health requires that the human will submit itself to something higher than itself. To function decently in this world we must submit ourselves to some principle that takes precedence over what we may want at any given moment."*

Scott Peck (1936-2005) American psychiatrist and best-selling author

We are body soul and spirit

It is not that we *have* a body, soul and spirit but all three are feeding into our experience of reality all the time. (1 Thessalonians. 5:23)

Through my body - my soma, my five senses, I can immediately be in touch with the world around me, that is assuming I'm well and my soul with its anxieties and archaic emotions does not intrude.

Through my soul - my psyche, my ego, I have a sense of myself no matter how distorted by my emotional history or tortured by the underlying exquisite ache demanding I do things to compensate for feelings of inadequacy. This part of me is on an endless quest to help me think well of myself.

Through my spirit - my pneuma - if my ego doesn't intrude I can have a sense of the transcendent, the big and awesome reality which is bigger than my sense of me. When I am attuned to my spirit the power of the need to think well of myself evaporates. I can have a sense of the eternal values that enrich life - love, beauty and truth - and that timeless sense of hope that draws me to an awareness of personal destiny and divine purpose.

The human awareness of a big and rich life waiting to be known

In Job 33:4 Elihu unveils the secret we all half know: *"The Spirit of God has made me; the breath of the Almighty gives me real life."* What is this real life?

In Latin the word *spiritus* means *life* and *breath*. There are two Hebrew words for spirit, *ruach* and *neshamah,* and we are told God breathed into man's nostrils the neshamah of life and man became the completed being. The breath of God is not simply the air that fills the lungs; it is the divine breath that fills and enlivens the soul and brings spiritual energy to the body. We're told in Proverbs 20:27, *"The spirit of man is the candle of the Lord."*

Dr J. Stafford Wright, a student of the human spirit said, *"The word spirit is never used of the animal world so we are quite justified in concluding that mankind's possession of spirit marks him off from the rest of the created order."*

It is this remarkable spirit referred to by Elihu that gives life meaning, puts a sparkle in the eye, gives life to the whole being and personality and helps us move forward with hope toward shalom or peace.

What is life and what gives life?

If I took a mosquito, pulled it apart then glued it together again with super glue,

would it be a mosquito? No, it may look like a mosquito but it would lack the unique life of a mosquito. It would have the external characteristics of a mosquito but would not have that unique X factor that makes a mosquito a mosquito.

The human X factor

Humans also have certain ways of being. At our best we have the capacity to be loving and compassionate and to see the bigger picture. We have a moral compass that enables us to know right from wrong and to choose right even when it's difficult. We have the capacity to look over our own shoulder and tell ourselves unpleasant but honest truths about ourselves and when we're integrated we feel fulfilled. Sadly, we're not always like this but if we could be convinced we could sustain it, it's the way we would love to live.

Three year study shows spiritual sensitivity is a common fact of life

A recent three year international study from Oxford has concluded that a sense of God is an essential part of our human nature - that we are naturally predisposed to have an awareness of a divine presence and that some vital part of us survives death. Co-director of the project Professor Roger Trigg Emeritus Professor of Philosophy at the University of Warwick said the research shows that religion is not just something a peculiar few do on Sundays instead of playing golf. *"We have gathered a body of evidence that suggests that spiritual awareness is a common fact of human nature across a whole range of different societies."*

He said, *"This suggests that attempts to suppress spirituality and religion are always likely to be short lived. Human thought itself seems to be anchored in spiritual concepts such as the existence of God, supernatural agents and the possibility of an afterlife or pre-life."*

We instinctively know there is more to life than human thought can grasp

We have been given great capacity for spiritual awareness and under-standing, not that we always use it. We have a remarkable sense of truth and justice. Nothing of the like is seen in the animal world and we ourselves are most conscious of these attributes when our own sense of self has been devalued, when we have been victims of injustice or deception.

Recovering a sensitivity to our spiritual intelligence

The Latin word from which we derive our word intelligence is *intelligere* which means to discern, to choose between. Spiritual intelligence is the capacity to choose between the ego - the soul, the basic uninspired self with its dominant self-absorbed survival instinct and this spiritual consciousness - the higher altruistic self with its yearning for shalom, self-transcendence and a good future for all. William Frank Diedrich (1949-) American speaker, executive coach and author wrote, *"We need to continually remember we are spiritual beings having a human experience."*

Spiritual awareness: how it helps with detachment - field independence

The great distinctive of Elihu is that he has a point of reference bigger than his own ego, emotions and defence mechanisms. This enables the best part of who he is to stay alert to what is good; it lifts him and enables him to keep the sensitivities of his spirit alive. It is how Elihu is able to avoid the psychological game-playing that is underway between Job and his so-called comforters.

Elihu exhibits what is called field independence. This is the level of autonomy that enables him to rise above the normal tendency to protect his ego by adapting and going with the crowd: it is another clear sign of his spiritual intelligence. He is more concerned with what the Divine Being thinks the truth is, and focused on grasping that truth rather than being supersensitive about what others think of him and his views.

Detachment: a sign of spiritual maturity and a necessity for spiritual intelligence

This spiritual discipline involves detaching one's sense of worth and well- being from all that the ego compulsively pursues in order to meet its need for significance.

It is what Jesus was trying to teach his brand new followers in the Beatitudes: Matt 5:1-5. It lay behind his statement *"Blessed are the poor in spirit"* i.e. those whose spirit is complete needing nothing else to find fulfilment. All the great spiritual teachers have taught the need to die emotionally to the grasping, insatiable and self-absorbed inclinations we are all prone to.

The need to believe in something bigger than your own ego

I have a feeling one of the reasons we find it hard to trust politicians is that we yearn to hear from somebody who believes in someone bigger than their own ego, someone who can inspire us. We know when we're hearing not undistorted truth but an angle designed to protect and enhance a person or their party.

Of the most trusted professions politicians usually come last or in the last three, competing for last place with used car salesmen and journalists. There is ample evidence to show neither the popular media nor our political system know how to handle the transcendent. We feel they're telling us what they want us to hear, not what we need to hear.

Those who look beyond the next edition and the next election are catching on

Recently major corporations, nations and the world itself have been taken to the edge of complete financial melt-down. People in high places lost their moral compass as greed and arrogance blinded them to the disastrous implications of their unethical choices. It is why the quest for spiritual intelligence is now being referenced and studied in those board rooms and corporate settings that have at last become sensitised to the need for a paradigm with a longer time frame.

The quest for spiritual intelligence turning up in corporate life

The likes of Nokia, Unilever, Shell, Coca-Cola, Hewlett Packard and Starbucks, to name but a few, are showing interest in spiritual intelligence. They are beginning to look at the triple bottom line - financial, social and environmental, to measure success. Why? So many brand names and institutions that fail to do this disappear overnight.

Steven Covey, who died in 2012 was an author, inspirational teacher and professor, holding 12 honorary doctorate degrees. Among his many awards were the International Man of Peace Award, and the International Entrepreneur of the Year Award. He was recognized as one of Time Magazine's 25 most influential Americans, inspiring millions with the power of his universal principles. He wrote, *"Spiritual intelligence is the central and most fundamental of all the intelligences because it becomes a source of guidance for the other forms of intelligence."*

Sometimes it takes some kind of ego failure to free our spirit from the tyranny of our ego.

A breakdown of ego control can provide opportunity for a breakthrough

It sometimes takes the collapse of the sense of self and identity to loosen the grip of the ego-validating mechanisms that support an inadequate sense of self. This is almost necessary before we can be humble enough to hear the inner voice of the spirit with clarity. Just when we thought we were going mad, bubbling up from deep within we hear the still small voice of peace and sanity, the voice of what Elihu calls our spirit.

The human spirit will always speak loudly enough for the humble willing to hear

I find it interesting to note that Oscar Wilde of all people, while reflecting on his tragic life from the perspective of Reading Gaol in 1898 said, *"How else but through a broken heart, may Lord Christ enter in."* For many highfliers it takes the collapse of their phony presenting self - their projected persona with its appearance of success and sophistication - to produce a genuine spiritual awareness.

Spiritual intelligence - the most fundamental of the intelligences

Cindy Wigglesworth is a trainer whose material has been used at the highest level of corporate operation. She said, *"Spiritual intelligence is the ability to act with wisdom and compassion while maintaining inner and outer peace, regardless of the circumstances."*

Sometimes those with type A or alpha personalities, because of the size of their ego and sheer energy, will gravitate to positions of corporate leadership. Many of them come from their left hemisphere and are so heavily into the need to control there is no space in the operation of their soul for the kind of reflection which alone can produce spiritual intelligence and wisdom. Hence, without intimate and honest companions both they and the business they lead will founder.

Paradoxically the shock of a moral and emotional breakdown can create an opportunity for spiritual illumination and success. When the ego's devices to hold itself together are demobilized strangely, there is then a chance for spiritual growth. A spiritual renaissance will often create an opportunity for the Divine Spirit to facilitate a fresh encounter with one's own inner voice of sanity.

Settling the inner chatter to uncover our own voice of wisdom and sanity

In us, as in Elihu, there is a part that enjoys being aware of the bigger realities. If we have ears to hear, this part is constantly in dialogue with us. If we are going to become aware of it, though, we need to learn how to settle the anxious chatter in our mind that most often sets our mental and emotional agenda.

There is a still small voice within that spiritual intelligence is attuned to

Ironically Kylie Minogue's 2001 hit song *"Can't get you out of my head"* was crowned the UK's most played song of the 2000's. Ironic because the Aussie pop star says she hears obsessive voices in her head that have her continually make detailed plans. She is not schizoid and my guess is we've all heard these voices from time to time but don't know if we should trust them.

Steve Jobs, founder of the Apple Corporation, said at a university graduation, *"Don't let the noise of other people's opinions drown out your own inner voice."* How can we discern our own inner voice, the voice of our spirit, as Elihu did? How can we isolate its pure wisdom from the rest of the chatter that is inclined to go on in our head?

Of all the inner voices which one should we take seriously?

Where do they come from? Our own healthy voice some have recognised as the voice of conscience, others as the voice of intuition. Eric Berne, the father of transactional analysis, recognised and named a number of voices or promptings. He used various names - the voice of our controlling parent or the voice of our nurturing parent. In some of these voices we may actually recognize the voice of our mother. He called others the adaptive child, and free child. These were recognised as the pouting and anxious child of our past, or the free child he saw as the giggling and happy child that surfaces when we are enjoying something.

Then there is the fascinating voice of intuition, the little professor

He recognised what he called the *"little professor"* - the mysterious voice of intuition amongst all those archaic voices. This voice is most often found to be the voice of gentle wisdom: it is also the voice of the human spirit that God speaks to and through.

The following story from my own family is a great illustration of how it works: My three year old granddaughter was chatting to her mother as she reflected on the huge event of turning three. Looking up at her mother she asked, *"Can I tell God I am three?"* To which her mum replied, *"Sure,"* as she continued with the family ironing. Looking down she was just in time to see her cute toddler go quiet, clasp her tiny fingers and silently move her lips in earnest prayer. After a moment of silence she looked up at her mum, beaming. *"He talked to me." "And what did he say,"* asked her mum gently. *"He told me he already knows,"* was the reply. *"Anything else?" "Yes,"* said the little girl with the most beautiful smile, *"He told me he loved me."*

We have the task of re-learning to recognise the inner voice of the spirit

From the voice of the spirit we hear the quiet and settling tone of messages that centre us like, *"Relax It's ok, I am with you,"* or *"Take your time until the issues are clear,"* or *"Be cautious here."* Sometimes we're admonished to *"Quietly back out of this situation; it's a bit of a trap."* When we're dealing with a child or a subordinate it might say, *"Gently; you're being driven and you're being unnecessarily hard on him now."*

At other times it will come as the voice of emerging self-awareness; the prompting of a truth you're avoiding or even a personal responsibility you are dodging: *"Come on you know what you should do. Stop putting it off."*

It may come as a moral reality beckoning you to commitment in which case it might whisper, *"Come on, we both know you're avoiding this. It's time to stop the excuses. It's time to commit yourself."*

You know when it's time to stop avoiding and start committing

Sometimes when we're consumed by self-doubt or inclined to beat ourselves up we'll find the spirit to be the voice of anchored sanity. If we can hear beyond our own inner accuser the spirit's voice will protest for us and say, *"No. Don't spiral down there. That may not have been perfect but it was good,"* or maybe, *"That was great, but don't indulge the part that wants to beat up on you; it's not from me."*

When you are drawn like a moth to the destructive flame

It may *say, "You are too close to this temptation now: Your immature archaic deficits and emotions are clouding your judgment."* At other times it might encourage with something like, *"In time you will be glad you stood firm,"* and yet again when you've wrestled with something and won, *"You met this moment well without getting yourself too tangled. Well done! In time you will know how important that was."*

The voice of the spirit is the inner mentor that lifts us from unproductive inclinations and impulses

In the past some have called this voice *"conscience"* but it is so much more. My goal in this book is to begin to show you how to tune into this remarkable part of who you really are because it does take some untangling from the other voices that constantly chatter away in the left hemisphere. This part bubbles from just below the level of consciousness. It will not accuse you or anybody else; it will be hopeful, not reactionary or vindictive. It will want honest peace.

Hearing the voice of sanity through the static

Problems arise from our narcissistic leanings, materialistic culture and old parent messages. They so clutter the airwaves of our personal and social discourse that most of us have lost the ability to recognise with clarity this voice of the spirit and the wholeness and sanity it brings.

It will always speak loudly enough for the humble willing to hear

Time and again those more spiritually discerning amongst us will recognise how often it was there protecting us from disaster like a guardian angel. There is story after story - many in this book - of people prompted to do something they would normally be too embarrassed to talk about but were so pleased they took the prompting seriously.

Once you become sanely attuned to it this voice is constantly and quietly whispering just loudly enough above the static for the humble willing to hear its life-giving truth. The more we reflect on it the more the flashes of this remarkable instinct will be recognized and it will move from the subconscious to the conscious.

This voice will always make itself known to those who want to know it

It is not a loud voice. Its work is to gently make us aware of the larger issues of our existence and to introduce us to the big picture and right values and relationships that will help us travel safely to our destiny. It will often though, take some kind of near death or personal or economic crisis to jolt us from the ego-shielding mechanisms of our left hemisphere's brain paths, the paths that set our inner agenda day after day.

Sometimes the rug has to be pulled from under the ego's comfort

The rug has to be pulled from under our ego's illusion of control before our spirit can get through to us with clarity. Perhaps this is why the book of Job, with its tragic back story, has fascinated so many intelligent and deeply reflective people.

Near death experiences, fits of depression, emotional crises and the like, all remind us that we are not in charge of the universe. Dr. Oswald G. Harding, in his book *"Near Death Experience - A scientific examination of all the most recent data on the subject"* said, *"The residual effect of NDE (near death experience) is a modification in the person's whole attitude toward life, and a reduction and/or elimination of the fear of death. These transformative experiences are like a religious conversion and seem to be permanent."*

People who have a near death experience speak of the emergence of a wonderful gift of unconditional love. They report that it sustains them with its qualities of compassion, tolerance and understanding, and often with a new kind of an inner knowing, all of which gives them an enhanced view of themselves and others. There is also a new sense of connectedness with life. All this sounds like the beginnings of spiritual intelligence.

You will find the stories in the next chapter are much more common than contemporary culture would have us believe.

Chapter 5

THE NEAR DEATH CRISIS THAT MADE A CONVERT

"The most beautiful experience we can have is the mysterious. It is the source of all true art and all science. He to whom this emotion is a stranger, who can no longer pause to wonder and stand wrapped in awe, is as good as dead – his eyes are closed. A knowledge of the existence of something we cannot penetrate, our perceptions of the profoundest reason and the most radiant beauty, which only in the most primitive forms are accessible to our minds - it is this knowledge and this emotion that constitute true religiosity."

Albert Einstein (1879 – 1955) German-born theoretical physicist who developed the theory of relativity

18 year-old with a song in his heart

We now know him as Yusuf Islam but he was previously known for his remarkable music and the name Cat Stevens. He'd already impressed the head of Decca records with *Matthew and Son* and *I Love My Dog* and had been fortunate to have as producer Mike Hurst who had worked with Dusty Springfield. Mike had seen this 18 year old with a song in his heart and had helped raise money to fund the recording session. It seemed life was opening up for the young Cat Stevens but two years later he was flat on his back with a life threatening bout of tuberculosis.

Can what seems like a disaster open the door of opportunity?

He lay on his back day after day looking out of his window at the rhythm of nature as revealed in the English woods. He said, *"Something happened within my soul. I knew that there was more to life than what I'd been doing; there was a part about the spirit."* By the time he recovered he had a whole new repertoire of songs and a previously unrecognized part of his personality was emerging. In 1970 he played his new songs to Chris Blackwell of "Island Records." There was a breath of fresh air in these songs that quite overwhelmed Chris who quickly signed him - and the rest is music history. Teamed with producer Paul Samwell-Smith and brilliant guitarist Alan Davies, young Yusuf (Cat Stevens) became an overnight success.

The battle between God and mammon

In Yusuf's own words: *"There was a lot of money around. Things became more and more commercial so I found it increasingly difficult to balance my spiritual quest with my musical one. Playing live in front of 40,000 idolizing people isn't conducive to much self-reflection."*

Time after time we see the challenge of celebrity, with the star becoming increasingly extrinsic - sensitive to appearances, and less intrinsic, attuned to spiritual integrity.

The wave that brought a second chance

Yusuf talked about the wave that saved his life. He'd been staying with a friend in Malibu California in 1976. It was a beautiful day and there was great surf. He swam out, got caught in a rip and found it impossible to swim back. What happened next sceptics are inclined to call an act of desperation, but it is typical of the spiritually sensitive. He said, *"My faith jumped right up to my heart and I called out, 'God save me and I'll work for you.'"* He reported, *"At that moment a friendly wave came from behind and swept me safely to shore. I felt like I'd been given a second chance."*

A spiritual quest

For some time he'd been searching spiritually reading all the philosophy and religious books he could get his hands on. He now became more committed in his spiritual quest. As he looked around the secular and spiritually cynical culture of England he couldn't see anything that would give him a moral and spiritual compass. In spite of the rich heritage of the Church of England he could see nothing with the intensity and discipline he could identify with.

"On the road to find out"

In his personal networks it was the Muslim people who seemed to have the level of absolute commitment and direction he yearned for; he knew he needed a framework of values and meaning that would enable him to manage and direct his now materially successful life. He said later of this experience *"It was hard not to follow the crowd but I started to swim in another direction."* In his song *"On the Road to Find Out"* he reflected on his life journey, *"Well, in the end I'll know but now I'm on the way to find out."* Many who are concerned about the identification of a growing number of Western young people being drawn to Islam would do well to reflect on this story. Every young person is in need of a narrative that is worthy of their life commitment.

Trans-moderns search for values frameworks

Times have changed. There was a time when most of humanity already had an organizing purpose in their lives, survival - in much the same way as a beetle on its back has a purpose - to get on its front and get out of the way before somebody stomps on it or has it for a meal. While survival is significant motivation for much of the developing world, many young people in the Western world are like the beetle on its front asking, *"Where do I go from here?"*

Narcissism will never feed the spiritually hungry but look at so many of the empty self-serving celebrities we are offering as life role models.

What is the culture of the West offering these spiritually hungry young people?

Repeatedly we see young sporting and entertainment celebrities fall prey to the very things that were meant to be the fruit of their success. No doubt you can bring many to mind. The media loves to feed on and then destroy those it first deifies and exalts.

Austrian psychotherapist Viktor Frankl said, *"I have clinical evidence to show, if we no longer know what we ought to do, we will no longer know what we want to do, and will find ourselves in an existential vacuum the clearest evidence of which is boredom."* So many young people from the developed world find themselves with the choice of either surrendering to the chaos of their dis-regulated appetites inclinations and ego needs or to surrender to the spiritual discipline of some kind of Level 2 religious fellowship.

Nowadays not so many are finding their way into the spiritual discipline, so how are we to help them give shape and form to their chaotic existence? Will the media and popular culture do it? Is modern education well placed to do it? What do they need to know so as to find an integration of their spirit into their awareness?

"The centre of me is always searching for something infinite"

Bertrand Russell (1872–1970) British philosopher, logician, essayist and social critic, was the loud atheist of his time. Even he had to acknowledge, *"The centre of me is always and eternally in terrible pain... a searching for something beyond what the world contains, something transfigured and infinite. The beatific vision – God. I do not find it, I do not think it is to be found – but the love of it is my life... It is actually the spring of life within me."*

It may explain why a growing number of spiritually hungry people are instinctively groping around in their search for spiritual nourishment and an appropriate spiritual home. Fortunately they haven't yet given up on finding it. For the time being, in the words of Cat Stevens, more and more of us are still *"on the road to find out."* This enlightenment is inclined to find us when we are least expecting it; it is likely to catch us in the most unexpected places at the most unexpected times.

More are on the road to find out than we would expect

As we move further into the 21st century we are finding that some of the most unlikely people are reporting an unexpected but profound rise in their level of spiritual awareness.

We are hearing reports from the likes of Denzel Washington through to *"Rush Hour's"* Chris Tucker and many others like Shia LaBeouf from *"The Transformer Trilogy"* whose movie *"Fury"* became something of a catalyst when he played a Christian Sherman tank driver in World War 2. Identifying with his role as an eccentric Christian soldier on the front line, it was in scenes depicting life and death battles that he found himself declaring, *"I really found God during the making of that movie."*

God was not lost

Doubtless God was not lost or needing to be found, however human beings can get lost amidst the ordinary affairs of life, until it gradually dawns - an awareness of a presence that had been there all along. In his book *"Against all Odds"* actor and black belt karate specialist Chuck Norris wrote, *"Funny, for years I simply went about my business, going through life doing my own thing, almost unaware of a divine presence in my life, and its mysterious workings in the lives of my friends. It was all there but it was as if I was deaf and blind to it. Now that I have travelled a few more miles in this my spiritual journey, I'm able to recognise the mysterious hand of God in ways I never have before."*

"I now recognise he's been working around me I just wasn't conscious of it"

Chuck Norris went on to say, *"Amazingly I now recognise he's been there all the time working all around me. I just wasn't conscious of it."* He talks about the surprise of it all: *"I've simply had to step back and say, 'Whew!' I didn't know that God could do such awesome things nowadays, but apparently he can."* This seems to be a common theme from people of all conditions and walks of life.

Spiritual awareness is no longer the domain of the religious or the deluded

Phil Jackson is known as the doyen of basketball coaches winning 11 rings as a coach and two as a player with the *"New York Knicks."* He is convinced that the secret of bonding and coaching an elite team of any kind is the spiritual dynamic. Of the critical ingredient he says, *"Above all things it is love."* He said, *"You have to move outside yourself and think about others."* His winning philosophy is based on the firm belief that when a single player surrenders self-interest for the greater good, he manifests his fullest athletic gifts, and *"selflessness will become the soul of teamwork."* He is convinced this comes from – wait for it - the human spirit!

The secret ingredient is of course, the activating of the human spirit

When asked whether he believed there is a God, he replied, *"Well, yes of course I do."* But he qualified it with, *"However I'm not so sure we use that word in the right context. I like all those other terms. Yahweh, or prime mover or, presence that there is, or whatever... I think we have lost some of the depth of our idea of it all, we have confused what is religion and what is functional spirituality."* He is convinced that functional spirituality is the life-giving essence of all positive human enterprise.

How spirituality cleaned up a football code

Australian Rugby League seemed to be such a dark area of testosterone and ego-driven excesses that a female psychologist facilitator was brought in to tame some of the sexual excesses. Families were keeping away from what they felt were the ugly aspects of the code's culture.

Change is happening though, as more and more Pacific Islanders with their Christian spirituality are rising to the top of the code. It is not unusual to see players huddled in prayer before a game. Many felt one of the highlights of the 2016 Rio Olympics was the Fijian's rugby union victory, whose team celebrated their gold medal with ecstatic prayer and hymn singing. Joy replaced triumphalism.

We are losing sight of religion and discovering a living form of spirituality

Different people use different language to describe it but for many otherwise normal people, what in the past seemed like the domain of the religious or deluded has moved mainstream. It is presently experienced as an unlocking of the mystery behind all things and it is not just the young who are finding the key to an integrated spirituality.

Another of those surprised by his own spiritual transformation is acclaimed movie maker David Putnam, the man behind the making of award-winning movies like *"Midnight Express," "The Killing Fields"* and *"Chariots of Fire."*

The movie that cleansed the soul of its producer

He had just made the dark movie *"Midnight Express"* and came out of America jaded and exhausted. The motivation for making the movie had been largely competitive – to prove to the Americans that the English could do better. Feeling cynical about the movie Putnam was shaken by its success, so when he got back to England he contemplated giving up on the movie industry. He felt the weight of his extraordinarily expedient career, so in reaction was ready to make a totally inexpedient movie.

Chariots of Fire was not likely to be a box office success

Chariots of Fire was a most unlikely plot - about a good man who ran fast and became a missionary - not an obvious box office draw. But Putnam said, *"For me it has been a very cathartic film. It has made me feel clean again."* Making this unlikely movie in his late 30's had him totally reassess his spirituality and religious beliefs. He said, *"Having survived the 1960's and '70's I am now absolutely convinced that we are not able to live without an injection of something additional in our lives. Four years ago I couldn't have said that. But now I believe absolutely in God."*

The pattern becomes clear

Putnam acknowledged that the remarkable story of Eric Liddell was part of his new direction and although other things also figured he has no doubt that it was during the making of *"Chariots of Fire"* his belief surfaced and was crystallized.

He wonders about the apparent coincidence of finding the particular paragraph about Eric that inspired him to do the movie. He'd been reading similar articles for years without ever noticing Liddell. *"Why at that time of my life when I had enough clout to produce a film like that, should I suddenly find this inspiring book?"*

Comparing his two films Putnam said, *"In Midnight Express the emotion was crafted into it by detached professionals who cynically calculated the impact of every scene, while in Chariots of Fire the emotion came from somewhere deep within."*

Spirituality - the great personal discovery of the 21st century

In the past people tended to be too embarrassed to talk about their spiritual and religious experience. It was meant to be private and all too often created division because of its ideological content - the religious ideas that often triggered dispute.

Currently we seem to have superseded the old authoritarian mindset and are more likely to be fascinated by real-life experiences we can share with another person. Today more and more celebrities and cultural leaders acknowledge their rediscovery of faith and the inner life, particularly its capacity to turn lives around.

Mel Gibson on the road to find out

This was dramatically demonstrated at the 25th Annual American Cinematheque Awards when Robert Downey Jr. was honoured. Formerly a Hollywood hell raiser he had moved to the top of his renewed career with the *"Iron Man"* franchise. Because of his chequered past the award organisers had difficulty finding a star willing to present Downey with the prestigious award so they asked Mel Gibson, who'd fallen from grace himself.

All were surprised to hear the unknown back story.

Mel spoke in a kindly tone of the star he'd famously helped make a comeback by paying Downey Jr.'s insurance bond so he could star in 2003's *"The Singing Detective."* On making the presentation Gibson shook hands and said, *"You are my friend,"* and went on in a heartfelt manner *"When I saw you all those years ago and got all those warnings from others about you, I just thought here's a man of promise, there's nothing so much wrong with this man that a friendship and helping hand won't fix. You're a good dude with a good heart."*

Robert Downey Jr.'s response surprised those who'd been holding Mel at a distance

The surprise came during Downey Jr.'s acceptance speech. He had even kinder words for Gibson, *"When I couldn't get sober, Mel here told me not to give up hope and he helped me rediscover my faith."* He continued: *"Mel told me it didn't have to be his or anyone else's brand of faith as long as it was anchored in forgiveness. At that time because of my reputation I couldn't get a part so he cast me in the lead of a movie that was actually a project developed for him to star in."*

The celebrity audience's jaws dropped as he went further, *"He kept a roof over my head and food on the table and most importantly he said if I accepted responsibility for my wrongdoing and embraced that part of my soul that was ugly – hugging the cactus he calls it — he said that if I hugged the cactus long enough, I'd become the man I was meant to be."*

"He didn't imagine the next guy would be him. He has hugged the cactus long enough"

He continued, *"I did it all and it worked for me. All he asked in return was that someday I help the next guy in the same small way. It's reasonable to assume at the time he didn't imagine the next guy would be him or that someday would be tonight. So anyway on this special occasion I would ask that you join me, unless you are completely without sin (in which case you picked the wrong industry) in forgiving my friend his trespasses and offering him the same clean slate you have me, allowing him to continue his great and ongoing contribution to our collective art without shame. He's hugged the cactus long enough."*

The crowd in the room exploded with enthusiastic applause

It was a rare and spiritually refreshing moment in a cynical and jaded industry. Mel Gibson was not the only person who teared up as people made contact with what lay below their phony presenting selves.

Mel's movie *"Hacksaw Ridge"* subsequently released, won him much acclaim for his directing. It is based on the inspiring true story of a young American soldier who, as a committed Christian, chose to go into battle without any weapons.

Tears rise as the heart overwhelms the mind - a reminder of the spirit

Currently, a significant percentage of the population is delighted to encounter others who resonate to their spiritual experience. It has become like some kind of secret society. A delightful sense of spontaneity and intimacy is often released when connection is made.

Not that all of these people have precisely the same religious views or that there is no chance of conflict in some cases. But Catholic or Protestant, there is relief to discover what they have in common is more profound and personally more significant than that which is different. There are still however a significant number of religious people with a Level 2 consciousness who are not able to accept difference.

The discovery of fellowship and a shared experience

As those on an authentic spiritual journey openly share their common experiences they find a parallel narrative with others on a similar journey. There may be different words used but as the words become windows to inter-personal experiences, mutuality and relief blossom. More often than not they discover shared gems of hard won truth about the inner disciplines necessary to keep their ego in check and their spiritual nature focused.

What they have in common is so much more significant than that which separates them. There are now enough veterans of the journey in all walks of life who see their lives as a vocation - a joyous shared pursuit of a divine calling.

Elihu would have many friends in contemporary society

William Johnson, in his reference book on religion wrote, *"To the surprise of many, the term spirituality has become democratised. Ideals that for centuries had been viewed as virtually unobtainable are now promoted as the path to spiritual growth for everyone. In a word, the spirituality revolution that has risen during the past 30 years has democratised the pursuit of holiness."*

The new awareness of the transcendent

Sandra Schneiders in the Santa Clara lectures said, *"Spirituality has rarely enjoyed such a high profile, positive evaluation, and even economic success as it does among Americans today. In short, if religion is in trouble, spirituality is in the ascendancy and the irony of this situation evokes puzzlement and anxiety in the religious establishment, and scrutiny among theologians.*

She discerned a note of self-justification among those who'd traded

"ideological correctness and doctrinal certainties of their past for the spirituality of the present."

All of life is coming home

The late Robin Williams in the opening soliloquy of the film Patch Adams said, *"All of life is coming home - salesmen, secretaries, coalminers, beekeepers, sword swallowers, all of us, the restless hearts of the world, are trying to find a way home."* He then defined home as the dictionary defines it: *"A place of origin or goal of destination."* Of course one wonders if he himself really made it home.

He was able to play Patch Adams yet needed help to find his own way home

It is as if the whole of humanity has been on an incredible journey and is now trying to find its way home to its intended pattern of life. Home is not necessarily a geographical place; it is a spiritual place where we can come to a settled understanding of what really matters. It is a place where we know and are known deeply and share a sense of alignment with the Divine Being's unfolding purpose, which leads us to what is called a state of shalom.

Peace is not about the absence of conflict; it is about coming home

Peace or shalom, is not about the absence of conflict but about all things integrating and moving into the pattern they were originally designed for. Some believe an outcome of the move to shalom is that many of us are subconsciously moving upwards to what is called an integral consciousness.

As people reach out for spiritual frameworks from which to recognise and understand their experiences a growing number are reviewing their lives in the context of non-materialistic values.

Prayer is more common than most would expect

80% of Australians say they pray while only 70% say they believe in God. Makes you wonder who 10% of them are praying to? While it may be true that fewer than half (43%) of all Americans regularly attend religious services, 90% pray and 96% believe in God or a universal spirit.

Deborah Howell Washington, bureau chief of Newhouse News Service, recently commented on the television industry, *"The news media is finally getting it. Religion and spirituality are the most important aspects of most people's lives."* It seems as the baby boomers get older and are confronted by their own mortality, they too are becoming sensitised to the spiritual dimensions of life.

Prayer under the microscope

A BBC survey carried out by the University of Nottingham found 37% of respondents said they'd experienced help in answer to prayer. Over the past 20 years researchers have put prayer under the microscope with rigorous clinical trials. One of the earliest was the 1988 San Francisco General Hospital trial. A group was invited to pray for certain coronary heart disease patients while other patients were not prayed for. The outcome was that the prayed for group needed five times fewer antibiotics, suffered a third less pulmonary fluid build-up and recovered with fewer complications.

The most critical issue

Dr. Peter Fenwick, consultant neuro-psychiatrist from London University said, *"We found that the attitude of the person praying was the most important variable. We call it the intention to heal."*

Harvard's Herbert Benson MD said the move to believing prayer was one of the most effective tactics of emotional protection. He showed that repetitive, hopeful prayer slows a person's heart and breathing rate, lowers blood pressure and even calms brain waves, all without drugs.

Of 5,600 surveyed in America, 40% said they prayed about their health all the time and 71% prayed about specific conditions such as cancer, chronic pain etc. It seems while we're travelling comfortably we are less likely to think about prayer but the moment the rug is pulled from under our ego through a health or life crisis our spirit is more likely to rise to the Divine Being in prayer.

What does this mean?

Viktor Frankl said, *"Every form of psychotherapy is based upon an anthropological premise, or if they're not conscious of it upon an anthropological set of assumptions."* In other words, whether they are aware of it or not every branch of psychotherapy smuggles into its method of operation a working philosophy of what a human being is.

This brings into view the fundamental question: Does man have a purpose, as Frankl asserted? If he does the therapeutic task is to help each person find their purpose. It raises profound philosophic questions. If there is a purpose where did the purpose come from?

Are humans essentially spiritual beings?

Viktor Frankl wrote, *"Diagnoses and treatment methods must of necessity be related to the essential structure of the subject of the application, which is man himself."* Author of the famous book *"Man's Search for Meaning"* Frankl believes that what he called *unconscious spirituality* is the origin and root of all human consciousness.

If he is right our subconscious is becoming more conscious and our unconscious is becoming subconscious and therefore closer to consciousness.

We will start becoming aware of the spiritual dynamics at work in our own existence.

The irony is that at the very time many atheists are becoming more vocal, even more of us are being taken by surprise by the rise of these spiritual promptings. Many would say this is what a spiritually anorexic generation needs to encounter as Elihu did when he discovered, *"It is the breath of God in a man, the spirit in a man, that gives him understanding."*

Chapter 6

HOW ATHEISTS ARE BEING LEFT BEHIND

*"There is an innate element in human nature ... that can grow
and develop through impressions of truth received in the
organism like a special nourishing energy."*

Jacob Needleman (1934 -) American philosopher, author and religious scholar.

What about science? Hasn't it relegated spirituality to the dust bin of history? No!
The latest thinking in neuro- science is that every time we recognise a truth, or are
validated or touched by the transcendent, endorphins are released into the
functioning of our brains' synapses. Agatha Christie's little Belgian detective Poirot
calls them his little grey cells. Healthy spirituality can now be shown to have a
positive effect on our cognitive functioning.

One's little grey cells seem to be nurtured by a healthy spirituality

It is paradoxical that while people in the Western world are inclined to be
embarrassed and hide their private religious experience from public view, the quest
for personal spiritual insight and the hunger for transcendence quietly continue
unabated. This in spite of recent crowing in the media about the decline of church
attendance, accompanied by the tirades of the new atheists. But then popular
culture always seems to lag five to ten years behind the latest thinking of those on
the frontiers.

Human quest for the transcendent continues

There is a remarkable insatiable yearning in modern people to experience and
explore, one way or another, the spiritual nature of their humanity. It is no surprise
to find that the quest to understand comes from the same part of the human psyche.
There is an almost symbiotic tie-up between education and spirituality in Elihu's
reminder of some thousands of years ago that, *"It is the breath of God in a man that
gives understanding."*

In our materialistic culture this connection has been trivialised and smirked at by
those pseudo-sophisticates who think they know. The sense of the transcendent has
been lost in the public square particularly among politically correct opinion formers
in mass media and politics.

Yet spiritual awareness and sensitivity continue to bubble up into the consciousness of modern aware human beings

This was evidenced when, during his presidency, Barak Obama requested that Christian Pulitzer Prize winning author Marilynne Robinson make time for him to have a long and expansive conversation with her. He said he wanted to explore with her what he called, *"the world of Christian thought."* According to Time Magazine he took the journey to see her because he had been stimulated by her most recent essay collection, *"The Givenness of Things."* Their intense deeply engaged wide-ranging conversation covered faith, morality and Christian humanism.

The quest for meaning and understanding continues at the highest-level

Until recently modern Western people had been led to believe there was a giant gulf between science and spirituality. This is in fact a 50 year old myth. A recent survey of scientists in the USA found that 61% identify themselves as Christian.

Noah Efron, senior faculty member of the Graduate Program in Science Technology and Society at Bar-llan University in Israel writes, *"One cannot recount the history of modern science without acknowledging the crucial importance of Christianity."*

Nancy K. Frankenberry is John Phillips Professor of Religion at Dartmouth College and in 2015-2016 was Senior Fellow at the Martin Marty Centre for the Advanced Study of Religion at the University of Chicago. She said, *"The historical titans of the scientific revolution – Galileo, Kepler, Bacon, Pascal, and Newton – were devout Christian believers to a man. All could inter-relate their Christian faith and scientific discoveries without difficulty."*

An emerging reality for me during research for this book was that most of the noisiest atheists were found to have a back story. Their position of unbelief seemed to have more to do with a personal history that produced a level 3 brand of thinking than with clear evidence-based logic. It was more like an understandable push-back against what had felt like a suffocating threat to their identity.

Modern science is now more open to right brain inspiration

At the time of his retirement Professor Roy Web, Vice Chancellor of Griffith University Australia, was the longest serving Vice Chancellor of any University and the recipient of many awards including the Order of Australia in 2003. During his tenure as Vice Chancellor over 50 specialised research centres, institutes and units were established at the University.

Referring to emerging attitudes in academic circles toward science and faith he said, *"In the past Australian universities have, with some important exceptions, largely seen themselves as secular institutions pursuing the preservation, transmission and development of knowledge without much reliance upon or regard for, and sometimes even with hostility towards, the religious and spiritual dimensions of life."*

The moral and ethical dimensions of life are now more evident

He went on to say, *"At its most severe, the secularisation of our universities proceeded upon the assumption that the paradigms of religion and of scientific rationalism were in fundamental opposition; that sooner or later the domain of religion would be crowded out by the ever-increasing explanatory power of rationalist endeavour. I believe that we can now say that the most extreme episodes of secularism have passed. The re-emergence of emphasis on the spiritual, moral and ethical dimensions of life is evident in the broad Australian community."*

Surprising change in thinking of modern people

Popular contemporary culture is always on a journey to catch up, and the assumptions and impact of what we now call left-brain thinking by the likes of Newton and Descartes' still linger. Unfortunately, though useful, this produced a more mechanistic view of the world that laid the ground for the assumptions behind Western education and thinking.

"I think therefore I am" replaced with "I shop therefore I am"

In a post-modern world Descartes' *"I think therefore I am"* is wearing a bit thin. We now know there is so much more going on in our minds than the early giants of science could have contemplated. Neuroscience has given Descartes' followers? so much more to think about. The fantastic worlds of quantum mechanics and neuroscience have shown that the so-called established laws of physics and medical science are not as absolute as we have believed for decades.

The intuitive mind will often tell the thinking mind where to look next

Nearly all frontline scientists are discovering the importance of intuition. As Jonas Salk, the famed discoverer of the Salk anti polio vaccine said, *"The intuitive mind will often tell the thinking mind where to look next."*

We are finding the old categories of thought and feeling, belief and unbelief are not adequate to represent the emerging epistemological reality as we're experiencing it.

Respected neuro-scientist and author Antonio Damasio believes he has clear evidence to show that what he calls emotion precedes thinking. For years Gestalt therapists have shown that we usually sense things long before we think them.

We sense things before we organise them into thoughts

This of course challenges what has become known as the thought versus feeling divide. Pope Francis, who as a young man studied chemistry and worked as a technician before entering the seminary, has embraced science as a way of learning about the world, while a recent cover story in Time Magazine carried a long article on brain surgeon and one time presidential hopeful, Ben Carson. The magazine article is framed with Carson's comment, *"While many struggle to reconcile a strong faith with a science background I believe one informs the other."* He continues, *"To believe that we evolved with the complexity of this brain from a pool of promiscuous bio-chemicals during a lightning storm – now that requires a lot of faith; a lot more faith than I have."*

The old secular mind-set is becoming threadbare

The frontiers of neuro-science are showing that we are wired for the intuitive and spiritual experience. The most aware and sensitive of us are at last becoming more conscious of what has been there all along.

Mark Worthing, author and historian of science and senior researcher with Lutheran Education Australia says of the new shift, *"There is little doubt that we are undergoing a paradigm shift of such significance that a new era in the history of science and theology is being heralded. Gone are the days when it could safely be assumed that theology and science had little or nothing to do with one another."*

Professor Andrew Newberg of Thomas Jefferson Teaching Hospital has made a study of what he calls the spiritual brain and has coined a new term to explain what he is doing - neuro-theology. It seems we are made to be very at home in the process of grasping for eternal truth.

Time for change of paradigm

There is a remarkable build-up of new evidence in the sciences with quantum physics, neuro-science and astrophysics all showing the scientific community that it's time to remove the blinkers of prejudice, for those who still have them, and to welcome the new world with its exciting emerging paradigm. It is time for a change in thinking.

Those academics who have been able to get past their old mindset are starting to see there is more going on than their old paradigms were able to grasp.

"There are clearly religious implications." Stephen Hawking

The late Stephen Hawking, well known British cosmologist and a man known to push against his first wife's faith, said in a rare moment of clarity, *"The whole history of science has been the gradual realization that events do not happen in an arbitrary manner but that they reflect a certain underlying order which may or may not be divinely inspired. The odds against a universe like ours emerging out of something like a big bang are enormous... I think there are religious implications whenever you start to discuss the origins of the universe."*

A spiritual understanding of the universe

This was just the kind of thinking that started getting Communist Party intellectuals nervous before the collapse of the atheistic empire of the old USSR. They found that the brightest young scientists were, on the basis of their science, declaring that they were beginning to believe in a spiritual concept of the universe. Stalin must have turned in his grave to hear this as well as President Vladimir Putin's chastisement of the West for not protecting the heritage of Christians around the world, particularly those of the Middle East.

It's as if the universe knew we were coming

In the words of Professor Freeman Dyson, research physicist at the Advanced Institute at Princeton, *"The more I examine the universe and study details of its architecture the more evidence I find that the universe in some sense must have known we were coming."*

Noted physicist, Professor Paul Davies who is hardly an evangelist for religion said, *"A careful study suggests that the laws of the universe are remarkably felicitous for the emergence of richness and variety. In the case of living organisms their existence seems to depend on a number of fortuitous coincidences that some scientists and philosophers have hailed as nothing short of astonishing. This causal order does not follow from logical necessity; it is a unique property of the world and one for which we can rightly demand some sort of explanation."*

New and active conversation between science and religion

The situation has changed remarkably. Scientist and theologian John Polkinghorne says there is now an active conversation between science and theology. He believes it had its beginning with the publication of Ian Barbour's ground- breaking book *"Issues in Science and Religion."* Published back in 1966 its influence has been unfolding and developing ever since.

The positive change in thinking was framed by Hungarian chemist Michael Polanyi (1890-1976) whose writing helped free science from the limitations of its empiricist prison. This made it possible for the two disciplines, science and theology, to enter into a mutually respectful conversation.

Those who missed the boat

Every now and then we come across the likes of Richard Dawkins, British evolutionary biologist and writer. Often referred to as the most famous atheist in the world in his capacity as a biologist, he seems to have completely missed out on this historic dialogue. One almost feels a little sorry for him as we discover videos of him debating those who are more than his equals, like Professor John C Lennox Professor of Mathematics at the University of Oxford. It becomes embarrassingly clear in these exchanges why many of Dawkins' academic colleagues are red faced at the thinness of the philosophic underpinning of his arguments. Dr Lennox has no trouble gently blowing away Dawkins' straw men - the empty assertions that he puts up as arguments.

The whole of science depends upon the predictability of the laws of nature

Nobel Laureate in physics Richard Feynman expresses the emerging position on the remarkable order that's found in the universe when he says, *"The fact that there are patterns at all to be checked is a kind of miracle. That it is even possible to find a rule like the inverse square law of gravitation, is some sort of miracle."* He admits, *"It is not thoroughly understood at all but because of its very presence it undergirds science, it leads to the possibility of prediction - that means it tells you what you would expect to happen in an experiment you have not yet done."*

The magic of laws that can be formulated

The very fact that those laws can be mathematically formulated was for Einstein a constant source of amazement that pointed beyond the physical universe.

Allan Sandage, widely regarded as the father of modern astronomy, was the discoverer of quasars and winner of the 1991 Crafoord Prize (astronomy's equivalent of the Nobel Prize). He said *"I find it quite improbable that such order came out of chaos. There has to be some organizing principle. God to me is a mystery but is the explanation for the miracle of existence, why there is something rather than nothing."*

The very miracle of existence has caused many academics to think again

All of these thought leaders have caused other academics like Mark Worthing to say, *"There is little doubt that we are undergoing a paradigm shift of such significance that a new era in the history of science and theology is being heralded."*

There is a burgeoning of associations of scientists and theologians interested in each other's disciplines. In Australia, to name but a few: The Institute for the Study of Christianity in an Age of Science (ISCAST), The University Science Faith Network, The

Symposium on Science and Theology of the Australian Theological Forum, and The Centre for Theology Science and Culture based at Flinders University Adelaide.

The dance between science and faith becoming more harmonious

In his book *"The Dance between Science and Faith,"* research scientist Dr. Nick Hawke writes, *"As science pushes its frontiers of knowledge, it is beginning to bump up against ultimate questions and this has helped prompt a new dialogue between the disciplines."*

This quiet build-up to a renewed interest in human spirituality became public with a Time Magazine cover story headlined, *"God is making a comeback."* It reported, *"In a quiet revolution in thought and argument that hardly anyone would have foreseen only two decades ago, God is making a comeback. Most intriguingly, this is happening in the crisp intellectual circles of academic philosophers."*

Science a subset of theology

Dr. Francis Collins has been director of the National Human Genome Research Institute since 1993, one of the most prestigious jobs in science. He has led the effort to decode human DNA, along the way developing a revolutionary method of screening genes for disease. Yet according to this widely respected scientist the newfound power to *"read our own instruction book"* is no obstacle to faith in the existence of God. He converted from atheism to Christianity in his twenties after seeing how radically his patients' faith transformed their experience of suffering, and after reading several works by C.S. Lewis. Some 30 years later he stands by his convictions, positioning science, not as substitute for theology but as a subset of it.

The ex-atheist philosopher who upset his Level 3 thinking colleagues

One man who was on the fore-front of the anti-God battle was brilliant academic Antony Flew whose 1950's work *"Theology and Falsification"* became the bedrock that most later atheistic writing was built on. However in 2004, much to the horror of his former colleagues, he stated that in keeping with his lifelong commitment to go where the evidence leads he now believed in the existence of God.

In 2007 he co-authored a book with Roy Abraham Varghese, called, *"There is a God"* subtitled, *"How the world's most notorious atheist changed his mind."* Author Francis S. Collins said of this book, *"It is towering and courageous, and Flew's colleagues in the Church of fundamentalist atheism are totally scandalised."*

"I am not an atheist" - Albert Einstein

Flews spends some time in his book putting the record straight about Albert Einstein whom atheists had dishonestly distanced from any form of belief in God. He quotes Einstein, *"I am not an atheist, and I don't think I can call myself a pantheist. We are in the position of a little child entering a huge library filled with books in many languages. The child knows someone must have written those books. It does not know how. It does not understand the languages in which they are written. The child only dimly suspects a mysterious order in the arrangement of the books but doesn't know what it is. That seems to me, is the attitude of even the most intelligent human being toward God. We see the universe marvellously arranged and obeying certain laws but only dimly understand these laws. Our limited minds grasp the mysterious force that moves the constellations."*

It is true that Einstein had some difficulty in comprehending what he called a personal God, but he clearly maintained that, *"God manifests himself in the laws of the universe as a spirit vastly superior to that of man, and one in the face of which we with our modest powers must feel humble."*

"Science without religion is lame; religion without science is blind." Einstein

Einstein is only one of the many significant minds that helped produce the new era in scientific thinking along with the likes of Max Planck, Werner Heisenberg, Erwin Schroder and Paul Dirac. All have made comments in similar vein to Einstein's.

Max Planck, who first introduced our age to the revolutionary world of quantum physics said, *"There can never be any real opposition between religion and science; for one is the complement of the other."* He also said, *"Religion and natural science are fighting a joint battle in an incessant, never relaxing crusade against scepticism and against dogmatism, against unbelief and superstition - therefore on to God."*

Paul Dirac, who complemented Heisenberg and Schroder with a third formulation of quantum theory said, *"God is a mathematician of a very high order and he used advanced mathematics in constructing the universe."*

The old wives' tale about science disproving the need for spirituality has been smacked out of the park.

We can now see the remarkable results that are achieved when science and spirituality respectfully work together

Some of the clearest evidence of this comes from the work of American neuroscientist Dr. Andrew Newberg, Professor and Director of Research Marcus Institute of Integrative Health, Thomas Jefferson University, previously an Adjunct Religious Professor and a lecturer.

He has made an extensive study of brain imaging and the study of religious and spiritual experience. One of his most published experiments was his work with Franciscan nuns in which he made a study of their brains while they were deep in what he called centring prayer. The nuns, who were most co-operative, allowed the good doctor to inject small amounts of radio-active material into their bodies so he could study the parts of their brain that were either more or less active.

The brain scans showed many changes in the brains of the praying nuns but most particularly in the part of the brain that influences the sense of self. As they prayed and worshiped God they became increasingly free of attachment to their sense of self – what Freud called the ego.

Freed of preoccupation with themselves

The goal of almost all religions is to save people from selfishness and self-obsession but one's sense of self often over identifies with a particular field of interest - from sport to science, from sexuality to spirituality. One's identity once obsessed becomes captive. It was the nuns' practice of prayer and worship that enabled them to become liberated thus demonstrating the paradox of authentic spirituality. Rather than lose their sense of self in an unhealthy way that would lead to some kind of breakdown, the nuns' prayers enabled them to transcend the limitations of their sense of self.

Discovering the source of an integrating peace and joy

With the sense of self no longer intruding something else seems to blossom, that which most people spend their lives looking for - peace and joy.

A commonly experienced phenomenon that attends the condition the nuns experienced is a profound awareness of a sacred presence that integrates with the whole of life and nature. Wordsworth called it *"the divine presence that rolls through all things."*

Those who reported experiencing an ecstatic experience like that referenced by Wordsworth were 29% millennial generation – also known as Generation Y (born approximately early 1980s to early 2000s)

There is a place of yearning in the human heart for the taste of eternity

An even more fascinating statistic has shown up during the period of what has been seen as a secular tsunami. There has been a whopping 81% rise in the reporting of these ecstatic spiritual experiences since 1987.

Of course many in this generation have been searching for artificial forms of peace and transcendence in diverse shadowy places including the misnamed drug ecstasy.

Later in this book we will look at the psychology of temptation and the many apparent angels of light that promise heaven but instead hijack our spiritual yearnings and lead us to hell. It is all tied up with an invisible phenomenon called our ego needs and the kinds of promises that seduce us.

Spirituality then is definitely not on the wane

This unsolicited letter sent in to The Religious Experience Research Unit in Oxford University graphically illustrates the nature of the new spiritual phenomenon. What is more, those conducting religious experience research, say the following letter is typical of those who have had a totally unexpected encounter with the transcendent.

"The following occurred at a time when I had no feeling for religion. It was not the result of religious ecstasy or a joyous heightening of the spirit. In fact a certain event had hurt and humiliated me. I rushed to my room in a state of despair, feeling as worthless as an empty shell. From this point of utter emptiness it was as though I were caught up in another dimension."

The letter continued, *"It was as if my separate self ceased to exist, and for a fraction of time I seemed like I was part of a timeless immensity of power and joy and light. Something beyond this domain of life and death. My subjective and painful feelings vanished. The intensity of the vision faded, but it has remained as a vivid memory ever since. Years later I read of Pascal's moment of illumination and was amazed by its similarity to mine."*

It seems the experience echoed that of French mathematician, physicist, and writer Blaise Pascal more than 300 years earlier, so perhaps there is something eternal and universal for those aware souls who are ready to welcome it.

A reminder that the inspiration for this book were Elihu's words in the book of Job, *"It's the breath of God in a man, the spirit in a man that gives understanding."*

So why don't we all get it?

The Oxford survey posed this question, *"Have you ever been aware of, or influenced by, a presence or a power, whether you call it God or not, particularly one that is different from your everyday self?"*

This was one response, *"I was walking across a field, turning my head to admire the Western sky and looking at a line of pine trees appearing as black velvet against a pink backdrop, turning to duck egg blue-green overhead, as the sun set. Then it happened. It was as if a switch marked ego was suddenly switched off. Consciousness expanded to include the beautiful expanded sense of being. The previously observed 'I' was now the sunset and there was no 'I' experiencing it. At the same time – eternity was born. There was no past, no future just an eternal now... then I returned completely to normal consciousness finding myself walking across the field in time ... but now with a profound memory."*

A chance of being freed from the destructive power of self-interest

Towards the end of the seven decades-long experiment of Scientific Socialism, a fascinating meeting took place between the Soviet President Gorbachev and much loved Pope John 23. At that encounter Gorbachev, made a remarkable admission: "We communists with our materialism have had too narrow a view of the significance of religion and spirituality. I now believe it's only as man's spiritual nature comes alive, does he have any chance of being freed from what we now know as the destructive power of self-interest."

No technology can transform human selfishness

As this book unfolds we will see the remarkable shift in culture as the shared human spirit has attempted to help the humble willing to make sense of truth in life, and our place in it. Yet we will also see how the ego's arrogance and tyranny have, time and again, taken us to the brink of catastrophe showing us that our problems are basically moral ones not scientific ones.

It was greed that triggered the global financial crisis and the clutching at power that turned the Arab Spring into a holocaust. It was arrogance that started the last two World Wars and brought us the Cold War with its nuclear arsenal. Blind ego-driven selfishness devoid of compassion is clearly our main problem. No amount of uninspired science seems able to address that.

As you read this book you will see how often the arrogance of the political, religious and yes even the scientific establishment, has stood in the way of the Spirit's drawing of our human spirit to the next stage of illumination and completion.

Sadly some of us may wake up too late, much like the late great atheist, biologist and advocate for the theory of evolution Julian Huxley who said on sitting up in bed wide-eyed at the moment of his passing into eternity, *"Oh dear It's all true!"*

Oh dear. It's all true!

Chapter 7

THE UNIVERSE IS THEOLOGICAL IN NATURE

"Discoveries that are at the heart of physics are showing that the entire physical universe is permeated at every level with a mystery that is fundamentally theological in nature."

Jeffery Satinover (1947 -) American psychiatrist, , psychoanalyst, physicist and author.

Jeffery Satinover is a practising psychiatrist with a doctorate in physics and if anybody is able to grasp what is happening in the amazing new world of both neuroscience and quantum mechanics it is he. He said *"I believe the discoveries that are being made at the heart of physics will make people aware of the fact, not just aware, it will make it second nature to them (in the way materialism is now second nature to them) that the entire physical universe is permeated at every level with a mystery that is fundamentally theological in nature."*

The latest thinking includes many fields of inquiry

We have finally arrived at a time in which the different disciplines are converging to produce a new understanding of the basis of our inner life and our place in the order of things. It seems at the very time secularism and atheism are most rampant in modern culture a surprising movement is building and those at the pointy edge of scientific thinking are producing results that evoke a deep awe about the very mystery and numinous nature of life.

The mystery of life itself is more and more respected

Research scientist Christopher Koch was the protégé of Francis Crick, British molecular biologist, biophysicist and neuroscientist, a man who was less than complementary about a non-materialistic view of life. Crick must have been a little startled to hear his colleague and protégé say on the issue of human consciousness, *"Throughout my quest to understand consciousness, I never lost my sense of living in a magical universe. I do believe some deep and elemental organising principle created the universe and set it in motion for a purpose I cannot comprehend."*

A new understanding of our inner life

The new perspective is not due to any single breakthrough but is part of the remarkable impact of the convergence of many discoveries in neuro-science, psychology, psychoanalysis and biochemistry. These disciplines are beginning to influence each other by offering a deeper understanding of how human beings become fully human. These apparently disparate fields of study all relate significantly to each other and to the world.

The great convergence leading to a new awareness

Wilder Penfield (1891 – 1976) American born Canadian, has been called the father of modern neurosurgery. In his quest to understand the mind he discovered more than his own mind could easily grasp saying, *"Through my own scientific career I, like other scientists have struggled to prove that the brain accounts for the mind."*

His thinking changed after he'd performed surgery on more than a thousand epileptic patients in the course of which he encountered concrete evidence that the brain and mind are actually distinct from each other though they clearly interact.

"The brain is not the mind." Wilder Penfield

Another neuroscientist intimately involved with Penfield's work, Lee Edward Travis (1896 – 1987) was one of the founding fathers of speech-language pathology in America. He said *"Penfield would stimulate electrically the proper motor cortex of conscious patients and challenge them to keep one hand from moving when the current was applied. The patient would seize this hand with the other hand and struggle to hold it still. Thus one hand under the control of the electric current and the other hand under the control of the patient's mind fought against each other. Penfield risked the explanation that the patient had not only a physical brain that was stimulated to action but also a non-physical reality that interacted with the brain."*

Penfield believed that man's spirit was a non-physical reality

To quote once again Penfield's own summary of his findings, *"To expect the highest brain mechanism or any set of reflexes, however complicated, to carry out what the mind does, and thus perform all the functions of the mind, is quite absurd."*

Penfield's conclusion that the mind cannot be reduced to the brain and his pointing beyond to the existence of the spirit, is a belief that is shared by other leading neuroscientists, two of them Nobel prize winners.

The world's pioneering neuroscientists are in agreement

Sir Charles Sherrington (1857 – 1952) was an English neurophysiologist, histologist, bacteriologist, and a pathologist, and was described by the British Medical Journal as *"The genius who laid the foundations of our knowledge of the function of the brain and spinal cord."* Just five days before his death he said, *"For me now, the only reality is the human soul."*

Australian neuroscientist Sir John Eccles was a former student of Sir Charles. Very early on he found the evidence pointed to a non-material source for what he was seeing turn up in the science. Though conventional wisdom equated the brain to the mind, he felt there was much more to it and that he had to go where the evidence led him. Consequently he developed a revolutionary alternative theory of the mind.

An Australian neuroscientist makes a fascinating discovery

His discovery disturbed many of his colleagues even though it accurately answered the questions the evidence was asking. The materialist mindset was confronted by his elegant solution - one that that recognized the functioning and influence of the human spirit.

Sir John's theory is known as dualist-interaction: i.e. we have a spiritual or non-material mind or self which acts upon and is able to influence our material brain.

He became convinced that there must be a non-material influence some-how in parallel to the physical world and that the two interact in ways he felt he could recognise but not fully explain.

He said, *"I am constrained to believe that there is what we might call a supernatural origin of my unique self-conscious mind, or my unique selfhood or spirit."*

Another leading name in the world of neuroscience felt that materialistic science had become more like prejudice than good science. Enough scientists now believed they had the tools to find all the answers they needed in order to make sense of this study of human consciousness. The answer was clearly spiritual.

At last the human spirit was being taken seriously

Now, for the first time, we have an integral understanding or holistic grasp of the wonder of the development of the human social brain and the spirit that illuminates it.

Here we begin the fascinating journey of the integration of the spirit with the human personality or soul. The spirit's deep intention is for love and truth yet there is an inevitable filtering and frequent distortion of these exquisite and unique human existential yearnings.

The foundations of the social brain are spiritual: It is why love and truth matter

It has become clear that the foundations of the social brain are shaped when an individual's emotional style is being established. The material make-up of the adult human brain is fascinating. It weighs 1.47 kilos and has the texture of firmly set jelly. It contains a hundred billion neurons, those tiny electrical cells that send signals to one another. We are born with nearly as many neurons as we'll ever have but as we mature we make new connections. However it is the shared meanings, when they give expression to the human spirit, that will build social cohesion and eventually a shared culture.

How a loving heart releases our spirit into our developing mind

In infancy thousands of new connections are made every minute. We now know that being lovingly held is the greatest spur to an infant's development, even more so than breastfeeding. In a mother's arms where the baby feels safe and warm, muscles relax and breathing can deepen as tensions are dispersed by gentle stroking or calm rocking. It is Erik Erikson the social scientist who believes that sense of security lays the foundation in the personality for trust. This is also the birth-place of hope and spiritual intelligence. It is fundamentally produced by self-giving love. Theologians of course believe it is an expression of our being made in the image of God

The remarkable synchronous heart and the intention to communicate

The baby's heart rate has been found to synchronise with the parent's heart rate. If the mother is in a relaxed, hopeful and coherent state so will be the baby. In effect the mother's autonomic nervous system communicates with the baby's nervous system, soothing it through touch.

As the baby looks at its mother's or father's face and reads their dilated pupils the sympathetic nervous system of parent and child is subconsciously aroused. The reward centre in the mother's or father's brain is activated and the baby's own nervous system reacts similarly, experiencing joy. The baby's nervous system becomes pleasurably aroused and its heart rate goes up as its will to engage grows. Even though it can't yet think in words its harmonious sense of attachment produces smiles and baby noises that show the blossoming intention to communicate.

The implications of growing spiritually-based attachment and connections

These processes trigger a biochemical response. First is what is called a pleasure neuropeptide called beta-endorphin which is released into the circulation, and specifically into what is called the orbital-frontal region of the brain. This process is known to help neurons grow in number and effectiveness, regulating glucose and insulin (ref. Schore). What is released in the process is a natural opioid which makes the baby feel good. At the same time another neurotransmitter called dopamine is released from the brain stem making its way to the prefrontal cortex, which helps new tissue to grow in the all-important prefrontal brain. It is this part of the brain that helps manage our inclination to impulsiveness and enables us to empathise.

Growing responsive people who are at peace with themselves

It all sounds very technical but it can be demonstrated that the mother's and the family's deep attachment and love, give space for the baby's unique spirit to surface and integrate. This grows the baby's capacity to be a happy, loving and responsive individual. As Carrington the famous clinician said in his book *Psychology Religion and Human Need*, "*Agape love is born into us by being loved that way.*"

Science can now demonstrate that if infants are to develop spiritually, they need unconditional love as a fundamental part of their nourishment. If any of us are to grow into the healthy and whole spiritual beings we are capable of becoming, we need unconditional love early in life, or failing that, later on a kind of spiritual conversion to lift us up from our defensive shield. It is also clear that human beings never grow out of the need for unconditional love be it from God or from others.

We never grow out of our need for unconditional love

Viktor Frankl believed that the human spirit lies deeply in our unconscious, and gains permission to surface when being loved and celebrated by significant others in our infancy. This it seems, is the remarkable place where body, soul and spirit become healthily integrated and the foundations of our personhood are laid down.

We now know why we need the agape kind of love for our healthy growth

We now know that lots of early positive and loving experiences produce a chemistry in our brain that facilitates growth of the pre-frontal cortex, which produces social and emotional intelligence. Unconditional love also develops more neural connections hence a more richly networked brain and central nervous system. These neural connections lay the foundation for all our higher intelligences. These are the developmental functions that lay the foundation for our becoming spiritually intelligent and emotionally integrated individuals.

At last we begin to see the complex tie up between body, soul and spirit and how they all feed into our experience of life: And why when actualised in a balanced way they are likely to manifest a purposeful sense of inner direction. Here we see how we were meant to have foundations laid that would lead us to our life's completion - our telos.

The most complex creation in the universe, the human personality

To achieve its rightful place in the shaping of a human person the brain needs to be seen as much more than a material phenomenon.

The human brain is thought to be the most complicated creation in the universe. At birth, unlike the rest of our body, our brain and central nervous system has all the neurons it needs. Our neurons may need the nourishment of new experiences to form the connecting synapses but unlike the rest of our body, we don't need to grow any more. Some believe it could well be the reason we have a lifelong internal sense of a non-ageing self. Ever asked how old you feel?

The brain is the only organ in the body that does not replace its cells

Unlike your brain, if you live to be 75 years of age, most of your body will be younger than you are. The cells lining your gut for example, are replaced every five days. The outer layer of your skin is replaced every two weeks; you get a new set of red blood cells every four months. In fact over time, your whole body gets a regular refit. The average age of bone cells is 10 years, muscle cells 15 years, the fat cells about 9 point 5 years. Your heart cells are six years younger than you, however if you've lived beyond 50, about half of the cells in your heart have been replaced.

But the spirit's engagement with the brain is unique

It is all very different with your brain. With the exception of the cerebellum and hippocampus your brain will stay with you through most of your life.

The essential feature of your brain's development is the neuronal connections, there to determine patterns of meaning. If you have been loved unconditionally or have some kind of spiritual rebirth, the spirit can dawn and be more active in your consciousness.

If you have become attuned to the spirit's promptings in your awareness you can discover a faith walk that will help you recognise your unique path; the path that will lead you to your telos - your spiritual completion.

However our neurotic self can lead us on a journey to delusion

Sadly the defensive pseudo self with great accuracy diverts us from the actualising of our highest self by leading us to attempt to meet valid needs in invalid ways. It gives new meaning to the words, *"As a man thinks in his heart so he becomes."* Or it may be why some say, *"What we are is God's gift to us but what we make of ourselves is our gift to him and the world around us."*

How do neuronal connections get made?

How do we proceed in the direction of our completion? How do we think and act in order for our neurons to be connected up so as to work more effectively in enabling greater spiritual integration? With more connections our spirit is able to use more areas of the brain to engage meaningfully and creatively with life and reality.

Spiritual integration and how it works

The Apostle Paul explained how it works in the book of Philippians 4:8-9, *"My brothers fill your mind with those things that are good, and that deserve praise, things are true, noble, right, lovely and honourable, and the God who gives us peace will be with you."*

If we grow up in an atmosphere of love, joy, peace, long-suffering, patience, kindness, goodness, faithfulness, gentleness and self-control, the very things the Bible calls the *"fruit of the spirit"* (Galatians 5:22-23),we will grow up as more whole and spiritually integrated individuals. Right here we catch a glimpse of the neurology of the spiritual life. This is the place the body and soul interact and overlap.

The Apostle Paul taught about the fruit of the spirit in the spiritual exercise of the mind that leads to peace and wholeness. He also taught about the double minded man, the Gollum of *"Lord of the Rings"* fame, that dwells in all of us. It's as if there are two dogs inside us continually fighting - a black depressive one and a white spiritual one. The dog that wins the fight is the one we feed the most. Which of course is quite problematic for a generation that has been labelled as spiritually anorexic.

The neurology of a dysfunctional soul

Chapter 8

THE GREAT PARADOX OF MODERN SPIRITUALITY

"What lies behind us and what lies before us are tiny matters compared to what lies within us."

Ralph Waldo Emerson (1803 – 1882) American essayist, lecturer philosopher and poet who led the mid 19th century transcendentalist movement.

In Great Britain, where the voice of the atheistic intelligentsia is dominant, the upper middle-class seem to feel they have outgrown their quaint old Church of England. Secularism in the media is strident and church attendance is thought to be in steep decline, so there was almost universal surprise when the research project *"Soul of Britain,"* found that over 76 per cent of people in the United Kingdom admit to having had a significant religious or spiritual experience. David Hay and Kate Hunt wrote about this research, *"If one looks at the figures on spiritual experience, they could well suggest that we are in the midst of an explosive spiritual upsurge."*

An explosive spiritual upsurge?

David Tacey, Associate Professor and reader in arts at Latrobe University Melbourne, is the author of five books on spirituality and culture and I interviewed him a number of times on my national talk-show *"The Conversation of the Nation."* In his book *"The Spirituality Revolution"* he suggests that the current hunger for spirituality is a sign of a new phase in the spiritual development of the Western World. He argues for a bridge between the old and the new to help us find meaning and significance as we attempt to chart the course of this new world with its as yet unimagined challenges and opportunities.

The need for a bridge between the old and new

Andrew Greeley (1928 – 1013): A Catholic priest, sociologist, journalist and novelist, was yet another academic who tried to build the bridge between the old and new in his attempt to probe the meaning of spiritual experience. In his book *"Ecstasy: A Way of Knowing"* the research he did with William McCreadie barrister and Teaching Fellow, shows quite clearly that profound and occasional mystical experiences are now quite common in Western society: *"The evidence suggests there are in fact millions of people in our society who have such spiritual experiences with some frequency."*

Spirituality is alive and well and living in the suburbs

In the past people who studied these experiences we now call states of heightened consciousness, tended to see them as transient schizoid or psychotic episodes. There is now evidence that these experiences are profoundly normal and human, that it is another way of knowing rather than a distortion of feeling. McCreadie says, *"If it is anything it is a heightened interlude in which the cognitive faculties of the person become sharper; they somehow know some things that they didn't know before. This is because they sense they are freed at least for a moment from their ego defences and its distortions."*

A real and permanent new way of knowing

Greeley asserts that many who have this spiritual experience and happen to read psychological and psychiatric literature become impatient with the insensitivity of the writers who they say, *"really haven't been listening."* This is because above all else, they have experienced a sharpening of their cognitive faculties. Their new capacity to see and know clearly is at the core of a rich and renewing spiritual experience.

A new spiritual awareness in the suburbs

Abraham Maslow, the late great student of human motivation, wrote that almost every one he studied had a similar peak experience of an intense feeling of unity with the universe, of their own place within it. According to Maslow, rather than feel fragmented or disorientated, these people then felt an incredible sense of wholeness, integration and clarity. There is growing evidence to suggest that this spiritual peak experience or mystical union is emerging as a common phenomenon. In fact Greely says that more than half of Americans report having had a profound experience that they label *"a union with a powerful spiritual force that draws me out of myself."* More than a fifth report these experiences as being frequent, though until now most have been too embarrassed to talk about them because the prevailing secular culture has not given permission for this level of consciousness to be comfortably disclosed.

The emergence of everyday mysticism in half the population

Maslow said, *"I don't equate this everyday mysticism with haunted houses, ouija boards, astrology, witchcraft, Druidism or any other New Age fad or anything like it. What stands out amongst these everyday mystical experiences is the noetic quality -*

the everyday suburban mystic reporting an overwhelming experience of spiritual understanding that makes them a better person."

Maslow's research indicated those who have peak experiences report seeing the unity of the universe and their own integration with it. William James working on these mystical experiences said they produce *"Insight into the depths of truth unplumbed by the discursive intellect. They are a source of wisdom that illuminates, they are revelations that usually have significance and importance for all, and as a rule they carry with them a curious sense of authority for all time."*

The delusion that science will lead us to a happy future has exploded

Andrew Greeley is amazed at how human consciousness has changed since his time in the academic world. *"When I was a graduate student in the sixties the serene confidence we had in the explanatory power of science would not have been questioned, I think, by either my fellow students, or by my teachers. Within a decade, however, came the beginning of the dramatic change. We were conscious even within the scientific enterprise itself that every answer generates new, more complex and difficult questions. But we also understand now that science cannot explain everything. Particularly the great mysteries: Why anything exists at all, and why there is the titanic struggle between good and evil in the universe, the human race, and in each of us. These are mysteries that can never be explained away."*

Coming to terms with the mysteries that cannot be explained away

As this generation sees man's impact on his environment, the global economic crisis, the water crisis and the disappearance of so many animal species it is clear that these mysteries can never be resolved by science. In October 2010 it was revealed that one out of every five of the world's vertebrates are threatened with extinction and that in the same month 600,000 names were cut from the world's plant inventory - gone forever! Our frail biosphere is in deep trouble. It is more than an intellectual and scientific problem we have. To all who are not morally blind it is obvious that something is terribly out of kilter and it is right there in front of us every night on television's evening news.

There has got to be a change of the inner world to save the outer world

We have been to the moon and back a number of times and worn out a couple of space shuttles taking multiple trips to outer space. We have created high-tech telescopes to enable us to look ever deeper into the cosmos, and have sent high-tech space probes further into the universe than ever before.

We have even experienced what astronomer Carl Sagan (designated by National Geographic as the most famous US scientist of the 1980's and 1990's) called the blue spot phenomenon which happens when we have gone so far into space that on looking back with high powered lenses the earth is little more than a blue dot, smaller than a pixel on a computer screen. Space exploration has shown us the uniqueness of life as we know it here on earth; it has also shown that there is nowhere else to go in our search for life in the foreseeable future.

Carl Sagan's blue spot phenomenon shows us our planet is unique in the galaxy

This is it folks! Yet we are depleting all the resources that make this unique life sustainable and we are confronted with questions about unsustainable growth. The global population is exploding while developing countries are asking for just a little of what the developed countries have.

Mounting evidence suggests that our ability to live together in peace is the biggest scientific, sociological, and spiritual question not of the next millennium, not of the next century, but of the next 25 years.

We have less than 25 years before it's all too late

While technological breakthroughs of the past 30 years have been important, of greater significance if we are to have a future is the human race's interior discoveries; one only has to look at the explosion of social sciences, particularly since the end of the Second World War. There's been the collapse of the Iron Curtain, the rise of the conservation movement and the impact of the women's movement. What brought about the collapse of the apartheid regime in Africa, the opening up of China and the coming of peace in Northern Ireland, however frail? None of these movements has been perfect but they have shown that the collective rise of a shared spirit can and will shift history.

It is a shift that takes us to a higher level of human consciousness

On looking at changes in human culture it is good to ask what is actually developing? We see the quality and quantity of connections between people in the form of shared meanings, experiences and agreements, relationships and groups of relationships, all of which constitute the organisms of a cultural revolution.

Through the Internet and Facebook I can now have thousands of connections around the world. While there is still no complete consensus as to what is wrong and what needs to be done this could still be the highest level of convergent thinking ever seen.

We have become aware of new intelligences - emotional, social and now spiritual. How did it happen?

In the book of Job the remarkable young man Elihu demonstrates that there have always been those who see from a broader, eternal and more intuitive perspective. Today more and more ordinary people are thinking like Elihu, increasingly frustrated and mistrustful of the media and political systems that seem to be mostly about the clashing of large egos and the manipulation of the appearance of things. They are frustrated with attempts by politicians to undermine the dignity and influence of their opposition rather than lead. Legal institutions too, seem to be more about winning than truth, justice and mercy.

Yearning for a new way of thinking

Bookshop shelves are bending under the weight of books written for people yearning to pursue a more spiritual frame of thinking. While many of them are New Age and many are *off with the pixies*, a greater percentage than ever are finding a strange prompting somewhere deep inside.

Australian social researcher Hugh Mackay once said to me, *"Most political leaders don't grasp the profound sociological reality that one third of the Australian population is spiritually sensitive and deeply cares about the future of their children and the direction the country is travelling in. They are willing to forego immediate comfort and pleasure for the sake of higher aspirations and they hate it when politicians try to buy their vote."*

He warned, *"It is also true that there's another third of the population that tends to be unresponsive, lacking discernment, and still another third that is positioned between those who are spiritually sensitive and those who are not so discerning; they swing either way depending on the current cultural climate."*

His conclusion? To create a positive future the secret is to recruit the third that cares with good clear policies that make obvious the connection between the sacrifices to be made and the social gains to be had. They then become confident in where they stand and where they're going, and will begin to influence those in the middle ground, gradually shaping the dominant position.

The economics of happiness

We now have the economics of happiness. We are told that a new fridge will give us happiness for two weeks and a new car for maybe two months. More and more research is showing though that love relationships and altruistic purpose, not possessions, matter most in our search for joy. Professor George Vaillant, psychiatrist and well known researcher on happiness said, *"Relationships are the secret if you want to live to a happy old age really enjoying your life. A good life is all about love, creativity, compassion and forgiveness, things that bring positive emotions to the fore and recognize the spiritual side of life. You will do a lot better emotionally going to a positive church than reading Richard Dawkins' book on atheism."*

A new consciousness is dawning with things seeming to get better and worse at the same time, but we are not so inclined to trust the future to others any more, particularly old style politicians.

"Every problem remaining in the world is derived from a poverty of consciousness." Steve McIntosh

You can no longer fool most of the people most of the time because more of us are sensing something deep within our heart. We have a desire to become complete and to find our place in helping our world complete its beautiful potential. We sense there is a tie-up between the two.

More of us than ever want to grow up spiritually and now care more for truth than our own personal comfort. The neurotic part of our sense of self wants safety equilibrium and control, whereas the spirit at the core of our soul knows its destiny is to positively shape the human future in a way that harmonises with the created order. So here we stand at the cross-roads of history: Our past may have shaped our sense of self but deep within our spirit there is a yearning that calls us to transcend the limitations of that self.

Our existential dilemma?

The machinery of the self that is continually defending its validity is in a process that inhibits our capacity for growth. It thwarts the kind of growth through hope that would focus our love and work to build an integrated faith imagination. Our spirit wants to lead us beyond this obsessive inner dilemma that exists below our consciousness. All the great teachers have recognised that getting beyond ourselves is our greatest spiritual challenge.

The good news: biography does not have to be destiny

Regardless of what our history has told us, the hope that rises from our spirit waits to lead us to the positive future that beckons.

Chapter 9

THE TRUTH WE KEEP QUIET ABOUT

"It seemed to be a necessary ritual that he should prepare himself for sleep by meditating under the solemnity of the night sky... a mysterious transaction between the infinity of the soul and the infinity of the universe."

Victor Hugo (1802 – 1885) French novelist, poet, playwright, dramatist, essayist and Statesman

We don't always feel comfortable talking about the things that matter most to us - things that move us to tears of joy or that evoke great grief and sadness. In particular, we Western people fear being swamped by our interior world so have tended to keep our deep beliefs and most profound feelings to ourselves.

A great discovery is taking place: the universality of human spirituality

All over the world, however, sensitive and aware people are discovering a great anchoring factor in the subjective rollercoaster of their lives. It is a renewed sense of the reality of the spiritual, the source of consciousness, and an awareness of this more hopeful dimension to life.

This awareness has dawned on us slowly because publicly it has been the atheists, cynics and sceptics who appear to be most convinced of themselves. They make the most noise and get the lion's share of media coverage yet any survey will show what a small percentage of the general population they represent.

As we move further into the 21st century a remarkable change is underway

An accumulation of scientific evidence shows that those with a functioning faith and active spiritual life appear best adapted to deal with the transition to the future.

After researching the connection between health and faith social scientist Tom Knox not only started going to church himself, but said in an article for London's Daily Mail that his research indicates it is in fact the atheists who are behaving irrationally. He finished his article by addressing the atheists, *"Sneer at faith all you like. Just don't for one minute think that science is on your side."*

Who owns the stage?

As we return to the book of Job we see young Elihu trying once again to process what is going on around him (Job 32:6-8). He waits silently while the older more opinionated people in the group speak first but listening to them, he feels distinctly uncomfortable. There is pressure on his sense of integrity and it is increasingly clear to him that he is in a very different place from those who seem to feel they own the stage.

He can remain silent no longer

When Elihu finally speaks it is because he's had enough of their empty clichés masquerading as insight. He can stay silent no longer and blurts out, *"It's clear that it's not only the grey ones that are wise. You've shown by your lack of wisdom you have run out of words that illuminate."*

Outwardly silent, he has been boiling deep inside as his spirit protested, *"These people seem to be clueless. They are living in a parallel universe. There is nothing they are saying that I recognise in my moral universe. They are not representing my experience of life and reality; they are off the planet!"* (paraphrase of Job 32:9-12)

It seems those who have the loudest voices have the greatest influence

Currently we have such a divergence of opinion and world view that it seems those who speak the loudest and with greatest confidence must be right. But what of those who like Elihu are silently watching the argument? They may not own the stage but their integrity tells them there is more to it all.

The distance between what noisily confident so-called opinion leaders believe and what silent observers sense to be true can create despair within the latter and an inclination to withdraw.

But where is Elihu coming from? In Job 32: 8 he says, *"It is the spirit in a man, the breath of God in a man that gives understanding."* The eyes never see; it is the mind and heart behind the eye that makes sense of what passes before the eyeballs.

Rip Van Winkle slept through the revolution as have many academics

There has been a revolution in consciousness but some older middle class academics who are blind to a new way of seeing are a bit like Rip Van Winkle who slept through the revolution. They are the product of their own secular patterns of thinking and their traditional paradigm seems to have them fear opening to the part of who they are that could register the transcendent. Lacking the sensitivity that would lead them to the source of spiritual illumination they seem more comfortable in trusting what they believe is reason alone.

How reasonable are we really? Where do our insights come from?

Some of these older intellectuals inherited a legacy from previous generations of philosophers and scientific thinkers whose goal was to be rid of what was often rightly regarded as a superstitious bias. Much of medieval religion was tainted with an authoritarian world view. A dogmatic grey cloud tended to clutter the mind, confusing the promptings of the spirit with idle emotion and inhibiting free speech.

This movement was called the Enlightenment and its followers trusted reason and the scientific method alone. Understandably, leading thinkers wanted to remove what they called emotion from the process of scientific enquiry.

Their error was to think emotion and spirituality could be eliminated by reason

Many were inclined to throw the baby out with the bathwater. They overlooked the spiritual source of inspiration for the many men of faith who had led the way into the scientific era. The list is a virtual who's who of those who helped lay the foundations for the modern scientific experiment and includes Pascal, Newton, Bacon, Descartes, Bayle, Kepler, Pasteur and Fleming, to name but a few. Almost all of these men would be bewildered by the so-called battle between science and God. Why? Because delightfully, they thought they were studying the very thoughts of God as revealed in his creation.

Immanuel Kant (1724 – 1804), is one of the most significant modern philosophers. He came from a profoundly committed Christian home, and was deeply influenced in his intellectual development by his mother's dictum, *"Two things fill the mind with ever new and increasing admiration and awe, the more often and steadily we reflect upon them the better: the starry heavens above us and the moral law within us."*

So what has this new awareness of spirituality got to do with choice thinking and knowing?

The paradox of choice and understanding

It is the modern neurologist who reveals where our thinking really comes from. We are now in the post-modern and trans-modern age with a return to centre stage of intuition and the truth it can bring. Once again meta- physics and issues of personal existence and subjective reality are centre stage.

Actor Jude Law captured the inner struggle of the millennials when he said, *"I was a great champion of the human spirit and I lost that for a time. However I feel like I have regained a bit of that in the last few years."* (Carole Cadwalladr interview in The Guardian July 2011)

Claims for science by many spokesmen and pronouncements of those who assert they are coming from a more rational framework - along with the darkness that haunts our daily headlines - would shake the most hopeful and confident.

Jude Law disclosed in the interview above, *"There was a period of my life in which I had a very low opinion of people in general."* Of course if spirituality is based on youthful idealism alone it inevitably leads to despair. Since the authentic voice of the spirit is the source of hope, loss of contact with the spirit inevitably leads to a dark place.

Science itself needs to be illuminated by hope-filled imagination

Most recently science has been a source of confusion and despair. It needs to be illuminated because rather than an anchoring source of hope and confidence, it has been turned on its head. The old certainties have been replaced by evermore bewildering questions.

The so-called law of gravity is now 20 different theories of gravity

The latest discoveries are in the exciting and brave new world of quantum physics. Black holes and neuroscience have forced the boffins to review many of their articles of faith because so many scientific conventions have been challenged and overturned by much that is essentially counter-intuitive. This has all been underway since before the collapse of so-called scientific socialism – communism. It actually became a cause of deep concern among the thought leaders in the old Soviet system.

There was a time that communist philosophers were convinced that the future was theirs because they believed their whole system was based on science. However towards the end of the communist era many of their best and brightest young scientists and philosophers were reconsidering the foundation of Marxism and were becoming drawn to a spiritual explanation of the universe.

The return of science fiction to modern science, quantum physics and neuroscience

Science fiction has returned like a prodigal from the occult themes it had wandered into because it simply could not keep up with the most recent plethora of specialist journals. Each scientific breakthrough would open up another ten areas of study.

Authors and script-writers have returned to modern science because the new scientific fields are so unworldly they seem almost unbelievable - entities that can be in two places at the same time, others that seem to change while you are observing them and entities that can have 11 different dimensions, to name just a few.

All scientifically viable options

The paradigm to do with our brain and what is happening while we sleep means our understanding of dreams has shifted as has our understanding of the human will and so-called free choice. In fact one series of neuro-scientific discoveries has shown that while many subconscious forces may be at work influencing our so-called free will, we have in fact been shown to have a *"free won't."* In other words while there may be many forces at work influencing our apparent will, it can now be shown that in the face of all kinds of pressure and temptation we human beings have the remarkable capacity to say no!

As we have shown, the brain is not the mind. There is much non-material evidence to show the role of the human spirit in our existence. For example the latest brain science shows us that even if we lose a large part of our brain, it can in time repair itself. The sense of self the real us, will eventually remerge. Nothing has to be the final story.

The unique human sense of meaning and cohesion we yearn for

Surprisingly, modern neurological research is revealing that when we begin to think, something other than reason comes first. World acclaimed neuroscientist Antonio Damasio (born 1944) calls this newly discovered dynamic *emotion*. It is not what we would commonly call feeling but a factor at work in our neurons that brings a remarkable - some have even said miraculous - sense of meaning and cohesion to our experience of life.

Coming to terms with our inclinations and predispositions

Damasio shows subconscious and unconscious forces are at work directing our thoughts, either fragmenting or bringing cohesion, but nonetheless bubbling up all the time. These invisible dynamics direct what we previously believed were our rational choices, and this can be shown to be true even of those of us who mistakenly think we are completely rational.

Time to review what is really happening when we make a choice

A recent television documentary about brain and choice showed scientists were actually able to monitor a man's mental processes as he seemed to make his choices.

They gave the subject a button to press when he was at the point of making a decision, then watching on a TV monitor they were able to read his brain processes and know six seconds before a decision was made exactly what the decision would be. They knew this before the man himself knew it, even though he was making the so-called rational decision. Amazing, because impulses from the brain travel at 170 miles an hour which is why you feel it so quickly when you kick your toe - but so much for rational choice!

Yet when they asked the man to choose but just before he chose to change his mind, there was no capacity to anticipate his saying no. It did not show up on any brain scan hence their belief in what they are calling a *"free won't."*

Spiritual intelligence, hope, and clarity of choice as derived from the human spirit

In working therapeutically with people I have become fascinated by great swings from love to hate. The swing from hope to despair can put a person's sense of wellbeing so at risk that suicidal ideation becomes a normal response to their reality. For this reason I have become much more interested in the clear voice of sanity that rises from the inner spirit with its sharp contrast to the dark forebodings that issue from an emotion-based script in which shadowy irrational forces can find a home. The archaic feelings in our life script shaped by emotional injury and inherited prejudice continually distort thoughts and attitudes and regularly discolour our life responses. These maladaptive distortions regularly frame the so-called choices we make.

Neurotic responses most easily predicted

Many of us become troubled by what we feel is our failing memory. That we are able to think and remember at all is amazing since our memory is a simple matter of our neurons firing off together when faced with a certain experience, then firing off again when something recalls the experience.

In an attempt to explain the dynamic that enables neurons to fire together so that we recognise and give meaning to our experience, the word emotion is now used. Little wonder that in an outburst of honest incredulity about the process, Baroness Susan Greenfield CBE FRCP (Born 1950) used the word miraculous. Baroness Greenfield is described as UK's foremost female scientist, a writer, broadcaster, speaker and CEO of biotech company Neuro Bio that she founded in 2013.

The miracle of what makes us human - the distinctive of human consciousness

This word emotion is used to show that something other than reason is operating and it precedes rational thought. Used technically by neuroscientists the word emotion is misleading because they say explicitly it is not *feeling* they are talking about.

The question arises: What is this miracle that precedes thinking?

"It is the spirit in a man, the breath of God, that gives him understanding."

Spiritually inspired intuition might be closer to the mark. The profound dynamic called spiritual intelligence increasingly surfaces amongst those studying inspired leadership. Albert Einstein was reaching for this when he said, *"Imagination is more important than knowledge. For knowledge is limited to all we know and understand, while imagination embraces the entire world, and all there ever will be to know and understand."* He recognized the spirit's leap of imagination that creates a functional and healthy future.

There is of course, a right place for reason. Reason needs to come along later and further test the leap of intuition, implementing and managing the faith imagination into time-space reality.

What is human consciousness? We know the brain is not the mind

In his most recent book *"Self Comes to Mind"* Antonio Damasio identifies the *"self"*,the inspired self not the brain in isolation, as the integrating force that helps us relate to and make sense of external reality and life. It could almost be said that this self organised by the left hemisphere uses the brain to help achieve its purposes.

The mind and ego use the brain in construction of memory

The way the left hemisphere shapes a sense of self out of our memories is an amazing phenomenon. The memories that shape the sense of self are distributed throughout the brain so if one part of an experience is lost many others will remain.

The benefit of this distributed memory storage system is that it makes long-term memory more or less indestructible. Memories are where we keep the stories we tell ourselves about ourselves; they are the source of a sense of identity. It is the particular task of our left hemisphere to round up these memories and construct our sense of self.

If memory is eradicated

If memories were held in a single area, damage to that place, for example a head injury, might eradicate the memory completely. It seems brain trauma and degeneration may whittle away at memories but almost never destroy them entirely. We may forget a person's name but not the memory of their face or perhaps the residue of some forgotten shared emotion.

The marvel of memories even when they stumble and falter

The marvel that so amazed Baroness Susan Greenfield is that memories are formed by a group of neurons firing together and if they fire together often they become permanently sensitised to each other - if one fires the others will also. But how is meaning formed?

It is not just the data but the recognition of the meaning of the experience that is the miracle. Remember the words of Elihu, *"It is the breath of God in a man, the spirit in a man that gives him understanding."*

On recalling a meaningful experience, in essence we recreate it by reactivating the neural patterns that were generated during the meaning, perceiving process of the original experience. This pattern of meaning has been encoded in our memory and we humans are uniquely meaning-shaping and discovering beings.

This means the mechanism we call the brain can have parts of it removed or damaged yet after recovery have the spiritually unique personality with its memories return. A study on the subject was recently published in the respected *"International Neuroscience Journal - Cerebral Cortex."*

The remarkable remodelling brain

Neuroscientist Dr. Tracy Dixon of the Menzies Research Institute said, *"Our data suggests that the cerebral cortex that is the brain's outer layer of grey matter surrounding the cerebrum, is capable of significant remodelling particularly following injury. The accumulated evidence now clearly indicates that damage to the adult brain causes some of the remaining healthy parts of the brain to remodel themselves in an effort to adapt."*

As wonderful as all this is, we now know that while the brain may be able to repair itself more often than not it is a misshapen self or ill-formed sense of self or ego that is likely to create its own distorted memories.

The misshapen ego

More than the physiological brain itself, it is the part of us we call the ego that simply has to look good and be right! When the ego uses the meaning-shaping facility to meet esteem needs without reference to the spirit emotional difficulties arise. Rather than use and respect the frail and beautiful brain-mind configuration to pursue truth, the brain is used as a kind of reality creation machine in both waking and dreaming states to serve the needs of the ego.

In recent times we have the phenomenon of so-called recovered memories

Many people reported in the media and some known to me, have recovered memories that never actually happened. The process was reported by Professor Richard J. McNally of the Department of Psychology, Harvard University, Cambridge, Massachusetts this way, *"The controversy over the validity of repressed and recovered memories of childhood sexual abuse (CSA) has been extraordinarily bitter. Yet data on cognitive functioning in people reporting repressed and recovered memories of trauma have been strikingly scarce."* This has had catastrophic consequences for innocent family members who were accused and vilified, often resulting in permanently divided families.

We now know that even when all is well we grasp only a tiny amount of what is going on so if we have experienced abuse as an infant it may be beyond our recall. If it really happened it is likely that the abuse interfered with the flow of glucose to the frontal cortex. This in turn will have given us a misshapen ego and an inability to recognise one's own truth which makes us vulnerable to suggestion.

At the best of times our own uninspired sense of self or ego, has been impacted by a large range of emotional deficits and bruises. This along with the normal limits of our awareness makes it almost impossible to see the external world as it is.

A profound spiritual link

Why is hope such a profound spiritual link? Weighing in around 1.3 kg the human brain is an accumulation of billions of neurons interconnected by trillions of synapses. Placed side by side these nerve tracts would stretch an amazing 3.6 million miles. Every second eleven million sensations crackle along these pathways in this highly complex organism.

Every waking moment the brain is confronted with an alarming array of millions of images, sounds and smells which it rigorously filters down until it is left with what seems to be a manageable list of about 40.

The result: 40 sensations per second make up what we perceive as reality

Our brain only delivers a fraction of what exists but it nevertheless manages to supply us with a seamless impression of reality. If not inspired, reality is really a construction made from sensory impressions combined with individually stored memories and emotional assessments.

In the space of just a few fractions of a second this construction passes through various areas of the brain. The process is the same for all of us whether we are making a purchasing choice or making a judgment about another person.

In the limbic system it all converges with the past to produce current perceptions

First optical stimuli arrive in the limbic system and are compared with knowledge and impressions already stored. Hostile feelings will be triggered if we have suffered similar negative experiences in the past while similar positive experiences will activate our reward systems.

Knowledge and feelings then converge in the prefrontal cortex and only now become our conscious perception. Our reality emerges at the end of this process. For this reason lack of forgiveness, unresolved love affairs and bruised need-satisfying attachments all feed into our distorted experience of reality.

Without our spirit attuned to the divine Spirit there is little chance of getting in touch with an undistorted external reality

The will, the inclination to push on against difficulty and the source of sane commitment (activities of the spirit), play an important role in the movement toward healing damage of the past and rising toward the high calling of who we are meant to be.

Perhaps Elihu has something to teach those of us trying to get to healing and fulfilment in the 21st century when he says, *"That which I see not, teach thou me."*

A leading scientist says, "I have seen the human spirit."

Wilder Penfield, the famous Canadian neurosurgeon, who was one of the first to map the brain, was called the physician of the twentieth century. He said, *"I'm here to tell you that the scientist has seen the human spirit. If you were to join all the computers in the world they could still not begin to reproduce what the human personality manages to know and achieve."*

There is a remarkable convergence of a significant number of sciences all throwing light on the human personality (when it is sane), and the unique spiritual life source that orders and gives meaning to it.

What is the relationship between Elihu's thinking, the human spirit and the new consciousness that is trying to surface in the first 25 years of the 21st century?

Chapter 10

HOPE: "HOPE IS PATIENCE WITH THE LAMP LIT"

"Hope is patience with the lamp lit."

Tertullian (155 - 220AD) Prolific early Christian author 155 to 220 AD in Carthage Roman province of Africa

Ex-President Obama's appeal may have faded but what did he appeal to when he first swept to power? He said, *"Hope in the face of difficulty, hope in the face of uncertainty. The audacity of hope! In the end, that is God's greatest gift to us, and the bedrock of this nation."* He quoted the New Testament book of Hebrews *"A belief in things not seen,"* and affirmed again, *"Our deep belief that there are better days ahead."*

Obama certainly bypassed conventional political wisdom by appealing directly to youth and hope rather than self-interest. Professor Michael McDonald from George Mason University said, *"Conventional wisdom has a name for candidates who rely on the youth vote - loser."*

Clearly this was different in Obama's first campaign which turned out voters 25 and younger in record numbers. The Washington Post reported that while the overall Democrat turnout jumped 90 per cent, the number of young Democrats participating soared by 135 per cent.

Perhaps the first election in which the youth vote played a decisive role

Political scientist Peter Dreier observed, *"The youngest generation of American voters has chosen a candidate and it may well be the first election in which the youth vote played a decisive role."*

The Trans-moderns had spoken. We have yet to see the level of their object permanence - how long they will stay focused?

Politicians usually do a balancing act between promoting their own policies and discrediting their opposition, basically saying, *"Let me do it right for you."* When Obama said, *"Yes we can!"* he was appealing to something more.

He called into the game the voter's own sense of hope commitment and responsibility. The title of his bestselling book *"The Audacity of Hope"* had first been used as the title of a sermon by the pastor of a church he used to attend.

He wrote, *"As I thought on it, it began to dawn on me that it represented the very best of the American spirit. The audacity to believe despite all the evidence to the contrary, that we could restore a sense of community to a nation torn by conflict; the gall to believe that despite personal setbacks, the loss of a job, or an illness in the family, or a childhood mired in poverty, we have some control - therefore some personal responsibility over our own personal future. It was that audacity, I thought, that joined Americans when they were at their best and made them one people. It was this all pervasive spirit of hope that tied my own family story to the larger American story, and I believed it also could tie my own story to that of the voters I sought to represent."*

Hope that lifts the human spirit is a force multiplier

Former Secretary of State and America's soldier statesman Colin Powell said, *"Hope is a force multiplier,"* which is exactly what Napoleon Bonaparte depended on. But where does hope come from and what is its personal significance?

Woodrow Wilson 28th President of the United States between 1913 and 1921 said, *"We grow great by dreams. All big men are dreamers. They see things in the soft haze of a spring day or in the red fire of the long winter's evening. Some of us let these dreams die, but others nourish and protect them; nurse them through bad days till they bring them to the sunshine and light, which comes always to those who are sincerely committed to the hope that their dreams will come true."* Sounds almost like poetry but it remains the secret of a rich and productive life.

What is hope and what is its significance?

Twentieth century sociologist and psychoanalyst Erich Fromm wrote in his book *"Revolution of Hope"*, *"When hope is gone, to all intents and purposes life has ended, actually or potentially. Hope is an intrinsic element in the very structure of life, it is the dynamic of man's spirit."*

Hope has been shown scientifically and psychologically to be at the foundation of all that moves us purposefully forward. The foundation of hope is our remarkable human spirit.

Hope is an intrinsic element of the dynamic of the human spirit

What inspires the brain? What illuminates it and makes the person with the brain get out of bed to greet the day with purpose and hope?

It all comes from this other place - the human spirit, where hope is born. We now know the human spirit is latent but can be nourished and developed by unconditional love - by the loving affection of significant others as well as by the inspiration of a role model either contemporary or from history. The significance of Jesus for his followers is that he embodies both unconditional love and inspiration.

The spiritual foundations of the human soul

Developmental psychologist and psychoanalyst Erik Eriksson (1902 – 1994) believes if we are healthy, hope is woven into the very fabric of the physiological dimension of our psyche. Hope rises as the default position in the emerging human psyche when a small infant is safe and loved. If an infant does not feel safe, anxiety rather than trust is the prevailing and ever-present life position, consequently the illuminating sense of hope will also go missing or if not completely missing, will at best be conditional.

Henry Krystal who died in 2015 aged 90, was a Holocaust survivor who went on to pioneer treatments for psychological trauma. In his book *"Integration and Self-healing - affect, trauma and alexithymia,"* we find this statement, *"We are looking here at the very foundations of the human soul, those developments which are as essential as the foundation of a house, and as invisible when all is well."*

The spiritual dimension is of central importance

Victor Frankl wrote, *"It is the spiritual dimension which is of central importance to the functioning of the human person, because it is the spirit which truly constitutes the core dynamic of the healthy personality. While it is proper to say that one has a psyche (soul) and a body, we must now say that a person is first and foremost a spiritual being. This spirituality is derived from what in logo-therapy I called the spiritual unconscious. Unconscious spirituality is the origin of the root of all consciousness."*

"In other words I know and acknowledge, not only an *'instinctive unconscious'* (as in Freud's instinctual drives, or ID) but also a spiritual unconscious, and in it we see the supporting ground of all conscious spirituality."

So there it is - the secret of what makes us and the reason we are such a mystery to ourselves. Spirituality is not simply a religious impulse; it is woven into the very fabric of all that makes us hopeful whole, and distinctively human.

G.K. Chesterton wrote, "Hope is the power of being cheerful in circumstances which we know to be desperate."

In her book *"Team of Rivals, The Political Genius of Abraham Lincoln"* by Doris Kearns Goodwin, we have the remarkable account of Abraham Lincoln's way of finding hope in the midst of his struggle with depression. As the 16th president of the United States of America he found himself in the midst of despair. The war was going badly and hope was in short supply.

September 1868 was the worst of times for him. John Pope, the impetuous general he had depended on to replace the cautious George McClellan, had turned out to be a bombastic incompetent. Pope had led the Union Forces to disaster at Second Manassas, and to avert a military disaster Lincoln had to turn again to McClellan.

Why was this a problem if the good general was competent?

Lincoln was determined not to let the Union be divided without a fight. In contrast General McClellan's political goal was to win enough battles so as to negotiate peace rather than win the war. Lincoln's determination to win brought him deep heartache, causing more death and destruction than he'd ever anticipated.

As well as that horrendous reality his depressive inclination was heightened by the death of his 11 year old son Willie who'd been the light of his life, and was also not helped by the incipient madness of his wife. To top it all off he was on the brink of his most desperate gamble, as powerfully shown in the movie Lincoln. He was about to make the proclamation which would declare all the slaves in the Southern States free.

American history at the cross-roads

This combination of pressures weighed on him physically. The Attorney General noted in his diary that the President *"seemed wrung by the bitterest anguish – said he felt almost ready to hang himself."* In this moment of dark despair Elizabeth Keckley, a free negro dressmaker who worked for Mrs Lincoln, recorded *"Mr Lincoln, coming into the bedroom looking deeply dejected was heard to say "No good news. It's dark, dark everywhere."*

According to Mrs Keckley, *"He reached forth one of his long arms and took a small Bible from a stand near the head of the sofa, opened the pages of the Holy Book, and soon was absorbed in reading them."*

After about a quarter of an hour Mrs Keckley glanced towards the sofa and noticed the face of the President had changed. He now looked more cheerful. She reported, *"The dejected look was gone and his countenance was lighted up with new resolution and hope."* Inclined to be a sticky beak, she looked at the Bible passage that lay open on the bed and discovered to her surprise that he had been reading the book of Job.

While not being a regular church goer Lincoln was something of a student of the Bible. I find it fascinating that he found hope from the source that was part of the very book of the Bible that inspired me to write this book, the book of Job.

Sometimes in our darkest moments, our spirit leads us to a source of hope

If we are free enough to respond to the promptings of the human spirit, they will lead us to our core hope. This is fundamental if are going to live a full and healthy life that will lead us to heights of positive achievement.

No wonder the New Testament tells us that this hope is an anchor

We are told in the New Testament we can have an anchor that will keep the soul steadfast in the face of the storms of life: it is called hope. In Hebrews 6:19 we are told that this deep spiritual reality hope not only gives us an anchoring point in crisis but from it springs those twin spiritual virtues faith and love that enrich our lives by helping us see the yet invisible potential (Colossians 1:5).

Hope, the DNA of the spirit that can bring illumination to every part of life

Because it is such a profound yet invisible motivating force for good we are told to be ready to give a reason for our hope, the gentle source of illumination that lies within us. The social sciences now show that hope is in fact the real yet invisible animating DNA of our humanity.

The transforming power of hope

Clinical studies indicate hope is both biologically and psychologically vital. We must have hope if we are to be fully alive and human. Martin Luther, who in 1517 forever changed Christianity when he nailed his 95 Theses to a church door, said, *"Everything that is done in the world Is done by hope."* Centuries later his namesake Martin Luther King Jr. took up the theme saying, *"We must accept finite disappointment, but never lose infinite hope."*

30 years of research are showing the health benefits of a hopeful spirit

A growing yet largely unrecognized body of scientific work has been amassed over the past 30 years showing that a rich, hope-producing spiritual life is medically, socially and psychologically beneficial.

In 2006 research by the American Society of Hypertension showed that churchgoers have lower blood pressure than non-churchgoers. In 2004 research from the University of California Los Angeles showed that college students involved in religious and spiritual activities were more likely to have better mental and emotional health and integration than those who weren't.

In 2006 population researchers at the University of Texas discovered that the more often one went to church the longer one lived. In their words, *"Our research has shown religious attendance is associated with adult mortality in a graded fashion:*

there was a seven-year difference in life expectancy between those who never attend church and those who attend weekly."

The *"American Journal of Public Health"* came to the same conclusion. After studying almost 2,000 older Californians over a period of five years, they found that those who attended religious services were 36 per cent less likely to die during the following five years than those who didn't. Clearly those who attend a place of worship regularly do better than those who never attend.

The spiritual significance of hope and its impact on physical well being

Professor Penny Schofield, Associate Professor at the Peter MacCallum Clinic for cancer treatment in Melbourne, conducted a fascinating study on the significance of hope on the prognosis of cancer sufferers. She found clear evidence that depression produced a negative health outcome shortening life and decreasing the quality of life.

Hope, on the other hand, had the effect of neutralising depression and making a profound and measurable difference medically. It not only lifted the spirits of the individual but made a marked difference to life expectancy and the quality of life lived. Other recent studies of the brain and neurology clearly demonstrate how negative thinking drains us while hopeful and positive thinking raise not only our energy and aspirations but also our bodies' capacity to function as it was designed to.

People with a strong faith recover faster

In 1998 the American Journal of Public Health found that depressed patients with a strong intrinsic faith - a deep personal belief not just a social inclination to go to a place of worship - recovered 70 per cent faster than those who did not have a strong faith. Those with spiritual belief also had more success with IVF than unbelievers.

You may well think this is just American research, and we all know they are a religious lot! But hold on!

In 2008 a survey of Europeans was conducted by Professor Andrew Clark, of the Paris School of Economics, and Dr. Orsolya Lelkes of the European Centre for Social Welfare Policy and Research. They found that compared with non-believers religious believers record less stress, are better able to cope with losing jobs and divorce, are less prone to suicide and enjoy their life because it has a purpose so are *happier* overall. It is interesting to note the Bible says, *"A heart at peace gives life to the body."* Proverbs 14:30

Academics find more than they are looking for

The most fascinating feature of this research is that the team didn't go looking for this effect; it surprised them. Professor Clark said, *"We originally started out to research why some European countries had more generous unemployment benefits than others."* He continued, *"Our analysis suggests that religious people suffer less psychological harm from unemployment than the nonreligious, and believers clearly had higher levels of life satisfaction."*

In 2010 Professors Robert Putnam and Chayoon Lim from Harvard published research showing clearly that religious people are significantly happier than non-religious people. They discovered that many of the health benefits of religion materialize only if you go to church regularly and have good friends there. In other words it is the organized part of organized religion that does a lot of the great stuff. The two Harvard scientists were so challenged by their findings that they considered altering their own religious behaviour. Professor Lim said, *"I am not a religious person but I personally began to think about whether I should go to church. And it would certainly make my mother happy."*

Could this mean atheists are a dying breed?

Spiritual life whether you went to church or not, showed up significantly in the study of nearly 4,000 older adults for the US Journal of Gerontology. It revealed that atheists have a notably increased chance of dying over a six-year period than spiritually active older people.

Significantly, religious people live longer than atheists even if they don't go regularly to a place of worship. The study clearly showed the benefit of spiritual life. One article on this research raised the question; given all this vast evidence that religion is good for you how come atheists are so set against it? Author Tom Knox wondered whether it is the atheists who are acting irrationally rather than those who are alive in their spirit. Since doing the research for his book on health and faith he himself started going to church.

The significance of life with purpose

Tennis player Anna Kournikova committed herself to win three grand slams in a single year. She won her three grand slams then burned out. Why? Her mission to win three grand slams had brought focus, but after she won, she didn't have an answer to the question, *"Why did I want to win three grand slams?"* She had had a mission but she did not have a timeless vision that would bring her long-term purpose and hope.

It seems then that our greatest fear should not be of failure but of succeeding at something that doesn't really matter. Purpose is significant. Victor Frankl said, *"It is amazing what people will put up with if there is a purpose in the pain, but if there is no purpose in the pain even the smallest aggravation becomes unbearable."*

We of all of God's creatures have a biological and spiritual need to know our life is adding up to something of consequence, something of significance. Animals don't care about it, neither do they care about justice or truth; they simply have instinctual drives that help them survive. Only we humans have the level of consciousness that can look over our own shoulder and ask, *"Why am I doing this?"*

Time to ask the important questions

When are you most inclined to feel bone weary? Is it necessarily after a hard day's productive work? No! You can feel tired after a day of hard work but the bone weariness that is a feature of the existence of contemporary human beings comes from a sense of futility, a sense that our life is adding up to nothing of significance and going nowhere in particular.

No longer like the afore mentioned beetle on its back struggling to get onto its feet before somebody steps on it, we are the generation which for the first time is like the beetle on its front.

Past generations were so busy surviving that all but a few did not have time to contemplate. We have had the rare and significant opportunity to ask the important questions about the meaning of our existence, questions like: Why am I here, and in what direction do I want to travel? At this stage we are discovering nagging questions but few real answers. Certainly very few of us have the tools and disciplines to find the answers we yearn for.

To mature we have to come home to the quiet of facing ourselves

We contemporary non-community people come home to the quiet of facing ourselves and ask, what was today really all about? If we switch off the computer, the television, the static in our minds and perhaps sit on our bed or lie down and stare at the ceiling and if we have the inner sense of security not to fear it but let ourselves focus, we will find something bubbles up from deep within.

The Bible says, *"Be still and know..."* If we can let the dirt settle in the fish tank of our small world for long enough we might just overcome our ego's battle for significance and mastery so as to become emotionally and spiritually aware.

We might hear promptings from our hopeful deeper self asking questions about our identity like, *"Why am I here,"* *"What am I meant to become?"* We might just begin to find our purpose, our story, and hear from the still small illuminating voice of our spirit.

Chapter 11

WHERE DOES THE MUSIC COME FROM?

"It is incontestable that music induces in us a sense of the infinite and the contemplation of the invisible."

Victor De la Prade (1812 – 1883) French poet and critic

There is art and there is beauty and they are not necessarily the same thing. Neurologists have seen what happens in the brain when people listen to music they consider beautiful: It is as if they had finally come home in the cosmos.

Johann Sebastian Bach was one of the composers whose music had this effect. By age 23 young Johann was very clear about his life's purpose which he believed was to create church music to the glory of God. Every time he sat down to compose he would scribble *"J.J."* on his blank page, *"Jesus Juva - Help me Jesus."* At the manuscript's end he wrote *"S.D.G., Soli Deo Gloria - to God alone be the glory."*

Clearly he was not composing music to feed his ego or to become rich and famous. In his life time he was not regarded as a success. His music was not well known and very little of it was published. He believed his job was to provide music for church or the royal courts week in and week out, and at the same time he struggled with ill health and the needs of a very large family. The music his sons wrote was often more popular than his own.

Bach's power to touch the face of heaven

Now more than 300 years later it is clear that the song he was to sing with his life, the narrative purpose he knew God gave him, was fulfilled. Many people say they begin to believe in God when they hear his music. In an interview with Time Magazine Aung San Suu Kyi of the Burmese National League for Democracy (Myanmar) - now State Counsellor - said of the earlier years she spent under house arrest for her activism, *"I would listen to the radio for news and the music of Mozart to make me happy, which is all well and good, but I must say I prefer Bach. He makes me calm and I needed calm in my life."*

A lady dying of cancer found comfort in playing all her favourite music, but when her illness progressed all she wanted was Bach. Australian historian, the late Professor Manning Clark, was asked by radio broadcaster Terry Lane if he believed in God. He reflected for a moment and said he didn't think he did, but there were some things that made him wonder about the mystery at the heart of things. He said, *"For instance, when I hear Bach's Mass in B minor, it certainly gets me wondering if there might be something mysterious going on behind life as we know it."*

The unique human hunger for the numinous

On my radio talk show I once asked Barry Jones, Australian intellectual quiz show giant and past president of the Labour Party, if he believed in God. His answer echoed that of historian Manning Clarke, *"I fear so. I mean I think that there is something profoundly mysterious about the universe; I don't think it is all cut and dried. I wish I understood more about it."* He went on to say, *"I mean I have a profound yearning for the numinous (mystical, spiritual, supernatural). I think in a way it's been argued that the work of Bach is one of those remarkable things that makes you think that really there is some sort of order in the universe and that the music of Bach is one of the factors that perhaps provides a kind of persuasive argument for the existence of a power that is beyond our own intellect, beyond our knowing."*

Peace beyond understanding

The Bible talks about the peace that is beyond understanding and it seems this kind of knowing is tied up with discovering our essential place in the universe. It prompted British statesman Benjamin Disraeli to say, *"Most people die with their music still locked up inside of them."*

Centuries before Christ it prompted Elihu to say, *"It is the spirit in a man, the breath of God, that gives understanding."* It is the part that moves us, in the words of Barry Jones, to *"yearn for the numinous"* in our lives - to work out who we are, why we are here and where we are going.

Religion: illumination or control?

Ecclesiastes 3:11 says, "God has set eternity into our hearts." All too often religion in general and Christendom in particular have pressed philosophy and theology into the service of power rather than illumination for the ordinary person. In doing so religion did itself and humanity a disservice.

Theology was often used to control not to liberate, to rationalise the prevailing point of view of the ruler, or to create a spiritual caste system rather than help people find their spiritual voice and their place in the eternal story. There have been many like Elihu who raised their voices against prevailing conventional wisdoms and were silenced or put to death.

True spirituality leads to freedom

In his book *"Rumours of Another World"* Philip Yancey wrote that religion in recent centuries has not served spirituality well. In the interests of control, religious institutions tended to confine the sacred to the *"fenced off area reserved for church activities."* He believes that many church people hardly give their spirit a second thought after they leave church on Sunday morning, saying *"They sing songs of praise, listen to a sermon and then re-enter the secular world as though passing through an airlock. Once the door closes behind them they believe they leave the sacred space, as if the world neatly divides between secular and sacred."*

Sociologist Robert Wuthnow in his book *"Creative Spirituality"* asserts, *"Artists, singers, dancers and actors, not theologians, have become the spiritual vanguard of our time."* He points out that in contemporary culture spirituality is increasingly focused on what he calls *"The inherently ineffable character of the sacred"*, or what Callas refers to as *"the divine mystery that lies behind all things."* He went on to assert *"Contemporary artists speak more comfortably about spirituality than about organised religion."* He further points out that, *"the human spirit is as much uplifted by the inspired concert on Saturday night as by the sermon on the Sunday morning."*

Art as an action of the spirit

The late Judy Cassab, arguably one of Australia's best portrait artists, said she was always trying to capture the spirit of the person she was painting. She believed the portrait painter has a rare opportunity to examine the human face for as long as they want; that they are allowed the deep penetrating gaze into character and personality that is usually reserved for those who love. In the best portraits we are able to discern something of the unique mystery of the person as divined by the skilled painter.

She described the moment when it all came together for her, *"When I was twelve I woke up one morning and I suddenly knew that 'I am,' and I also knew all I wanted to become was a painter. While that was a moment of awareness, I had a belief I was born with, that I believe is a gift like my gift as an artist. I had nothing in my upbringing to make me a believer. On the contrary my father was an atheist, and the whole family was not religious. I however prayed every night all my life. I feel that I have a higher power within me, and that we all have it within us if we recognise it."*

It is one thing to have our spirit; it's quite another to own it and recognise it

Cassab said, *"To people who want to know about my belief I simply quote the motto in Franz Werfel's book, The Song of Bernadette, 'For those who don't believe, every explanation is in vain and for those who do believe, every explanation is unnecessary.'"*

It seems the inner eye that could see the spirit of the person she was painting was also the same eye that could see the eternal. It takes courage to welcome and not fear the eternal - something bigger than we can grasp.

Inspiration and creativity

The artist, the poet and the musician have his or her rules. It is the conscious mind that works on the material the artist is creating but unless that elusive something from the depths of their unconscious spirit is present the work of art will be no more than a design in colour or a piece of verse in the form of a tune. The framework, the skeleton and the flesh are there but what gives life is not there.

Many have tried to write a poem that didn't work. We choose a subject decide on a theme select a meter and express our thoughts in the most poetic words we can find but the result is disappointing because we know the thing is utterly dead and uninspired. In the process though, we have experienced something of the poet and creative writer's struggle to take a flash of inspiration and craft it so that others experience it as inspiring. Many people have had a love of poetry killed in them by having to read it for exams or by never having seriously tried to find anything inspiring in it.

The poem and its attempts to reach for the reality beyond the words

Those open to exploring the realm of poetry find some poems appeal strongly while others leave them cold; all they know is that they have either been moved or not moved. In the same way a sunset can make you go *"wow,"* while at other times you are so preoccupied you don't even see it. If you are moved in a particular moment you have been touched by something that lies beyond rational analysis.

In the words of Keats:

> *"Heard melodies are sweet,*
> *but those unheard are sweeter.*
> *Therefore, ye soft pipes, play on;*
> *not to the sensual ear, but, more endeared,*
> *Pipe to the spirit ditties of no tone."*

Ode on a Grecian Urn

John Keats, English Romantic poet who was born 1795 and died of tuberculosis at age 25, said he was often unaware of the beauty of some thought or expression until after he had written it down, then *"It seemed rather the production of another person than my own."* Evan Thomas, American author, historian and journalist wrote of the power of poetry, *"Poetry is what in a poem makes you laugh, cry, twist your toes, twinkle, wriggle, be silent, know you are alone, and yet not alone in an unknown world."*

Yes, good uplifting poetry carries within it echoes of the transcendent. The heart alone resonates to the deeper meaning behind the obvious that the mind can't quite define. Good poetry is the face of the invisible in the visible. Life is more fulfilling and rewarding when you can tune into and read spiritual poetry.

Of course the greatest delight is to discern the mind of the *"great poet"* behind it all who helps us see that in and through and sometimes in spite of the traumas, all things really are working together for good for those who can respond to love in operation.

The poetry beyond the trauma

Ancient Greek poet Pindar wrote that, *"A discourse lives for a longer time than deeds, which a tongue seizes from the mind's depths with the Graces' favour."* 19th century novelist Robert Louis Stevenson humorously referred to his *"brownies"* who he said did the main work of composing his stories for him. Mozart described the phenomenon of hearing the parts of some new composition not sequentially *"but as it were all at once."*

Handel was sent a compilation of Bible verses to set to music and at once it gripped him. He finished the enormous work of the Messiah in 22 days, with another two days on the orchestration. For him it was like a spiritual visitation. He wrote in a trance; food, sleep, ordinary life passed him by. He never left the house. Time ceased for him and when he finished the great Hallelujah Chorus he sat for a moment, the tears in his eyes, *"I did think I did see all heaven before me and the great God himself!"* he cried to his servant.

The mystery of the creative impulse

The artist, poet or musician is one whose mental and spiritual sensitivities have him experience the stream of life at a dynamic level. From somewhere he grasps the soul of things then struggles to present that core meaning to others. As we contemplate a finished inspired work, if we are aware and sensitive we find a resonating response rising within us. This usually puts us to work internally.

Music and art realign us with the music of the spheres

Research indicates that we are the only species that spontaneously sway, move and dance to the rhythm of music. Music seems to be programmed into the very place that body, soul and spirit meet. It also brings an automatic release of endorphins but only when we surrender our ego and move with the music. When we restrict our movement by choosing with an act of will or by letting an archaic restriction inhibit us, the endorphins do not flow. Of course when we refuse to groove we rob ourselves of that other spiritual sensation, joy.

Realigning our narrative to the big story

Indigenous Australians in many tribes believe that God sang the world into existence, so whenever a baby is being born the women gather around the mother and sing to the child as it comes into the world. They may sing then: You are being born under the shade of the gunyah tree, while the stripes are still on the baby emus; you came into the world looking at the blue sky and the ancestral mountain. You were your mother's special boy child.

Later on the child will sing this song. It becomes the song of his identity and when the family gets together they will sing the song of their own spirit together. When the clan gets together they will sing their own songs - the song of the family and the song of the clan. These are the songs of their spirit, individually and collectively.

When the mind is attuned to the spirit, or following the heart's leading, it is normal for a song to rise from deep within. Watch it next time you're alone and inclined to hum or sing to yourself in the car. When the deep inner harmony begins to rise from the core or spirit, there will be a gentle expression that brings with it a healing sense of validation, affirming one's sense of individuality. Children who are still free from imposed inhibitions are most likely to show us how it happens.

Uninhibited children are often our best teachers

Thanks to our Western education and culture, overdevelopment of our brain's left hemisphere alienates us from our spirit so we lose touch with our spontaneous core, our heart's song. When adult indigenous people become too involved in the white man's world they often become alienated and feel the need to go walkabout. They may be working as a builder's labourer and will just put their tools down and walk off until they have caught up again with their souls. Sadly, this response to alienation is not accepted and is viewed on the same level as getting drunk. White bosses think going walkabout is irresponsible but it's a shame they are so driven they cannot learn from it.

Many marriages and families would be a little richer if the music of life was not choked off. This is why British Statesman Benjamin Disraeli's comment has echoed so powerfully down the generations, *"Most of us will die with the music still locked up inside of us."*

In harmony with the life we've been given

The part of Elihu that prompted him centuries ago to say, *"It is the spirit in a man, the breath of God, that gives understanding,"* is also the part that prompts us to find our song and work out the answers to the big questions. Questions like: Who are we? Why are we here? Where, ultimately are we going and how can we harmonise with the life we're given?

For centuries religion has been used to control people. Even Christian doctrine and dogma was pressed into service of the brain's left hemisphere to rationalise and promote a prevailing world view.

In contrast, Christianity's founder was more of a level 4 thinker who came with a non-legalistic way of seeing the world. He came with a message of liberty and grace that expressed itself in a lifestyle of awareness, intimacy, spontaneity and joy. He said "My joy I give unto you." His message was a threat to the religious authority structures of the day.

The result? He became the victim of those with a Level 2 mindset who were threatened by his capacity to see past them. As is so often the case they moved to get rid of the source of their discomfort.

Too often those with vested interests wear psychological blinkers

Why were they threatened? They saw him as a danger to their ego's constructed certainty. There is none so blind as those who refuse to see! They would rather stay in their current world view with its limited, joyless, black-and-white preconceptions than join in the adventure of a new way of knowing. The attitude of Level 2 thinkers is, *"Don't confuse me with facts, my mind is already made up."*

Chapter 12

THE SILENCING OF THE NEW SONG

"To see what is in front of one's nose requires a constant struggle."

George Orwell (1903 - 1950) English novelist, essayist and critic most famous for his novels *"Animal Farm"* and *"Nineteen Eighty-Four"*

The effort to see beyond one's nose is something Level 2 thinkers are not so inclined to make. This makes life difficult for those who have spiritual intelligence and are therefore innovative thinkers. Throughout history there have been many like Elihu who could see more; who raised their voice against prevailing conventional wisdom and who were ridiculed silenced or even put to death.

There is none so blind as those who will not see

Jesus himself could be said to have been crucified by the Level 2 mindset in a religion controlled by a prevailing cultural mindset.

There is a tendency for the neurotic part of all of us to be more interested in a comfortable equilibrium than in a challenging life option. Fundamentally, there are two orientations, one that's designed to defend and convince itself of what it already thinks it knows and another that has the ego strength to be open to new insights. The paradox is that those with weak egos are most inclined to be ego-centred and inflexible.

We don't necessarily learn from experience, but by reflecting on experience

In the book of Isaiah 28:23-29 God speaks to the human spirit to give it wisdom. It is how he teaches the farmer to use different methods with regard for the different nature of crops and it is this kind of insight we call spiritual intelligence.

As the text shows this insight does not necessarily come in a blinding flash of revelation but usually dawns on us in the ordinary processes of life. One could almost call it common sense but this kind of humble insight is not actually so common.

This is Elihu's kind of humility - *"that which I see not teach thou me"* (Job 34:32) and it is how we are given the grace to see the patterns of meaning inherent in the data before us. Gestalt Psychology believes this capacity to sense the shape and form of the reality is present long before reason is able to comprehend it.

Elihu shows us what is called "the wisdom of the farmer." (Isaiah 28:23-29)

Here we see beyond the intellect's capacity to observe when we are permitted by our heart openness, thus freeing our intuition to be educated by the instincts of the spirit. When observing the ordinary affairs of life we are led by the spirit to glimpse the universal insights that lie behind everyday events. These insights can equip us when we are thus inspired. I firmly believe this part of us can as it were, glimpse eternity. I see these moments of inspiration as the functioning of hope filled, faith imagination.

This is, of course, the inspiration and real secret of human progress.

A teachable spirit has Elihu say, "That which I see not teach thou me."

This is precisely why James in James 4:6 says, *"God resists the proud but gives grace to the humble."* Contrary to conventional understanding wisdom does not come from experience. If it did we would never make the same mistake twice. Wisdom comes by *reflecting* on experience and permitting the spirit to illuminate.

Because the uninspired ego always wants to look good and be right, if not silenced it will intrude into the spirit's delightful quest for understanding and wisdom.

Life without ego blinkers enables one to see even an inconvenient truth

Hungarian obstetrician and medical pioneer Ignaz Semmelweis (1818-1865) was the first to discover that doctors going from patient to patient without washing their hands were causing the death of 20 percent of all mothers and their newborns. Unfortunately his germ-ridden colleagues did not take kindly to his suggestion that they were responsible for the death of their patients by failing to wash their hands between examinations.

Semmelweis and his medical breakthrough destroyed by arrogance

In a nearby hospital run by nuns who washed their hands regularly there were far fewer fatalities. His theory however was new; it was unheard of! The entrenched medical community refused to believe this radical new theory.

In an effort to curtail deaths due to childbed fever Semmelweis instituted a strict hand washing policy amongst his medical students and physician colleagues in Division One. Everyone was required to wash their hands with chlorinated lime water prior to attending patients. In Division One mortality rates immediately dropped from 18.3% to 1.3% and between March and August 1848 not a single woman died from childbirth. Despite this dramatic reduction in the mortality rate Semmelweis' colleagues and the greater medical community greeted his findings with hostility or dismissal.

His dramatic results were greeted with hostility

Even after presenting his thorough research on childbed fever (more technically referred to as puerperal sepsis) to the Viennese Medical Society, Semmelweis was not able to secure the teaching post he desired. In a state of grief he returned to Hungary. There he repeated his successful hand washing attack on childbed fever at the St. Rochus hospital in Pest. In 1860 he finally published his principal work on the subject of puerperal sepsis but this too was dismissed resulting in thousands more mothers losing their lives to infection.

The years of controversy and repeated rejection of his work by the medical establishment weighed heavily on him. It was excruciating to know so many lives were being lost because of ignorance and arrogance. It took its toll on his health. Semmelweis eventually suffered a mental breakdown and died in 1865 in an Austrian mental institution before his work was vindicated.

Galileo's cosmology

Galileo (1564 - 1642) was an Italian astronomer, mathematician, physicist, philosopher and professor who made pioneering observations of nature with long-lasting implications for the study of physics. He was sacked because he confronted the prevailing cosmology which asserted that the earth was at the centre of the universe. He asserted that the earth moved around the sun and the authorities refused to believe him despite his clearly presented evidence. He was forced to recant, saying that his discoveries were not true, a crushing experience for one's integrity.

I refer throughout this book to the four levels of consciousness and where they come from (see Appendix). The Level 2 traditional thinkers are usually the anchoring point and give a culture stability, often however they are also the inhibiting point and work against the breaking-in and acceptance of the new.

The genius of Mandelbrot's fractals

Benoit Mandelbrot (1924 - 2010) was a Polish-born French American mathematician universally known as the father of fractals. He is a classic example of the stultifying effect of conventional wisdom. Confronted with 2,000 years of geometry with its limiting misconceptions he showed that the triangles squares and circles that frame the way we think about the world existed more in textbooks than they did in reality.

He showed that simple rules used by nature are the cause of repetition and generate the seemingly complex and chaotic patterns we call fractals. Just as branches look like small trees, small parts resemble the whole.

Many are starting to realise that few people in history have had as broad and practical an impact as Mandelbrot. His contributions affect physics, engineering, arts, music, linguistics, biology (blood vessels and lungs are fractal) and medicine. He went unheeded though by the very field in which he started, economics.

Had we listened to Mandelbrot there might never have been a global financial crisis

Back in the 1960s he proved that most financial theories underestimate market risk, the very underestimation that caused the most recent global economic crisis prior to the pandemic. Recent history shows us that more often than not it is the prevailing wisdom that is wrong. Mandelbrot, who died aged 85 on October 14 2010 was, according to a Time magazine obituary, *"self-taught and fiercely independent"* - the very things that work against acceptance by traditional thinkers.

He produced his famous Mandelbrot set when he was in his fifties and did not get tenure at Yale until he was 75, the age most people have retired. To this day older mathematicians resist his geometric and intuitive methods.

After his death others have received awards for proving his theories to be true.

In 2006 the Fields Medal, the top prize in mathematics, was awarded to someone who proved one of Mandelbrot's most significant theories to be true. *"I have never done anything like others,"* Mandelbrot said not long before he died.

There are countless stories of misunderstood Level 4 thinking pioneers. Like Einstein, Mandelbrot's intuitive or right hemisphere's intelligence opened up worlds and horizons from which to launch a new generation of scientists. Too often, though, young radicals become old conservatives. In this so-called rational and scientific age the community of scientists is as likely to reject a new position that confronts their conventional wisdoms as did the community of theologians in another era. The ego's need to look good and be right always trumps reason unless truth is more important than reputation.

A cure for ulcers

A classic example is the work of Australian scientists Robin Warren and Barry Marshall who won the 2005 Nobel Prize in medicine. In broad Australian slang Barry Marshall said he was thrilled to be recognised but their discovery was *"As bloody obvious as the nose on your face."* The two scientists described how they were initially shunned for insisting stomach ulcers were caused not by stress as was commonly believed but by bacterium.

It took 20 years for the medical establishment to accept it

They made their discovery in the early 1980's but it took 20 years to convince the medical community which initially viewed them as an eccentric pair of Aussies with a bee in their bonnet. Barry Marshall said, *"The idea that stress was the cause of ulcers was just so entrenched nobody could really believe that it was bacteria."* He went on to say, *"I think you have to come from a weird place like Perth, Western Australia, because I think nobody else would have even considered it."*

When he could find no other way to test his theory, Barry Marshall, who his wife says has a dreadful sense of humour, eventually decided to swallow the bacterium they believed to be responsible for the stomach ulcers (Helicobacter pylori). When she enquired why he was so ill, he laughed and said, *"I couldn't get any other guinea pigs silly enough to do it."* Fortunately he proved his point by curing himself as well as tens of thousands around the world who were sufferers of life-threatening and disabling stomach and intestinal ulcers. The 20 years that elapsed between discovery of the cure and its acceptance meant many thousands of people suffered unnecessarily.

Why the delay? It can be attributed both to a Level 2 traditional mindset and vested interests of multi-billion-dollar pharmaceutical empires. It is haunting to realise that the uninspired neurotic part of the human psyche is always more interested in equilibrium than creative change.

Truth or equilibrium? The choice that stands at the door of tomorrow

The left hemisphere of the brain is the part most inclined to think sequentially and in straight lines. Most IQ tests evaluate the left hemisphere's capacity to function. It is also the part that shapes our ego with its need for validation and sees us highly rewarded for academic achievement. What a combination! It explains so many of the stories in this chapter.

Too often it is our ego that blocks our spirit from helping us see what we haven't seen before.

We can have a high IQ but low spiritual intelligence

Spiritual intelligence is shown in the way Elihu prays, *"That which I see not, teach thou me."* (Job 34:32). Remaining open to what you can't see is the clearest example of humility and spiritual intelligence. It is the best chance we have of seeing what lies before our eyes without the distortions of the ego. Of course the historic danger of traditional Level 2 thinking is that in its mole-like blindness it is sure that what it is seeing is all there is to see.

It is easy to see why, until the time of the Reformation, the social order in the Christian West was quite stable. Kings ruled and the church was the most significant opinion-forming agent. The temporal rulers told you what to do and the church told you what to think and of course you knew it came straight from God. It was the discovery of individual conscience during the Reformation that would start a revolution.

The conscience discovered in the Reformation was the voice of the spirit

A dominant new factor during the time of the Reformation was individual conscience informed by the word of God. People were now taught to tune in to an inner voice that may or may not stand in the face of conventional wisdom or theological orthodoxy. It was a huge challenge to the state church's authority.

It has always been profoundly important for those with a prophetic voice to speak truth with courage to those in power, even though at times it has meant standing against contemporary paradigms and power structures.

As many now had access to the Christian Scriptures people could form their own point of view. They were autonomous enough in their conscience or spirit not to need authority figures to tell them what truth was. For those in power there was the valid concern that everyone would do what was right in their own eyes and chaos would rule.

This is why it was such a radical and historic moment when Martin Luther, a key player in the Reformation, said before the Pope's own emissary and all the nobles, *"Here I stand, I can do no other!"* In other words, *"Kill me if you like but I can't go against my inner voice of conscience, because it's the real me."*

Luther is released to discover a spiritual attachment to a loving God

Luther was inspired by the New Testament book of Romans with its revelation about the potential freedom and dignity of the human spirit and the way God's Spirit speaks to the human spirit. This connection with God is such that our human spirit responds deeply with *"Abba"* meaning my father (Romans 8:15-16), or in other words, *"I am connected to you as is a trusting child to a wise and loving parent."* Martin Luther's relationship with his father was less than happy so to discover he was loved by a divine and heavenly father who gave him spiritual freedom was revolutionary for him.

Theology went through a drought with respect to the third member of the Trinity, the Holy Spirit. The significance of this has been profound and there is evidence to suggest the whole of Western Christianity has misunderstood ideology and seen it as belief.

Werner and Lottie Peltz wrote a book called *"Your God is No More."* Their central proposition is that Western thinking and theology has systematised its understanding and in so doing conceptualised God making him no bigger than our concept of him. Philosophers found it easy to dispense with this God. Swiss Protestant theologian Karl Barth tried to re-awaken a sense of the profound mystery by saying that God was *"the wholly other"* - whatever you imagine or conceptualise him to be he is wholly other than it.

Religion and spirituality in conflict or harmony? Love or war?

A growing number of thinkers and theologians are starting to believe that much of the Christian church has lost contact with authentic spirituality and has failed to take note of the insights of those we call the desert fathers of Cappadocia. The desert fathers believed the essence of God - what makes him unique - is that he exists as a sort of continuous and indivisible community that expresses itself as love. The desert fathers lived in community and understood oneness and its spiritual significance.

Humanity is male and female. As C.S. Lewis wrote, *"Jointly the two become fully human. 'In the image of God created he them.'"* When the male, out of his deep love and yearning for unity with the beloved female is inspired and drawn, not threatened by difference, new life comes into being. Paradoxically, consummation comes both through appreciation of difference yet yearning for unity. Here we begin to understand what the left-brained person is never likely to get; oneness comes out of a loving desire for unity through appreciation of the other. Healthy sex is not simply about carnal desire but a spiritual yearning for completion.

We all yearn for oneness and completion

The God-head is Father, Son and Holy Spirit who appreciate each other. In the Bible the Father is recorded as saying, *"This is my beloved Son in whom I am well pleased."* The Son says, *"I only do those things that please the Father"* and the Spirit's task is to help mirror and create these loving and appreciative relationships throughout humanity. This is where our spirit's ache for unity is derived from.

As the Desert Fathers also believed, we won't understand humanity unless we have a working knowledge of the God-head in whose image we are made, and we certainly won't understand the strange human phenomenon we call falling-in-love.

A living spiritual experience or mental assent to certain doctrinal ideas?

Western Christianity has for many people been about giving mental assent to certain theological propositions which became increasingly untenable with further education. In the words of Australian Doctor Peter Holmes, *"Conversion was not so much about a transformation of the spirit that makes us more Christ like, but Western dogma saw it more as some sort of legal transaction, a once off forensic act."* The very faith and spirituality that should have helped us become more spiritually complete became a conceptual proposition, a source of control alienation and division.

A spirituality attuned to a bigger cosmic story

There have always been those attuned to a bigger story whose spirituality helped them rise above the controlling conventions of their time from Francis of Assisi through to Martin Luther and more recently Mother Teresa.

There has been a discovery of insight that brings a unifying illumination and coherence between truly Biblical thinking and the latest thinking in quantum physics and the social sciences and neurology, producing an integral spiritual consciousness.

The narratives are coming together

In the words of B.J. Lee, "Put simply, God's spirit is where God's deep story is. Our spirit is where our deep story is. Through the immanence of God's Spirit with and in the human spirit, the big story that is intended for history is transmitted and realised."

The narrative deep within us from which we derive our sense of purpose and joy is to be found within our spirit. The main task of the Holy Spirit is to lead us to community where we become an authentic human being in fellowship with other pilgrims on the journey, and thus discover our unfolding story.

The deep narrative that wants to lead us to our happy ending

In the Narnia stories C.S. Lewis tried to convey the deep story by calling it the deep magic. At the heart of all things lies a tantalizing mystery and part of us senses it, knowing there is more to know. When we are at our best we are inclined not just to protect what we know but to say enthusiastically with Elihu, *"That which I see not teach thou me."*

For those unable to utter these words this heart-sourced illuminated response and insight went missing from the more dogmatic forms of religion. The outcome of this Level 2 attitude is not only alienating but deadens the natural quest for authentic spiritual exploration of life.

Left brain dogmatism in the name of religion has diverted us from real life

Theologians fought and rethought theology in the context of the great battles of the Reformation and Counter Reformation and in the process of arguing from their left hemisphere lost sight of their heart and therefore the significance of the human spirit.

Theology was shaped in universities rather than by life

While the Holy Spirit has been neglected down the centuries by Western theology we have now had the Charismatic and Pentecostal movements sweep the world and redress the balance, though this movement of the Spirit has been funnelled into a certain section of the Christian world.

The spiritual discipline of becoming attuned to the inner voice of the spirit as a channel of divine illumination has not only been largely forgotten, but its legitimacy still waits to be recognised. The result? The driving force for illumination in changing human consciousness and modern society has been driven from the stage of history. No wonder we're feeling a little lost as we go looking in all the wrong places for that which would satisfy our deepest yearnings.

Chapter 13

AN IMBALANCE TO REDRESS

"It is now clear to me, spiritual thought transcends matter ...
the power of what is in you permeates the world around you."

Barbra Streisand (1942 –) American composer, actress, director and producer was
the first major female star to command roles as a Jewish actress.

A classic case of not being able to see the wood for the trees

Elihu alerts us to the fact that there's another imbalance waiting to be redressed -
our lack of awareness of the remarkable and ubiquitous human spirit and the kind
of influence it has on us. It's as though we are so close to it that we are functionally
blind to it.

In his book *"Proof of Heaven - A Neurosurgeon's Journey into the Afterlife,"* Eben
Alexander wrote, *"Our eternal spiritual self is more real than anything we perceive
in this physical realm, and has a divine connection to the infinite love of the Creator."*

Our eternal spirit is more real than anything we can touch and feel

We are body, soul and spirit and we need to recognise we have impulses and
influences from every one of these three sources and there is a remarkable
interaction between these three discrete influences. For some time now we've
recognised how the body influences the soul and the soul influences the sense of
well-being of the psyche. In medicine it is called the psychosomatic phenomenon.

For centuries the most sensitive and creative amongst us, particularly in the Western
world, have been aware that something has been missing from our existence. This
awareness of an absence has fuelled some of our greatest works of literature and
art. What is this existential ache, and what is the role of the spirit in our almost
unconscious quest for completeness?

Are we too close to see the most profound factor in the human personality?

The recognition of this animating dynamic within our personality will bring an
awareness of the unique place it should have in our study of sociology, psychology,
medicine, theology and philosophy.

Scott Peck in his book *"Further Along the Road Less Travelled"* said of psychiatry and the healing of souls, *"We are all spiritual beings, and I believe that a psychiatry which does not regard humans as spiritual beings may be largely missing the boat."*

The spirit has a special place in informing our conscience and our finding a sense of fulfilment and purpose. It is the location of our unique *telos* or path to completion and well-being. Our spirit gives us the capacity to identify with the general source of spiritual intelligence, the kind of wisdom that illuminates the human experience.

Discovering our source of human illumination

As Elihu says, *"It is the spirit in a man that gives understanding."* This source of wisdom has significant implications for the way we engage with the whole of life; the way we manage everything from our families right through to economies. It should be foundational in the way we think about how we do business, education, politics and therapy, and the way we work with communities and nations. It will inform the way we work productively with people who have been in disasters as well as the way we help people survive emotional trauma and the way we rebuild hope in communities.

The internal source of strength and resilience in the face of catastrophe

As people become attuned to their spirit and its intuitive wisdom they find themselves becoming aware of an internal source of strength and a heightened sensitivity to truth. They acquire a key reference point in realising their own autonomy in the face of that which threatens to destroy. In the face of the darkest threats they will find their own authentic voice and the capacity to represent it even when all about them seem intent on resenting and speaking against them.

The spirit's role in finding and representing ourselves to others

Our conscious mind is immersed in a range of intuitive impulses and emotional needs that come from a semiconscious awareness of the higher yearnings of the human spirit as it wrestles against the deficits that inflame and drive our lower nature. It is time to acknowledge the significance of this inner struggle and to bring it out into the open.

It is time to recover an understanding of the function of the human spirit in the shaping of a healthy and resilient identity, in the shaping of visionary thinking for strategic leaders and in the building of a healthy shared culture. An understanding of the spirit's integrating role will not only promote freedom from destructive grasping self-focus but will also facilitate what our world needs so desperately, the growth towards transcendent community through the celebration of our unique shared humanity.

Going back to the dawn of the human spirit and what defaced it

In this journey of discovery we will go backwards through the centuries to show how this significant part of us has been there since the emergence of mankind itself. In the story of creation we are told man was created from the dust of the ground and the Almighty breathed the breath of life into him: Only then he was declared complete. However subsequent experiences of bad faith, deficits and emotional bruises skewed mankind's orientation away from his natural place of peace and home.

We see this referenced in Zechariah 12:1 by its author, the post exilic prophet, *"This is the word of the Lord concerning Israel. The Lord who stretches out the heavens and lays the foundations of the earth, **and who forms the spirit of man within him."*** (emphasis mine)

The breath of life = the spirit = the source of understanding

In the ancient book of Job we hear Elihu say, *"It is the breath of God in a man, the spirit in a man that gives understanding."* Why is this so noteworthy? The distinctive of Job is that it was written before the other Judeo-Christian Scriptures and is part of what are called the Wisdom Books of the Old Testament. Unlike other parts of the Old Testament the Wisdom Books do not focus on the rise and decline of the Hebrew people.

The Wisdom Books focus on questions that usually stump us

They focus on existential questions that every thinking human being has had to wrestle with at some time in their lives. As previously noted, they have been called the *"how to"* books of the Bible.

Job : How to make sense of suffering

Psalms : How to connect with your spirit and God in worship

Proverbs: How to make sense of yourself in everyday living

Ecclesiastes: How to find lasting purpose and fulfilment and joy

Song of Songs: how to discover authentic love beyond infatuation

The Psalms were written by King David and the last three, Proverbs Ecclesiastes and Song of Songs, were written by King Solomon. Why is the book of Job so significant? The dialogue in the book wrestles with the great existential question of human suffering, a question as old as human literature itself.

Why do good people suffer? And why me?

Job's story was probably written at the time Joseph was managing the economy in Egypt which would place it before Moses compiled the first five books of the Judaeo-Christian scriptures. It is interesting then to see the themes that arise - that bad things happen to good people and that there is evil in the world. These are issues that confound the capacity of reason alone.

When reason has no answer

As we look closely at the characters in this ancient story we find that Job, who is disclosed to us in Job 29, is a remarkable human being - something of a cross between Francis of Assisi and Mother Teresa.

In the face of the multiple tragedies that have befallen him (Job 1:6 to 2:10) we realize it is no wonder he feels he is tottering on the edge of sanity. Then come the three friends whose traditional Level 2 left hemisphere mindset prevent them from empathising and building a sense of community with him. They have a closed attitude of, *"Wow, what bad thing did you do to receive this punishment?"* Their response would push most mere mortals completely over the edge.

Elihu turns up with the stuff that makes people legendary

Then comes Elihu, the central figure of our book. He is the young man with uncontaminated vision and a pure heart, the stuff legends are made of. He is like a young King Arthur or Frodo, the small hobbit entrusted with the burden of the fateful ring in Tolkien's great epic *"The Lord of the Rings."*

In this oldest piece of human literature known to man we catch a glimpse of a good young man not yet contaminated by compromise. He has another way of knowing and his communication cuts through the fog. He has the clear intention of bringing restoration and life, unlike Job's three friends who are out to prove Job's moral failure. Elihu says, *"Job, speak up, for I want you to be cleared."* (Job 33:32). It is the voice of truth with grace.

The spirit of Elihu is everywhere

Once we crack the code we recognise it. In contrast to the three friends Elihu has a more gracious spirit working in him. Today we can see the same spirit in young men and women who like Elihu, are sensitive to issues of truth, justice and mercy. In their early years both David and Solomon, authors of the other Wisdom Books, were like Elihu, but they lost their way.

Learning from those who lost their balance

In their youth David and Solomon saw with the clarity of a good heart. In his Psalms we often see David try to get himself sorted out after losing the plot but being swamped by fear. Psalm 73 is a classic example of his feeling lost and depressed then rediscovering his spiritual intelligence. (It's worth a read.)

The circumstances of life tend to swamp us all, but some find a special place within; the spirit. Others might call it conscience but it is the part of us that chooses not to react emotionally to what is happening but to face oneself and see the truth in the situation. This is what I am calling spiritual intelligence. David does this often in the Psalms as he seems to talk to himself. We see it in Psalm 42:5 when his spirit asks his soul, *"Why are you downcast, O my soul? Why so disturbed within me?"*

The inner dialogue the key to self- regulation

From deep in his soul David's spirit shows him how to re-encounter his lost peace, *"Put your hope in God"*, then, *"for I will yet praise him."* He continues in Psalm 42:8 in the reassured tone of somebody who is now more spiritually integrated, *"By day the Lord directs his love, at night his song is with me."* We are hearing the inner dialogue of a person becoming re-anchored in the place where spiritual intelligence is born.

The anchored soul and the source of wisdom

King Solomon started out well. When asked to choose what he most wanted, he said he wanted understanding and wisdom. Guided by his spirit he became a remarkable young scientist examining and naming the natural world. In the beginning he was like a young Elihu but his own reputation seemed to divert his focus to his ego needs and they eventually claimed him. He enjoyed the reputation and identity, the self-concept (shaped by the left hemisphere) of being a wise man which paradoxically, meant he lost sight of the source of his wisdom. He no longer had a heart attuned to God and his creation.

Solomon's sensitivity to his reputation for wisdom was his slippery slope

Like his father David before him Solomon got entangled with women - 700 wives and 300 concubines. (Some people collect stamps but this is a little over the top!)

We believe Solomon wrote the love poem we call *"The Song of Songs"* when he was a young prince trying to work out the nature of true love, and in his early manhood the book of Proverbs so as to give his young sons some kind of foundation in spirituality and common-sense.

He wrote the book of Ecclesiastes when he was older and fighting off despair about what had become a self-absorbed and wasted life. Between Ecclesiastes 1:12 and 2:11 there are more than 60 personal pronouns. He had become full of himself. He was a celebrated success but as for many celebrities, this caused him to lose contact with his intrinsic spiritual nature.

The rediscovery of the integrating principle

As we redress this imbalance, the neglect of the human spirit, we may find a new understanding is being formed, one that will unite the latest understandings of psychology, psychiatry and neurology with a practical understanding of the ancient wisdom that makes sense of our personal existence. It might just lead us into to a new era of knowing ourselves and to the healing of souls. Once we crack the code we may well find words for something humankind has half known all along.

Becoming a double minded person

Back to David: In Psalm 51 we saw him wrestling with himself and God after being found out by the prophet Nathan. (You will find the dramatic story in 2 Samuel chapters 11 and 12). David is in a state of psychological and spiritual devastation. Many of his Psalms are really poems and songs that rise from his core yearnings as he tries to make sense of various crises he finds himself in.

In Psalm 51:17 we see him doing therapy on himself in the presence of the Divine Being. He is asking for help for his human spirit as he seeks a way back to the same sense of divine connection spoken about by Elihu. In this Psalm there is only one mention of the Holy Spirit and that is in verse 11, but in verse 12 David prays that God will grant him a willing spirit to sustain him.

Powerful deficits and what they produce

We all have powerful deficits that draw us into situations that can make it feel as though we have another will within us. In Psalm 51 verse 17 David says, *"The sacrifices of God are a broken spirit; a broken and contrite heart, O God, you will not despise."* In Verse 10 he prays, *"Create in me a pure heart, O God, and renew a steadfast spirit within me."*

Renew a right spirit within me: help me be realigned with my real self

David knows that because of his affair with Bathsheba he has lost contact with the purity of intention that gave him his steadfastness of spirit. He knows he needs a willing spirit but he knows his path to a sense of wholeness will only come through a *"broken spirit and a broken and contrite heart."* In Psalm 51 we see him doing soul work. He's separating his higher self, his spirit, from the neurotic dynamics of his soul produced by emotional deficits.

Hebrews 4:12 says, *"The word of God is living and active. Sharper than any double-edged sword, it penetrates even to dividing soul (ego) and spirit... It judges the thoughts and attitudes of the heart."* This battle between soul and spirit had the apostle Paul cry out in anguish, *"Who will deliver me from my own duplicity? The good that I want to do I don't do; the bad things I hate and don't want to do, I do. God help me."* (paraphrase of Romans 7: 14 – 25.) He feels he is doomed to live his life chained to an impulsive stranger.

David knows he has lost his authentic voice

This produces what is called the double-minded man. David, like Paul, can see how far he has moved from a single-hearted love relationship with God. It is interesting to note in verse 10 of Psalm 51 he says, *"Create in me a pure heart, O God."*

In the Beatitudes Matthew 5:8 Jesus said, *"Blessed are the pure in heart for they will see God."* This is a heart free from secondary motives and from the combination of an inner exquisite ache of psychic need shielded by an ego that's got to look good and be right. It is an amazing level of awareness on David's part.

We all have mixed motives but theology tells us that a pure heart is a miraculous phenomenon. As this book unfolds we will see that a pure heart also brings clarity and peace to one's whole being and personality. We are so caught up in the battle between the spirit and the soul (ego) that usually we can't tell whether the soul is usurping the pure intention of the heart.

At the end of time I have no doubt that the greatest creation of God who spoke and whole worlds came into being, will be celebrated. What is it? It is most likely to be those frail human beings who have a pure heart. Psalm 51: 6 most clearly shows the human spirit in operation yet it does not even mention the spirit, *"Surely you desire truth in the inner parts; you teach me wisdom in the inmost place."*

Knowing truth at the core, the inmost place, the spirit

This is where we do our soul work; when we journal, when we pray, when we communicate we listen to our own thoughts with an inner ear. If we really want to we can tell if we have mixed motives. We can tell if we are being phony, if we are exaggerating or if we are telling a story that is just a bit more colourful and a little larger than the reality we experienced. No animal knows or experiences the sense of integrity that can come with honest self-examination. It was that sense of integrity that David had lost and he yearned for its return.

The human spirit is the source of our conscience and sanity

It is the human spirit that informs our conscience. It sensitises us to truth and cares about justice. From the human spirit comes the yearning to be freed from the internal distortions external structures and false paradigms that prevent us from seeing from our heart clearly.

This part of our humanity is to be treasured by us, nurtured not tampered with in children, kept alive in marriages and respected in cultures.

It will have to be of the spirit if we are to save the flesh

General Douglas MacArthur, when accepting the surrender of the Japanese on the battleship Missouri, reflected on the devastation caused by two atom bombs and the devastating years of war, *"It must be of the spirit, if we are to save the flesh."* After the destruction and suffering of Europe, the bloody conflict of the Pacific caused by the Second World War and the monstrous nuclear weapons that brought it to an end, Macarthur recognized that the human ego at its core needs a transformation if civilisation is to survive.

The human spirit is one of the highest creations of God

Back to Zechariah chapter 12:1, *"This is the word of the Lord concerning Israel. The Lord who stretches out the heavens, and lays the foundation of the earth, and who forms the spirit of man within him..."*

The human spirit is one of the highest creations of God, a profound motivating dynamic in our personality. For it to bring all of its potential illumination it needs the grace of God to lift it to its highest expression - that of a pure heart, something the human mind however educated simply cannot create.

This is why the Christian Gospel story and what God is doing in it will always appeal to those human spirit is honest enough to recognise they are not truly free but yearn to be.

Our spirit is a core aspect of who we are as human beings and as we will show, is usually subconscious.

Chapter 14

WHY IT NEEDS TO BE OF THE SPIRIT IF WE ARE TO SAVE THE FLESH

"It must be of the spirit if we are to save the flesh."

General Douglas MacArthur (1880 – 1964) Commander of the Southwest Pacific Theatre in World War II, administered post-war Japan during the Allied occupation that followed and led United Nations forces during the first 9 months of the Korean War.

Throughout this book I have referenced what I believe to be the key insight that potentially illuminates our personal existence. It is the insight referenced by General Douglas MacArthur when he said, *"It must be of the spirit if we are to save the flesh."* We can now get a handle on the nature of this spirit and the remarkable continuum of sensitivities it can produce in us if we are aware of its promptings.

Spiritual intelligence

There is a back story that frames the Elihu narrative, a narrative that is the key reference point in helping us make sense of ourselves. It focuses the core humanising quest of the human heart and is in fact the dynamic behind the revelation of the whole Bible.

When Elihu says in Job 32:8, *"It is the spirit in a man, the breath of the Almighty that gives him understanding,"* he reveals one of the most remarkable and distinctive features of human consciousness at the same time referencing what will become the peak revelation and major insight of the special sub-theme of the Bible.

We can be spiritually dead yet breathing

As we explore the various themes that tend to surface when the transcendent aspect of our human consciousness is expressing its innate spiritual nature, we discover something just a bit beautiful.

Real human life is meant to be beautiful

The Biblical story holds a mirror to our highest nature and the focus of this book has so far been on this higher aspect of our human nature. Experience shows us however there is so much more to the story.

We see exactly what happens when the inclinations of the spirit are subverted into the service of power, greed and selfishness, all of which produce a dark insatiable vacuum. No matter how strong our ego defences, in the words of Swiss psychiatrist and psychoanalyst Carl Jung, *"Deep down below the surface of the average conscience a still small voice that says to us, something is out of tune."*

We cannot be completely happy because our spirit knows when we are disconnected from its influence. When this occurs we are often, at the very least, left with a low level sadness, if not a depressive flatness.

Where does the human inclination to be destructive come from?

The illuminating and generous life-giving nature of the spirit can all too often be quenched, thus inverting the normal characteristics of the spirit's turning light into darkness. Its absence leaves an insatiable yet exquisite ache. The Rolling Stones' classic song *"I can't get no satisfaction"* could easily be the tragic insignia tune of a self-absorbed generation that has become spiritually anorexic. However it doesn't stop there. This dark absence will tend to contaminate everything it touches becoming a pernicious and destructive force. A core question: How come supposedly rational human beings who know to do good, still choose to do evil?

The transcendent life of the human spirit if quenched can have a dark side

Something so profound to our human nature as the spirit, should not have only one story to reveal its situation. And of course it doesn't.

An exploration of the Biblical record soon reveals that Elihu is not the only one in the Judeo Christian scriptures who talks about the breath of God in a man, the spirit in a man that gives life and understanding. There are many passages that talk about the spirit of man and the Spirit of God and three special events explicitly tell very similar stories about a divine breath that brings life.

The spirit's relationship to human life and death

All these narratives have profound personal implications for all of us. They are not just a series of religious tales but they reveal the secret of what holds things together, particularly the key to experiencing the rich fulfilled life all human beings were originally designed to have.

The latest research on the human mind reveals profound forces behind the thoughts that bubble up into our mind. Dr. John Bargh (born 1955 in America), is a social psychologist working at Yale University where he formed the Automaticity in Cognition, Motivation, and Evaluation Laboratory. In his book *"Before you Know It,"* he shows clearly the unconscious factors that influence how we think and act, writing that in fact, *"The unconscious can lead us astray if we are not aware of its influence."*

The unconscious can lead us astray if we lack awareness of its power

 Most of us are something of a mystery to ourselves so there are important disciplines to help us discern where our spirit is in the midst of it all? A recent volume on psychotherapy presents 36 different therapeutic approaches and it is believed many of these paradigms will be sub-divided yet again.

36 different approaches to psychotherapy

Victor Frankl warns, *"Every psychotherapy is based upon anthropological implications."* He goes on to say *"Diagnosis and treatment methods must of necessity be related to the subject of the application - man himself... thus the question, what is man? needs to be squarely faced. And the second question must also be confronted, what is the meaning of his existence?"*

Some philosophers believe that mankind has the task to design itself or discover itself, but Frankl believes *"Mankind cannot discover himself or design himself."* He asserts, *"The true discovery of our essential humanness or the inventio hominis occurs only in the Imitatio Dei - imitation of God."*

We uncover the authentic self as we identify ourselves with Jesus

Victor Frankl believes that while we don't create ourselves we do discover our spiritual nature and integrate it into our conscious sense of self. His view is that this is the only way for us to transcend our neurotic self and the unconscious dynamics at work in us. In the Book of Romans, 7:15, the Apostle Paul says *"I don't understand what I do .. For what I want to do I don't do and what I hate I do."* He goes on to say that he feels as though he is doomed to spend much of his life chained to a stranger - his other self.

And don't we all feel a bit like that from time to time?

In the very next chapter of the same book of Romans, 8:16, Paul has learned the secret of his own spirit's liberation through being identified with the Divine Son and sensing through that identification his own spiritual family attachment. It should not take us by surprise.

For centuries we have been told there are non-rational forces at work in us

For over 5,000 years the Bible has been trying to help us sort out internally, what is worthless from what is the precious: Similarly the father of Greek Philosophy Socrates, tried to seek for virtue.

In this book we can see through the fog of a person's current consciousness that this kind of moral clarity is possible. This kind of awareness can however, only become available via the facility of a yearning and receptive state of heart and mind.

The Divine Being speaking in the Bible says, *"If you seek me with your whole heart you will find me."* Deuteronomy 4:29

On the edge of life's mystery: Finding the key

All these stories are profound, but if you can first locate your spiritual yearning then let yourself be led by it down the path to awareness of the truth that's waiting, you will find an existential dimension poised to unfold. Only then will you find you have been brought to the edge of a place that Elihu's consciousness or what I have called *"Elihu's key,"* can alone unlock, hence the title of this book.

What lies at our core waiting to be discovered?

As we unpack the following stories we will be led to glimpse our best selves. If we stay with it we will find it's a bit like unpacking a special gift. What are these stories? And how do they work in revealing to us our spirit's intelligence and most normal orientation?

The surprising sources of this illumination

1st The creation narrative is found in the first three chapters of the Bible. I encourage you to read it lightly as one would savour a favourite poem or piece of music. Look for expressions of what is distinctive to the human spirit. In doing so you might find places where truth, love, responsibility, creativity and agency become visible.

Looking for the human spirit, keep in mind what seems so obvious we rarely think of it - that dogs and cows don't care about truth or beauty, that there is no evidence that animals can even see a beautiful sunset let alone be inspired by it.

Most of us fail to recognise how profound it is for us humans to hear our psychological birth story for the very first time. This is why Viktor Frankl was so captivated by it all. For him it revealed emotionally satisfying answers to the following existential questions that science and psychology have no adequate answers for:-

- Where did we come from?

- Why are we here?

- What does an inspired human being look like?

- What is the distinctive nature of how we relate to life and all we connect to?

- What is the nature our connection with our world and all we have some kind of a relationship with?

- Finally, how come we humans seem to have a big and fatal flaw?

This is not meant to be a technical exposition of human biology

The brief bold strokes of this narrative reveal it was never meant to be the final word about the technical aspects of human physical and biological development. Similarly our place in the pattern of creation left work for we inspired human souls to grasp. Yes, we have been given to inquire and to reach for understanding so as to find our role in participating in the creative process. It seems our spirit was given space so that its God given inclination to name, discover and create would be free to participate in the unfolding nature of creation. It would do this by working at probing the mysteries of the universe to find yet more answers to the as yet unknown.

The creation narrative has at its peak moment, the creation of humankind

Remember Elihu's contribution, *"It's the breath of God in a man the spirit in a man that gives understanding."* This was a gift, given so man could explore and recognise what lies at the deepest point of human existence and creation. (More of this later)

2nd The story of the dry bones is found in Ezekiel 37:5 where God says *"I will make breath enter you, and you will come to life."* Many of us are willing to acknowledge modern non-community human beings tend to look increasingly like emotionally empty shells. It is possible to exist without being alive psychically. Why the sex, drugs and rock n' roll if we're not trying to trick ourselves into believing we are truly alive. Many contemporary economies are largely driven by the relentless psychological drive to feel alive.

The dead bones of one's own soul need to be brought to life

One only has to observe commuters in peak hour traffic to see many on trains and buses hiding behind newspapers or retreating to their iPhone and digital music. Too often we arrive home to the safe harbour of our primary relationships - spouse children and family dog, only to find, regardless of how much we love them, emotionally we feel like an ironing board. No matter how hard we try we find we simply cannot be emotionally present. We have nothing to give.

At these times we know what we long to do but in spite of all the clichés confirming guilt and failure in our head, the dead bones of one's own soul need to be brought alive. We need the divine breath.

3rd In John's Gospel Chapter 20:22 is a narrative in which we see a bunch of Jesus' defeated followers who probably felt like the emotionally lifeless skeletons of the book of Ezekiel. It is this event that will lead them to transformation - to get a new lease of life. Authentic spirituality does not mean we have gone *off with the pixies* but that we have in fact become profoundly anchored in reality.

Spirituality is not about avoiding life but engaging tenaciously with it

Stay with me as we take the journey because at first glimpse these stories may not look so inspiring. As you let your spirit lead you down the path that Elihu's key can unlock you will eventually find you have come upon a door to a new way of understanding - an understanding you probably vaguely half knew but the significance of which you have never fully grasped.

The divine breath promises a new life orientation

As we come to these narratives that have important significance to our mental health we will find we are not the first. A number of schools of psychiatry have been exploring this realm for years. Carl Jung spent a lot of his time probing what he called the collective unconscious, looking below the presenting story, reaching for what he called the profound archetypal stories. Where did they come from? And why have they inspired almost all who have plumbed the depth of what they are trying to reveal to us?

It was Antonio Machado the Spanish poet and philosopher who said, *"Under all that we think, lives all we believe, like the ultimate veil of our spirits."*

Where do our deepest and heartfelt motivations come from? We're not as cognitive and rational as modern secular education tries to tell us. The whole of the thought and culture of nation states and civilizations is made up of what are called shared symbols of meaning.

It is our shared belief systems that bring social cohesion

Societies put together stories from their history that tell them who they are. These are called social myths. A myth in sociology is not a fairy tale - quite the contrary! It is effective in uniting the consciousness of the people only to the extent it is uncritically believed by them to be a true reflection of things as they are.

Bronislaw Malinowski (1884 – 1942) born in Poland and died in America, is often considered to be the most important anthropologist of the 20th century. About the powerful belief systems that hold civilizations together he said, *"Myth is not an explanation for the satisfaction of scientific interest, but a narrative of primeval reality, told to the satisfaction of deep religious want, moral cravings, social submissions, assertions, even practical requirements. Myth is thus a vital ingredient of human civilization. It is not an idle tale, but a hard-worked active force. It is not an intellectual explanation of an artistic imagery, but a pragmatic charter of primitive faith and moral wisdom."*

Whenever you see human beings questing for meaning and practical truth you know the human spirit is behind it and driving the quest.

It is easier to destroy what is beautiful in a culture than to create it

The civilizing values that inform a heathy culture have usually been shaped by crises and historic events that have helped people separate the worthless from the precious. Stories and parables are an attempt to put into memorable form the life lessons a people believe should never be forgotten. At its best this process helps people make sense of their lives in the face of the raw and contradictory evidence that confronts them daily.

The best way to unravel a culture's civilizing values

It is a dangerous time for a culture when a group of committed social revolutionaries attempt to undermine it. They often do this by seeking to get the ear of the vulnerable and alienated pointing out inconsistencies in the prevailing narrative. They will also attempt to focus those who are marginalised on what supposedly victimises them thus justifying a latent anger and turning those who feel like victims into self-righteous persecutors. At the same time sympathetic souls are invited to identify with those who look like victims inclining them to become rescuers.

Psychiatrist Stephen Karpman (a student under father of transactional analysis Eric Berne) conceived the social model that maps this type of destructive interaction that can occur between people in conflict; it now bears his name, The Karpman Drama Triangle.

In this process those committed to undermine a culture seek to trigger archaic emotions and thus bypass reason. It is all subconsciously designed to undermine the prevailing narrative with the undergirding values and the world view and beliefs that come from it.

A long history of those wanting to unravel the hold of the Judeo-Christian story

Few realize what chaos will be released if they manage to unravel the complex web of self- limiting choices that hold our society together. This is why it has been said that every social revolution eventually becomes a failed revolution. The Russians tried to do it for over 75 years in the Soviet era.

While social fads come and go there is something about the beauty that springs from the human spirit that will in the long run, demand recognition and transcend the trivial fads and fancies of most eras.

Regardless of how they are attacked, those values anchored in the Judeo Christian story have a resilience because they have been found to be true over many centuries. How have they survived?

Their survival stems from the reality that the values are anchored in the eternal sweep of the cosmic story and echoed in the moral yearnings at the very core of the human spirit.

Some things are based on foundations that can outlast the transient

These stories have their roots deep within the mystery of the human spirit's unique sense of the eternal.

Why? While not every person is sensitive to it, the human spirit with its sense of the eternal has the capacity, like the in-love experience, to rise up and disturb and confound the most settled and rational of people. The prompting to faith has at times risen up and made itself known unexpectedly, even to those who may have been among the loudest of atheists. C.S. Lewis in his book *"Surprised by Joy"* described himself as *"the most dejected, reluctant convert in all of England, dragged into the kingdom kicking, struggling, resentful, and darting his eyes in every direction for a chance of escape."*

Was it like this for Moses? We don't know, but it is fascinating to ask

Did Moses get some kind of clue from the book of Job since it was probably written earlier, or did he independently find inspiration from the rich oral tradition that may have illuminated an inspired writer of clay tablets?

Transcribing the story that reflects the music of the spheres

It probably doesn't matter so much how a piano is made and tuned. The real inspiration lies in the fingers that glide across the ivories bringing the music alive to the receptive spirit.

In a similar process the human author illuminated by the Divine Being was an active participant in the moment of revelation. As the chosen scribe worked faithfully on the sacred task of giving shape and form to the profound story, for him as for the musician, the experience may have seemed that he was transcribing the music of the spheres.

Something of the same inspiration was expressed by George Frederic Handel after he'd written The Hallelujah Chorus when with tears streaming down his cheeks he said to his elderly servant, *"I did think I saw heaven open, and saw the very face of God."*

Where did the God breathing on man story begin?

Ezekiel who brings us the story of the dead bones knew that he was probably under the same spirit of inspiration borrowing images from Elihu or Moses. We have every reason to believe that Jesus himself had studied them all and was very alive to the eternal message they conveyed. The *breathing story* in John 20:19-23 provides the climactic communication event.

For those who can hear its subliminal message this is transforming

Why? Because in using it as a metaphor the master communicator Jesus of Nazareth provides a capstone for the whole Bible. In doing so he reveals an amazing multi-level insight into human existence and the existential ache that motivates us. For the humble willing he provides the resolution to the central question lingering in our soul. He also brings into focus the non-rational psychological drivers which alone are able to explain the complex dynamics behind the mystery of our human motivation.

How does Jesus weave together these stories and in so doing also profile what was implicit in Elihu's insight?

Let's take the disciples down from the fairy-tale shelf of our mind

The John account of *the breath* that focuses our thinking is found in the all-important passage John 20:19-22. I encourage you to read it.

The secret of understanding the Bible is to get inside the mind of the hearers and ask what they understood from what they heard, and also to get inside the mind of the communicator to ask what he was intending to convey. This is called the science and art of hermeneutics and if we do this we will find there is so much more going on than first appears. Some of it is quite revolutionary.

Let's first get inside the skin of the hearers. They were shattered

The disciples were a bit like Ezekiel's dancing bones. They believed themselves to be attending the wake of a much loved leader when the person they thought had been executed turned up and said, *"Peace be with you."*

The Hebrew word for peace, shalom, while being a common greeting in Jesus' day also carried a sense of everything finally coming together in an integrated way. It was not simply about the absence of conflict but the profound theological hope and insight that promised progression towards an end-time sense of completion, nothing less than a universal telos - an ultimate climax of history.

The climactic coming together of the whole created order

Remember the situation? They had thought they were following a leader who was about to bring in the climax of the ages only to have one of their own betray both him and them. Stinging their minds forever would be the memory of Judas' kiss of betrayal.

Then Peter, another one of their own who had been marked out to be a leader among them, denied any knowledge of Jesus at the very time he was being brutally interrogated. They had all scurried off leaving this Messiah unsupported to face an unjust and unlawful trial for his life. Not too much to be proud of here.

To cap it off, the very next day he had been executed on a cross between two criminals with the crowd howling for his blood, and not one voice known to have been raised in his support. All of them had expected him to be hailed as a messianic hero yet they hadn't even had time to say sorry or goodbye.

Death was not the expectation as they had arrived in Jerusalem

They were expecting to be leading the armies of this Messiah in a glorious coup; one that would kick the occupying force of the Roman Army into the Mediterranean Sea.

Jesus had not led them astray. In Mark's Gospel, the earliest of the four Gospels, he had told them he was going to Jerusalem to die but had also made it clear he would be coming back from the dead. It is recorded in Mark 8:31,32: 9:31,32: 10:32. Take a look!

However they did not want, or were unable, to hear it. It is not the kind of thing one hears every day but it was very likely a case of: don't confuse me with facts because my mind is already made up. From this distance it is difficult to show just how committed they were to the emotionally satisfying shared vision of their expected future.

For decades young Jewish men had been yearning for a brawl that would enable them to push the occupying army into the Mediterranean Ocean. Of course an executed Messiah was certainly not in their play book. Neither was this spooky arrival just when they were coming to terms with the horror of the ghastly execution and the ignominy of their crushed dreams.

"Well boys. Shame you didn't listen to me. Will you believe me now?"

This other-worldly upper room encounter with the previously dead Jesus not only shook them but in time would change the way they saw the world. When the realization finally dawned it had them replay all they had said and done over the previous three and a half years.

What did they, in time, understand about the meaning of this other-worldly encounter? We know that initially they were fearful, expecting a knock at the door any minute and a bunch of soldiers to burst in ready to carry them off. We are told of their fear of the Jews and the temple guard and along with this there would be lingering guilt about leaving him alone to be executed in front of an angry crowd. All this would have been accompanied by despair at the collapse of the dreams they had been so committed to. They would be likely to fall into a dark pit of depression and something of a huge identity crisis.

Who are we now?

In the account in John 20:19-23 when Jesus looked into their eyes after their desertion and his death, his first words carried no hint of blame. They were, *"Peace be with you,"* the very same words they had heard him use to calm the storm on the lake of Galilee. At this point it was likely that their identities were being tossed about in an emotional turmoil redolent of such a storm.

"Peace be with you."

Initially these words were no doubt deeply comforting after those huge depressive waves that had pounded the shores of their delicate sanity. (It is interesting to note there are 366 *"fear not"* and *"peace be unto you's"* in the Bible). After calming their internal world with this gentle and empathetic tone however, he then showed them his hands and side. Hardly an act likely to make them feel good!

There would have been nail marks in his wrists where the weight of his body had left horrible stretch marks, as well as the ghastly gaping wound left by the Roman executioner's spear thrust into his side so as to be absolutely sure Jesus was dead. This Roman officer would, with all others present, have seen that when the spear pierced the Nazarene's side, what they believed to be blood and water leaked from the wound. We now know the centurion's spear must have pierced the pericardium-sac around the heart.

Eye-witness to the first ever autopsy in human history

In reporting this we are seeing something of an autopsy because when a person's blood separates into its constituent parts he will have been dead for some time. Only John, the women - the so-called weaker sex - the quaternion and the centurion who led them, would have seen it. The darkness over the scene seems to have scared most of the bystanders away. Judas, who had betrayed them all including himself, was making plans to end his life. Apart from John, the rest of the bewildered disciples seemed to have cleared out and were cringing under stair wells. There were still though more than enough eye-witnesses to prove the truth about his death in any reasonable court of law. This was no product of an exhausted imagination.

Not a fairy tale! He is now here talking to them

How could one's frail mind make sense of it? How could they compute it all? The impact was profound. Eventually it would give them a new lease on life, literally. They would no longer be the defeated little crowd they'd been up till this moment. They had experienced an encounter with another dimension of reality, one so profound and illuminating it would transform them from a cowering huddle of fearful men into a confident and assertive bunch.

It was an encounter that would lift them, inspiring them to initiate a global movement that would eventually challenge the whole Roman Empire and spread throughout the civilized world. It is a movement that has seen off the communist empire of Russia, and in atheistic China, despite decades of persecution, there are now more followers of Jesus than members of the monolithic Communist Party. In spite of constant talk about this being a post-Christian era with countless rumours of its demise, Christianity is a growing global movement to this day.

Christianity is growing everywhere except among those who think they know what it is

The story of what the event meant was called the gospel, which means the ultimate good news. The palpably real, concrete and historic manifestation was of course a real mind-bender. No doubt it would take time for the rest of what it all meant to sink in, not only for his followers but also for many in the West who think they know what the essence of Christianity is.

Many who presume their outdated fifty year old memory of a poorly taught Sunday School lesson defines it all, have failed to face up to some of life's most remarkable and fundamental questions. They are therefore unable to recognise the difference between an immature attempt to indoctrinate them with their family tribal religion and the radical life and insights of Jesus of Nazareth. As a result there are many who fail to comprehend what is essential in order to anchor their existence deep within the spiritual framework of the Christian faith's brilliant and living way of knowing.

The moment the profound meaning of what it is all about is revealed

In referencing the divine breath of the Genesis story Jesus echoes Elihu's *"breath of God in a man"* and the dead bones of Ezekiel. He is pointing to what life is and what it is not: It is not merely existing!

Too often we have been barely existing; have merely been human-like things

We have all come across friends and acquaintances who seem to have gone – who have disappeared into an emotional cave; the lights seem to be on but nobody is home! We have all had those moments when the body is present but we have disappeared.

Little children know it all too well. When mum is exhausted that is when they tend to play up the most. Why? They would rather have negative feedback than be left in a vacuum. Whether it is exhaustion, or the mind working on some conscious or subconscious unfinished business we and those with us realize there are times we may be physically present but certainly not all of who we are is there. We have become like Ezekiel's bones, lifeless human-like things. It could be said that the great threat of our times is dehumanisation and alienation.

Spiritual intelligence means all of who we are is present, body soul and spirit

When spiritual life and all it signifies is deeply grasped it will lay radical and new foundations to all we know about psychology, sociology, education and what it truly means for humans to be whole.

What does it mean to be whole and really alive?

It is spiritual intelligence that will also make clear that there always were more profound philosophic and theological dimensions to what was afoot in the Book of Job and the comments from Elihu, as well as in the three narratives in which we see the metaphor of God breathing on his people.

They were important and revolutionary clues to show us the full human life

They were in fact important, revolutionary signs and symbols intended to introduce us humans and our society both to our fatal flaw and to its remedy.

We will also find what it is that draws us to these highest expressions of ourselves, the unique and transcendent aspects of our humanity that grip and inspire us in the best moments of our lives. It is in these uplifting narratives we are reminded that we were meant for something more. These stories uplift us because we see the triumph of our own best selves reflected in them.

Of course these stories also remind us that we were originally created to be deeply attuned through the spirit to the profound awareness of the divine mind.

Chapter 15

DISCERNING BETWEEN IMPULSES OF THE PSYCHE AND SPIRITUAL PROMPTINGS

"You have to leave the city of your comfort and go into the wilderness of your intuition. What you'll discover will be wonderful. What you'll discover is yourself."

Alan Alda (*1936 - *) *Actor, director, screenwriter, comedian and author. Six time Emmy award winner and Golden Globe Award winner*

Missing the moment

How does it work? Because of our special creation if we are attuned to the promptings of our spirit we have the capacity to tune into a divine frequency. It is as if our human spirit is a radio receiver so if we are alive to its continual communication remarkable things can happen. Most of us however, miss out on some of the significant and pivotal moments of our lives that we have been made for.

Response to a prompting that averted a tragedy

She'd been looking forward to this holiday for a long-time. The children were playing in the river that ran all the way to sea and, using the book she was reading to insulate herself from the stresses of the previous year, she quietly luxuriated saying to herself, *"This is me time."* The voices of the children at play were a pleasant background sound when bubbling up from somewhere deep within, came a feeling of apprehension. She thought to herself, *"I'm not going to be distracted from my moment of recreation and comfort."*

The foreboding became more insistent. Would she engage with the real world and look up and see the children? It took a significant amount of moral energy to do it. Telling me this story in a radio interview she said, *"For the rest of my life I will pay much more attention to these promptings."* Why? Because on this occasion she looked up just in time to see the dorsal fin of a shark heading toward her children playing in the shallows. She screamed out a demand for them to leave the water and reached out to grab them as the shark lunged.

Too often we miss the promptings

As vivid as this story is I am now convinced similar stories are played out in most of our lives in any given year. This case is so vivid because it sharply contrasts the soporific frame of mind she was in with the profound danger to her children.

How do you think she would have felt had she remained what I call spiritually lazy? How would she have lived with herself for the rest of her life? In this instance it would not just have been an archaic parent tape in her head beating her around; instead she would have had to live with the fact that her selfish orientation had her miss the moment in which she could have protected the precious lives of those most dear to her.

I believe we are wired by our spirit to be tuned to a larger life-giving reality, however our self-absorption and the impulses of our lower nature tend to set our agenda and shape our immediate level of thinking.

Sometimes we have to unlearn some of our first habituated responses before we can be confident of the message from our spirits.

The day 140 passengers on board Batik Air were saved by a spiritually sensitive pilot

Extensive News coverage Oct 2 2018 -BBC, CBN, Fox Telegraph U.K.)

On September 28th 2018 a series of earthquakes struck central Sulawesi Indonesia with magnitude 7.5 on the Richter Scale. It was a big one.

Soon after the main shock a swirling tsunami struck Palu City. It was a nightmare! This dreadful event was the deadliest earthquake to hit Indonesia since 2006 and produced over 4000 casualties.

A few minutes before this great tragedy a strange event took place. One that made headlines around the world and was many believe, an amazing miracle.

Central to this event were the promptings experienced by the pilot

Pilot Ricoseta Mafella of Batik Air felt a strange awareness surface and demand his attention. He recounts that during that Friday he had felt a strange prompting in his spirit that led him to praise God in song.

A strange prompting to sing out loud in the cockpit

As a Christian it was not uncommon for him to hum hymns quietly to himself but being a Christian in a predominantly Muslim country meant he felt a certain hesitation to be so demonstrative about his faith.

A few minutes before the tragedy what many believe is a miracle happened for Captain Mafella who, during the whole of that Friday, had been feeling a little uncomfortable.

A strange feeling that was a mixture of joy and apprehension began to rise

At the beginning he was inclined to push the feeling away so as to focus on the task of flying the plane. He couldn't help wondering though, if he should pay attention to this feeling? However strange it was he felt a prompting to sing songs out loud to God finding it brought a sense peace and resolution.

He now needed to concentrate though as he was circling to land at Palu. The airport was known by pilots as the *"valley of death"* because it is situated dangerously between two difficult mountain ranges. As he was coming into land a part of his mind was already gearing up to fly to his next destination Ujung Pandang from Palau.

A sense of urgency began to push him and with it, to the surprise of his crew, he says *"I felt impelled to praise the Lord unashamedly."* As the plane swung in to land he says, *"The Lord whispered into my heart to circle again before landing. The words of Psalm 23 verse 4 came to my mind 'Though I walk through the valley of the shadow of death I will fear no evil for you are with me.'"*

He felt a strange sense of peace and urgency

As he landed he sensed there was not a moment to waste. He instructed his crew members to make haste, *"No time for a long break. Get the passengers off and the new ones seated."*

The plane was to return immediately to Padang

The captain requested the control tower permit him to depart at least 3 minutes earlier than the scheduled time and on receiving permission he prepared immediately for take-off.

He noticed the plane beginning to sway and wondered why. Just a few minutes after taking off he attempted to communicate to the tower but received no response and on looking down he saw something strange. The seawater seemed to be boiling and rushing to fill a large hole.

It was certainly turning into a strange kind of day

Upon landing at Pandang airport he was shocked to hear a huge earthquake had triggered a destructive tsunami. The strange events of the morning became clear but sadly the air traffic controller Anthonius Agung had been lost. Had the captain not been prompted to get away 3 minutes earlier than scheduled all the passengers aboard the plane would have died.

Both Captain Mafella and Air traffic controller Anthonius Agung were hailed as heroes for saving the 140 passengers on board that tragic day. Captain Mafella said later, *"Whatever happens, we must be calm and not in a panic so that we can clearly hear God's instructions coming to us through the Holy Spirit."*

The Bible says, *"Be still and know..."* We are able to recognise clearly what the Bible calls the still small voice right there when we tune in to hear the voice of God whispered to our spirit by the Holy Spirit.

The bullet proof chaplain

In his book *"The Man the Anzacs Revered"* author Daniel Reynaud reveals *"Fighting Mac"* - William Mckenzie, Chaplain of the AIF in the First World War. Fighting Mac was a larger than life character and many of the soldiers believed he was bullet proof - that he led a charmed life.

"Wherever he served he was extremely popular with the troops."

For the Aussies who were usually a bit leary about attempts to impose any kind of religion he was different: they felt he was one of them and they knew he would do anything for them – a comfort in this hell on earth where there was not a lot of respect for the English Officers.

The thing they most appreciated though, was that unlike most other chaplains and officers, he would be actively with them in the heat of battle, sometimes comforting and praying for the wounded and dying, at other times bringing food and ammunition to those on the front line who were trying to survive the hail of bullets and bombs.

They all knew nobody would die alone on his watch

Whenever there was a lull in the battle without hesitation he would go into no man's land to tend the wounded and dying or whenever possible to give the dead a Christian burial.

All this in plain sight of enemy sharp shooting snipers

When asked how he managed to survive it all day after day and how he kept up his positive and hopeful demeanour he said that both his faith and what he called his guardian angel, were the secret. But how did it work?

On one occasion he wrote, *"I had just buried seven of these fallen heroes, when my Guardian Angel said, 'Get away from here quickly.' I obeyed instantly and had got away 25 yards in the slanting direction from the enemy's fire when a big artillery shell landed right on the spot I had been standing only minutes before. I only got a shower of dirt.*

At all the times of great danger I'm quietly conscious of this Guardian Angel's presence while engaged on such work. I cannot see him nor can I tell who or what he is like, but I hear his voice sometimes saying – 'Do not go there,' or 'Get in here,' 'Lie down in that shell hole,' 'Be careful,' 'You are quite safe,' 'Wait 5 minutes here,' and suchlike messages."

"I could give at least 6 instances in the past week where prompt attention to his instructions has saved me from those big shells."

In Jeremiah 15:19 we are given a clue as to how it works. The Spirit says it is as we learn to separate the worthless from the precious that clarity will come.

Whether it be speech or action, with clarity comes confidence of spirit. Hebrews 4:12 shows us how the good Chaplain Mac through the discipline of years learned to stay in touch with the voice of his spirit. The passage says, *"The word of God is quick and sharper than a two-edged sword, able to penetrate between the soul and spirit... It judges between the thoughts and attitudes of the heart."*

Right here is our challenge

How do we discern what the Bible calls our soul, our ego, our lower self or rather, the pure voice of our spirit? In Australia we have many stories of explorers who died of thirst under the shade of trees that would have quenched their thirst had they been aware of the resource right in front them from which they could have had access to the life-giving refreshment.

Later: How the archaic deficits and bruises in our emotions clamour for our attention.

Chapter 16

A LITTLE LOWER THAN THE ANGELS

"As a child I received religious instruction both in the Bible and in the Talmud. I am a Jew, but I am enthralled by the luminous figure of the Nazarene ... No one can read the Gospels without feeling the actual presence of Jesus. His personality pulsates in every word. No myth is filled with such life."

Albert Einstein (1879 - 1955): German born physicist and author who developed the special and general theories of relativity.

What does it mean we were created to be "a little lower than the angels."

One may well wonder why Albert Einstein was so moved by the words of the Nazarene. For those who listen with their heart something strange and beautiful is likely to unfold.

The God-breathing narratives we are about to reflect on are to some extent our human story. They are meant to signify nothing less than the richness - the loss and return of what is distinctive to our human soul.

This distinctive tells us why it is that in our highest nature we have an innate sensitivity to love, truth, creativity and a yearning for agency.

It is nothing less than a reflection of our souls when we are at our best

In these expressions of what some call our better angels we find the illumination of the human spirit at work in a healthy human personality. This shared common spirit reaching for the truth is also the genius and redemptive power in healthy human groups.

Here is the context for shared spiritual intelligence. It is right here we discover a manifestation of what the Gestalt therapists call, *"The whole being more than the sum of its parts."*

"They were all in one place with one accord."

There is nothing quite like being with others of like mind whose spirit has transcended their ego. When this happens people are able to experience what it means to be truly human together. When there is good will, there will also be a natural tide of spiritual lubrication releasing an inter-personal tide of positive vibes. These in turn create a social climate in which it is normal to be loving, truthful and spontaneously creative, giving rise to a shared culture which it seems is almost magically arrived at.

All have found internal permission to have responsible freedom

Of course one can't be truly responsibly free without being consciously committed to the business of freeing others.

It is clearly observable that when we are collectively committed to these higher objectives we will also find ourselves - surprise surprise - un-wittingly rising to the business of completing our authentic selves. Consequently this is how we will find ourselves fulfilling our transcendent life purpose.

Nothing less than the unique and rich purpose of human existence

Of course it will also mean finding our place in what it means to be a productive human person in this the 21st century.

So this is what was in Jesus' mind when he breathed on his disciples in that upper room! It was also an exposition of the meaning inherent in the first three breathing references. (Chapter 14) In doing this Jesus showed his disciples and anyone willing to listen, the fascinating path to human completeness.

Carl Jung famously said, *"To strive for perfection is futile but rather strive for completion, however remember the path to completion passes through the doorway of self-acceptance."*

"The path to completion passes through the doorway of self -acceptance."

One of our self-defeating inclinations as human beings is our constant gravitation to operate from the thousand and one sub-conscious ways we use to think well of ourselves. This though all along the Divine Being has found a way to liberate us if we can only find within us the humility and gratitude to say thank you for the grace that has been extended to us.

It is right here in this grace that's been extended to us, that we have the chance to find the unique and profound human self we are invited to come to terms with.

How can these stories reveal our complex highest self to us?

Many Biblical students have misunderstood the Biblical injunction that seems to say, *"Be ye perfect as I am perfect."* The Bible was not commanding the impossible: It was actually saying, *"Become complete in yourself as I am already complete in myself."*

What does it mean to become complete?

It means nothing can be added to your sense of self-worth or taken from your esteem by any external action. We are told that Jesus had life in himself and I believe we humans are called to have life in ourselves.

Temptation usually comes from our attempts to become completed

A famous Australian athlete said, *"If I am not complete as a person without a gold medal I will be no more complete with a gold medal."* Deficits and emotional bruises from our past set up a psychic agenda that dictates our key drivers. It is almost impossible for these not to morph into yearnings that set up subconscious dynamics that contaminate our feeling worlds and set our inclinations.

This is why we are admonished to avoid seeking any external source to enrich our internal world. It is why Jesus said, *"Blessed are the poor in spirit"* - ie those who don't seek the illusion of spiritual enrichment in anything other than a relationship with the Divine Being.

We are too prone to feed our hungry deficits on the fruits of fame and fortune. This always disappoints because real and permanent joy can never be gained by any attempt at emotional trading. I will give you if you will give me! This is why we are so uncomfortable with undeserved favour- ie grace. We feel it places us under some kind of obligation.

How myth becomes historic and lived reality

The God-breathing narratives were a classic illustration of how myth works. The stories were nothing less than an invitation to engage with a paradigm that would shape one's world view; a paradigm that focused a meaning that offered a framework of understanding enabled the aspect of the human spirit a place to know itself.

The breathing stories were a profound metaphor that would, if received freely by the heart, become actualised as a personal, social and historic reality. It is nothing less than a reflection of our souls.

It is nothing less than a reflection of our souls

A parable is meant to be an earthly story with a heavenly meaning. History has shown these parables triggered a social and spiritual movement that eventually became a global revolution.

Professor Edwin Judge of Sydney's Macquarie University believed that in the late 20th century history demonstrated that this Christian paradigm of what a healthy society should be, became a benchmark for all cultures and religions to measure themselves by. From atheism to Buddhism there seemed to be a consensus of what a productive person looked like.

While Elihu may have been the first cab off the rank he was meant to remind us all .

The book of Job in which we find Job and Elihu was one of the earliest books of the old book we call the Bible probably written about the time Joseph was managing the economy of Egypt, which makes it all very fascinating because this puts it before Moses who put together the first five books of the Bible we call the Torah. Why reference it again? Because in these early books of the Bible we find the first God-breathing event mentioned.

How does this work?

When inspired one often can sense the shape and form of truth

While the author of the book of Job recounts in chapters 32-37 the story of Elihu and his inspired insights about the breath of God in man that give understanding, we know the book was written earlier than Moses' time. We think that Moses as an inspired poet or a songwriter under God's inspiration, sensed the shape and form of inspired truth in the narrative. As he looked at the clay tablets he recognised in Job and the words of Elihu and the other creation stories truth that has been illuminating human hearts through the ages.

The inspired heart can recognise eternal truth

What Moses drew together from the clay cuneiform tablets is a narrative that had been around for centuries. It expressed the collective human spirits' attempt to give shape and form to the narrative that explained their lived experience. This is likely to be the reason for the inclusion of the book of Job. Moses, in a state of inspiration and guided by God's Spirit through his own spirit, teased out from previous inspired attempts the sacred story of creation that has now come down to us.

This is why there is a part of us that seems bigger than life itself

It is the remarkable story of human beings being made in the image of God himself with an exposition of what that infers. The implications are profound because in our modern secular attempt to move away from this creation story we have unwittingly contributed to a rising tide of dehumanization. Many, myself included, feel this has hastened the slide into our current graceless political and cultural malaise.

As Victor Frankl wrote, *"At first mankind understood itself a special creation, and to be sure made after the image of its creator, God. Then the machine age came and soon humans began to understand themselves as creators, and strange to say, they began to understand themselves after the image of their own creation, the machine."*

Not only has the understanding that we were made in the image of our Creator humanized us but it has alerted us to those dynamics in history that were inclined to dehumanize and depersonalize us. Hence the American constitution reminds us that we have all been endowed by our Creator with certain self-evident and inalienable rights.

This sacred Creation Story has inspired deep thinkers over the centuries

Most remarkable in this historic process is that the sacred creation story has resonated so deeply throughout the Western world. For decades it has fascinated serious thinking people like Carl Jung, Robert Campbell, Robert A. Johnstone and others, all of whom have pondered deeply on what makes our human consciousness unique.

We can also find in the Creation narrative a story in which if we look closely we can discern the special spectrum of humanities' spiritual features that act like a mirror to our soul's current and most profound yearnings.

What is human? What are its distinctives?

How do we recognise the great distinctive of human spiritual intelligence?

The Creation Story at the beginning of the Bible in Genesis chapters 1 and 2 carries a narrative in which as C.S Lewis would say, we find the *"deep magic"* of the human soul.

In this narrative not only are we introduced to the meaning of our human existence but various stories in those two chapters reveal universal characteristics at the deep core of our humanity. Also revealed is the human spirit we derived from the breath of our Creator that is clearly shown to be of a different order and quite distinctive from purely animal life.

The great divide between man and the animals

Human life is distinctive in that it is hyper-sensitive to, and clearly resonates to, certain aspects of God's own nature. We have been told that just as God is love, God is truth, God is creator and God is king, we are also different from the animals if we are healthy and alive in our spirit. This is indicated by the fact that we will be deeply affected by issues to do with love, truth, creativity and the nature of responsible freedom (agency).

Two tiny chapters but in them we are told, *"it is not good for man to be alone"* - love. Man had the privilege of naming the animals - creativity; he had a unique relationship with spiritual life and death because of the forbidden fruit and the ensuing choice - truth and knowledge. He was to work in the garden to keep it ordered and in a state of shalom.

The story highlights what happens when those wholesome spiritual characteristics go missing and become inverted.

We see the grim spectre of all that makes our life miserable

The narrative also reveals the tragedy that took place when we lost our desire for the love relationship with God that we were created for. Paul writing in his letter to the Colossians reminds us we were originally *"created by God and for him"*. When we stepped out of that sustaining relationship the full life also went, leaving the spiritual hole it used fill.

We are now haunted by the great absence

We were left with an exquisite ache inside our soul - our psyche. This ache is now the profound source of our obsessions, anxieties, deepest fears, addictions and all our destructive inclinations and yearnings. It has all the hall marks of a personal hell. No wonder there is such a rise in mental illness and youth suicide, often among the most aware and sensitive of us. Strangely, it is happening at the very time Christianity is being pushed to the margins.

The toxic absence that takes on an evil existence and destroys life and joy

20th century philosopher and political scientist Hanna Arndt in her controversial write-up about the trial of Adolph Eichmann coined the term *"the banality of evil."* She was referring to the great absence in Hitler's henchman Eichmann. She had expected to see a dark monster. It was he who had been responsible for the transportation of hundreds of thousands of European Jews to their death. Instead she saw a moral weakling simply following orders. He did not give the moral implications of his efficient transport system a second thought.

Hannah was haunted that in that same sense most human beings are pale grey; they simply go through the motions of living without really reflecting the significance of their life choices or lack of them.

Not good enough to be good or brave enough to be bad, just pale grey

We are all a bit like the dead bones described in Ezekiel 37, not even beginning to realize we need the life-giving second breath ourselves. Our self- justifying ego defences keep us blind to the fact that we are not quite fully alive spiritually.

We are all more inclined to be aggravated by the spiritual blindness of others than to have the wisdom to be aware of its source in ourselves. In contrast, in the book of Job we see Elihu crying out *"That which I see not teach thou me."* Why? Because he fears he is, like most fallen humans, prone to the arrogant blindness that plagues Job's friends.

Every time you point the finger it is good to remember the three fingers pointing back at you

In contrast in Elihu's prayer we see a more completed human being whose spirit is still alive in its responses to both God and truth; he is therefore able to bring that illumination to his daily discourse with life.

His spirituality is not otherworldly but clear-eyed and he has an anchored awareness that is deeply engaged with the real world. This is spiritual intelligence and the source of joy. Of course Elihu is exhibit A and the demonstration of where we are all meant to be, but sadly seldom are.

Spiritual intelligence that makes life engaging

Elihu is an expression of what is now being looked for in the kind of leadership that is hungered for in liberal democracies: Wisdom that is able to transcend its own identity needs and a faith vision that has the moral compass that can direct to the better tomorrow. It is called spiritual intelligence.

The source of spiritual intelligence and joy

While the Bible does not claim to be a final scientific and detailed description of human biology, it does give us the kind of realistic hope that inspires a remarkable sociological, psychological and philosophic insight into what makes life an exciting and healthy adventure, well worth the living.

Why this higher human journey our spirit beckons us to is worth taking

The spirit beckons us to our own story, one without regrets. We are also shown the path that leads us to our completion (telos) - our happy ending - and in so doing gives our existence the magic of joy.

Conventional happiness is when happenings are going the way our frail ego wants them to go. In contrast joy comes from the inner conviction that things are unfolding according to a divine plan even if circumstances are uncomfortable and it is hurting at the time.

The anchoring effect of joy in the human spirit

This kind of intelligence, if included in our daily discourse with life and taken seriously, will not only illuminate the central questions we wrestle with on a daily basis, but also shed light on the whole dilemma of our human existence and its meaning.

It will shed light on the sense that something is missing in our life and what we need to do if we are to remedy it.

The most aware of us know we humans are a dilemma to ourselves

Why are we here? What are we meant to be doing? Where are we meant to be going? What is our unique existence all about?

It can seem our life is some kind of puzzle to be solved and a high IQ tends only to exacerbate the situation. In fact, if we lack spiritual intelligence it can feel as though we're caught in some kind of existential riddle without enough clues.

Why we are similar and yet so different from the animals

We know evolution may be able to answer some of the questions to do with the soulless part of us, the part of our nature we share with the animals, though instinctively we know there is more. We know we have a part of us that is beyond the grasp of our reason. The more aware of us know that there is a part of us that is bigger than time and space, a part that hungers for transcendence. That unique hunger for transcendence is directly tied up with our yearning for love, truth, creativity and intelligent agency.

Why is it so?

We can't always articulate its source but there can be a dawning in our heart that leads us to a deep sense of knowing that these yearnings are of a different order to the instincts that drive animal life. We also know that the things that make life worthwhile are essential to our sense of being in a state of shalom - our sense of fulfilment, wellbeing and integration.

This is the path we need to tread if we are ever to become fully human. According to Victor Frankl it is because we not only have instinctual drives but also a spiritual unconscious. He believed the boundaries between the conscious and the unconscious are fluid, thus we are always looking for symbols that make the unconscious conscious; hence the power of the Biblical narrative.

These are the spiritual yearnings that give our lives meaning,

Chapter 17

THE SOURCE OF THE ETERNAL YEARNING

"The time has come to proclaim to a nobler humanity, the freedom of the spirit..."

Friedrich Wilhelm Joseph Von Schelling (1775 – 1854) German philosopher and educator, a major figure of German idealism.

Russian political and Christian religious philosopher Nikolai Berdyayev (1874 - 1948) said, *"Freedom is a positive force... flowing up from a spring of boundless depth. Freedom is the power to create out of nothing, the power of the spirit to create out of itself."*

What is the source of this spring that seems so boundless? What is this mother lode from which both freedom and creativity spring?

Playwright Henrik Ibsen (1828 - 1906) once recited in a poem he had written for Norway's Independence Day

> *"Freedom is life's finest treasure".*
> *Only he is free who boldly aspires forward,*
> *Whose deepest craving is the deed,*
> *whose goal is an heroic act of*
> *spirit..."*

We use the word spirit so generally that its meaning has become fuzzy. In this book we are using the word spirit in its etymological sense of the non-material animating principle in human existence. Its root is *"spirare"* which also means breath and is the root of our word aspire, aspiration, inspire and inspiration. So Rollo May, in his book *"Freedom and Destiny"* says, *"Thus, spirit is the breath of life. God breathes into Adam."* He explains further, *"Spirit is that which gives vivacity, energy, liveliness, courage and ardour to life."*

The human spirit is the animating distinctive that enables us to be whole

It is why there is a clear tie-up between clarity of vision and a pure heart. It is why Jesus said, *"Blessed are the pure in heart, for they shall see God."* Matthew 5:8. It seems we are not only able to see God but to also see things from an eternal perspective which is why it is called spiritual intelligence!

Where we gained our mind and lost it

In the wide sweep of the creation story in Genesis chapters 1, 2 and 3 we find the spiritual meaning of our unique human consciousness. It also outlines the nature and distinctiveness of our personal and corporate existence. Amazing as it seems we come across these profound keys to our existence in what is probably the most examined part of the whole Bible.

Only three short chapters at the beginning of the Bible

These three short chapters became the inspiration for the creative greats of Western culture. They inspired one of the greatest ever works of art in the Western world - Michelangelo's Sistine chapel. That same creation narrative inspired and became the source of spiritual illumination for much of the art of the whole Western world.

Those inspired included Leonardo da Vinci, Johann Sebastian Bach, George Frederic Handel, Leo Tolstoy, Dostoyevsky and many other sensitive souls. They and their ilk glimpsed patterns of meaning in the Biblical accounts and tried to reflect and sometimes even grasp, the revealed sense of transcendence.

Whether it be music, poetry, novels, painting, sculpture or any other form, they all seemed to be driven by an attempt to reach for transcendence - to make the unconscious spirit conscious and in doing so to give expression to a sense of the sublime.

Hence our eternal fascination with beauty

We have been told that in the process of our unique human creation God has made *"everything beautiful in its time"* and has also put eternity into our hearts (Ecclesiastes. 3:11.) But how do we begin to realise this in our daily lives as did these inspired icons?

A pattern in the created order

It all begins to unfold in the Creation story in Genesis chapter 1. Initially the text is about the development of living things.

There are two things to note:

1 There is a clear pattern in the created order. First, the heavens and the earth, light, the oceans, vegetation and dry ground etc. : We then find the development of living things with each one named and ending with the qualification, *"after its kind."*
2 In the creation of human beings there is a break in the process where we are then told it is to be *"after our kind."* We hear the Creator say, *"Let us make*

human beings after our kind." The big question is, in what way are humans created unique?

In what way are we distinctive? In what way are we made after God's kind?

We find the narrative all quite intentional and deliberate. What is it trying to say to us?

3 The special creation (Gen 1:1-2) - It is why there is a clear tie up between clarity of vision and a pure heart.

4 It is why Jesus said, *"Blessed are the pure in heart, for they shall see God."* (Matt 5:8) It seems we are not only able to see God but also to see things from an eternal perspective. It is why there is a clear tie-up between clarity of vision and a pure heart.

5 In the development of living things before human beings arrive we are first told that God makes everything *"after its kind."* We are then told that God saw that it was good.

6 Then at verse 26 there is a clear break in the creative pattern when we come to the unfolding of the human part of the creation story. The brakes are applied to the narrative.

The unique creation of mankind seems to be the peak event in the creation process. We hear the words *"Let us make man in our image, in our likeness."* (Gen 1:26). In the following verse we are told that man is to have a special authority and function (Gen 1:27) hence our personal need for significance and agency.

The very remarkable moment of personal creation

In the next chapter we are not only given the moment of creation but in subsequent verses we are shown the unique expressions of this form of life.

In Genesis 2 verse 7. *"The Lord formed man of the dust of the ground and breathed into his nostrils the breath of life and man became a living (nephesh) being - personality or soul."*

He/she became the full personality or person: i.e. all that persons are meant to be

Mankind became the full thing he was meant to be. There are three parts to this creation event:

1 The material - the dust of the earth.
2 The in-breathing of the divine breath.
3 The outcome: a living being (and then the profile of what a living personality thus created does).

However in chapter 3: disaster

It is in chapter 3, "the fall", where this pattern is turned on its head.

The inference is that subsequently human beings are no longer the pristine beings they had originally been. They had been designed to be a reflection and expression of the person who breathed his life into them. When that life and the divine attachment that flowed from it was jettisoned, all that was left was the exquisite ache where the full life used to be.

The result? We now see the human soul existentially driven to find its sense of transcendence in all kinds of quests that never fulfil their promise.

The book of Ecclesiastes says the human soul is consistently chasing after the wind. (Ecclesiastes Chapter 1:14)

Hence the human dilemma, the constant quest to transcend ourselves fuelled by fantasies that spring from deep within the human soul; the source of the thirst that was previously met by the spirit's constant attachment to God.

Here we have the source of most of our addictions, crushed hopes and lingering fears. The experienced deficit of spirit in the soul that only the sensitive and aware are conscious of can either be a subterranean driver of creativity or a depressive abyss that most are blind to.

This loss of shalom we try to compensate for in a hundred ways

From self-medication with a variety of drugs from alcohol and pills through to porn and loveless and obsessive sex we discover too late one never gets a relief from a severe itch by scratching it.

In a thousand ways we blindly try to compensate for our lost shalom. Few discover that it can only - and naturally - come from a spiritual and emotional reorientation that springs from a trusting attachment to the Divine Being. Right here we find both the dilemma and the answer to the great human question: so simple yet so profound.

Human consciousness without comfort and resolution

Right here we discover why these later breathing events in the Biblical narratives are crucial to our social cohesion and sanity. Far from being a simple story about Adam and Eve, they are the language that reveals the human blue-print of our personal and collective harmony and wellbeing. It seems this is the blueprint designed to restore the humanity that was lost - to fill the post fall existential vacuum and moral void.

In the original creation story man became a living and conscious being. But what now?

Where does human consciousness come from? How does it work now?

The Biblical narrative explicitly shows that humans initially became different kinds of beings able at the beginning to relate comfortably to the Divine Being, to each other and in harmony with themselves.

They were beings characterised by the same personal features that were typified by the Divine Being who breathed His very life into them: Self-aware, creative and able to have an uncontaminated I-thou relationship with other persons.

What we humans currently experience as life is not the full thing

What is currently available for us to see as the state of existence of human-kind is not in the full and vibrant form of the pristine original. Hence our personal dilemma. The most aware of us can tell something is missing.

In the words of John O 'Donohue (1956 -2008) Irish poet, author, and priest, *"...Outside us, society functions in an external way, its collective eye does not know interiority, if it sees at all it sees only through the lens of image, impression and function."*

Yet even in this fallen state we are much more than the animals

We can have a consciousness that is quantitatively a huge leap from that of the animals we are supposed to have evolved from. We are unique human beings with souls that have a yearning for freedom and a capacity for agency.

But still something is missing. In the beginning our spirit enriched our soul and illuminated our existence and relationships. This illumination brought awareness and a satisfying harmony into these relationships.

Originally we were created into a profound network of relationships

In the beginning mankind had an intimate and primary relationship with God. We could call that the theological dimension of his consciousness. From this fundamental relationship with God mankind derived a relationship with himself. We could call this the psychological dimension of his consciousness. This deep and pristine kind of self-awareness led to a rich authentic and intimate relationship with the woman. We could call this the sociological dimension to his existence which revealed the nature of real love.

Where the distinctive human expression of love came from

From this loving and creative relationship between the man, the woman, and God grew a cherished relationship that permeated the whole natural order.

This natural order into which they had been placed became the matrix of their conscious existence. We could therefore call this the ecological or environmental dimension to their shared existence. All of these flowed into a deep and harmonious appreciation and consciousness which explains why our enjoyment of nature and intimate relationships reaches our spirit and is a reminder of what has been lost.

The sense of wholeness that was lost

This harmony in the created order produced what the Bible calls shalom. Captured beautifully in the old hymn that says *"Oh What peace we often forfeit oh what needless pain we bear..."* It reminds us of the current human predicament. We may still hunger for that love-based set of attachments we were created into but we have left our original place of Creation. We are no longer in the garden.

The wholeness we still yearn for was lost when the original attachment was lost

All was at peace in these spiritually illuminated relationships until we stepped out of the life-giving foundational relationship.

We hear God explaining our current situation in the book of Jeremiah 2:13, *"My people have committed two evils: They have forsaken me, the fountain of life and tried to quench their thirst for real life in the broken cisterns of their own making."*

While the yearning for harmony and beauty still lingers and still expresses itself in many fascinating ways we know we have lost paradise. The original may have departed but the quest for spiritual completeness and shalom continues.

The missing piece of our existential jigsaw found

This is important to reflect on because throughout history thinking human beings have tried to understand our human paradox: Are we evil or just a little lower than the angels?

We are told that Socrates was inspired to take up his life quest when an associate came back after asking the oracle of Delphi who the wisest person in the whole of Athens was, to which the oracle replied, *"Socrates."* On hearing this Socrates thought, *"It can't be me; I know how ignorant I really am: but then maybe that's it: At least I know I am not wise!"*

He was like Elihu who prayed "That which I see not teach thou me."

As he looked around Athens he saw the hypocrisy and reflected, *"So many arrogant men blindly think they know."* He then plagued the people of Athens, particularly those who were happy with themselves, who universally thought they knew. He set about the task of challenging them; in fact he seemed to enjoy revealing the emptiness of their pride.

He genuinely wanted to know what virtue and goodness were

One thing he was certain of; he did not have it. He would ask everyone he met what they thought was the most important question in life, *"What is the life of goodness? What is virtue?"* Many people felt plagued by him particularly those who were living a double life. His persistent questioning created great anxiety among them. The result? Many young men gathered around him then began asking the same question of their elders. For this he was put to death.

What is a good life? A great question

After seeing the death of Socrates and collapse of democracy in Athens following its lost war with Sparta, Socrates' student Plato was highly motivated to make his life's work the discovery of how to create a *"good society, one that will create good people."*

The human paradox: are we good or bad or both. And how come?

This quest has set many fine thinkers and philosophers to work for centuries, particularly thinkers of the Enlightenment including Rousseau, Machiavelli, Marx Freud and more recently Victor Frankl.

Philosophers and social scientists have swung between optimism and despair when trying to grasp the nature of mankind. Brian Cox, the brilliant Scottish actor who has played many complex characters, when asked about the human condition said, *"The human condition is essentially quite a tragic condition."*

The missing piece of the human jigsaw puzzle

Caught between tragedy and hope, what is the real source of the human predicament and condition? Let's go back to the narrative that seeks to explain it to us to answer the questions, how did we end up here and what is our purpose for existing? The questions that have troubled philosophers and intellectuals for centuries.

We are told in the foundational creation story that God himself breathes into humankind those unique characteristics of his own life-giving person-hood.

The original organic nature of the Creation and our integrated part in it

The divine breath, the life giving-natural order it brought into being, and the cohesive networks that are derived from it grant us a glimpse of the wonderful world we were meant to be part of - what wholeness looks like and where it is derived from.

As we look closer we find there are unique aspects to all life and our relationship to it. There are characteristics that not only echo the beauty of the Divine Being but are also typical of what we now know to be emotionally healthy humans.

We have a kind of consciousness that is inclined to be thinking and caring

Similar to the Creator we too became thinking, communicating, creating and caring beings. A *"nephesh"* - Hebrew word for completed soul, the full package.

However after the events in Genesis 3 where we see love replaced by blame we also see the curse and its fruit – the tortured, human self-consciousness. In place of the natural inclination for love and truth (the source of intimacy), we now see the fallen human inclination is to project a persona so as to avoid the ego pain of failure and guilt: thus starts the never-ending anxious work of the business of thinking well of oneself.

The beginning of self-absorption and the loss of a moral compass

Before what we call *"the fall"*, we not only had those distinctive pristine echoes of divine personhood but unlike the animals we had a unique capacity and inclination for empathy and moral choice that came from an uncontaminated will. This is the distinctive of the divine spirit that was breathed into us (the Hebrew words for breath and spirit are interchangeable).

To have real human life - unlike the animals - is to be able to have a sense of the big picture - spiritual agency and moral direction.

There may be disfigurement and confusion but the yearning remains

There remains a profound residue of this spiritual yearning in our soul. But there is more!

The great student of human motivation, American psychologist Abraham Maslow (1908 1970) concluded at the end of his life, *"The spiritual life is part of our essential human essence. It is a defining characteristic of human nature without which human nature is not fully human. It is part of the real self of ones identity of one's inner core; of ones species-hood, it is an expression of full humanness."* What did he mean?

Our spiritual core - our highest self, yearns in unique ways

Our human spirit yearns in particular ways when, as Maslow showed in his study of human motivation, we rise beyond our *"safety, biological and esteem needs."*

Spiritually unlike the animals, we have the remarkable capacity to rise above these basic needs. So with inspiration we humans are able to lay down our lives for a transcendent purpose and in fact we are nearly always inspired - even moved to tears - when we see it happening.

Our desire for meaning makes us constantly bored with the trivial

We have a deep and fundamental need to know that our life is adding up to something of consequence and a significant need to know our life is making a positive difference. We catch glimpses of this when we spend a day of futile activity and feel exhausted at the end of it while alternatively, after a long and productive day we may feel tired but we're often psychologically lifted and refreshed.

Our spirit was designed to be meaning-focused and caring

As we recognize this residue of the spirit in the yearnings of our soul we will also uncover the rich treasure waiting to be discovered. It's what others are calling our archetypes – the deep and illuminating frame works that make sense of our collective human experience. It is believed that they are a profound subconscious dynamic at work in our psyche, also believed by some to be our spirit looking for frameworks so as to emerge into our consciousness.

A universal story is being shaped by what looks like the ordinary affairs of life

It is all captured in the words of Hannah Arendt who said of humans *"...Our story-telling reveals meaning without committing the error of trying to tie it all down and define it."* This is because we know that our brain's left hemisphere always wants to define and thus control our thinking, but our heart or spirit wants to travel with emerging meaning, and thus lead us to glimpse its telos - the path that leads to its satisfying conclusion.

The key that unlocks the secret of the reason for our very existence

So let's do away with talk of monkeys and so-called common ancestors! This Biblical narrative reveals the rich story of the meaning of our humanity, a rich story about the *why* of our existence and the shape of our soul. It is a totally different scenario from that revealed by the exploration of the mechanics of our physical creation, the *how.*

Not limited to the physical and material nature of our human past, this narrative is able to reveal to us what motivates the highest aspects of our lives. It is about the spiritual prompting that evokes hope and enables us to aspire spiritually to become the best model of who we can be within our current set of life options.

Becoming the best model of a human being we were designed to be

This illuminated spirit is meant to become the moral compass that gets us to our happy ending. Unlike the animals, our inspired spirit can lift our thinking so as to enable us to focus on realistic aspirations that can be derived from hope.

The story of how this spiritual part of our humanity was shaped

In a perfect and pristine world vital life options were presented. In the original and perfect setting we are told that there was only one thing that was not perfect; only one thing that was not good. In Genesis 2:18 we see, *"It is not good for the man to be alone."* How come? Didn't he have a perfect relationship with the creation, also with the Creator? Yes, but we are also told the woman was made to be bone of his bone and flesh of his flesh. (Gen 2:23-24) How could man love as God loved?

So God's response? I will make a helper suitable for him. At the level she is human she is the same as him, but at the level she is female he will find she is different; however together, when they are one, they will be the blueprint of humanity.

Humanity is male and female

God says we need someone to share in caring about what matters deeply to us. This of course infers something profound. We are meant to be social beings. We then find what life actions are normal after procreating.

We are shown that the first two persons after the apex of creation are given various tasks as a way of expressing their unique shared nature :

1. To care for the garden and in doing so learn to enjoy the science and art of nurturing life. (Gen 2:15)
2. The naming of the animals. (Gen 2:20) It could be said this was the beginning of taxonomy which lies at the base of all scientific endeavour. Naming and knowing means human beings know in different ways from the animals.

Different way of knowing and engaging with the world

In this we see the distinctives of the unique human mind at work in the creative process. They didn't simply say we'll call that one a monkey or that one a hippo. In the style of Hebrew thinking they synthesized both the nature of the animal and what would be their relationship with it, thus producing its special name.

The special human process of naming and knowing

In a fascinating part of the story it seems God stood by and waited to see what names they would come up with. They had totally free agency in it all. (Gen 2:19)

Knowing and naming accurately is the essential mark of a high functioning human being. The ability to know and understand the qualities of what is being named before your eyes is a profound human capacity.

Just note the delight in a toddler's eyes when it names something accurately, and as well, the shared moment of recognition of the process with the parent.

Here we have both creativity and communication

Knowing naming and categorising is called taxonomy and taxonomy is an essential part of the process in any scientific endeavour.

In the Biblical account man is put to work tending the Garden and naming the life forms that are flourishing there. It is almost as if human-kind is participating in the ongoing process of appreciation and realizing or recognizing with God the process of the Creation itself.

Mankind had a role in the ongoing creative process

We are told mankind was placed in a beautiful and perfect world in which to live with everything provided so as to enable them to enjoy a rich, full and delightful life. For example we are told that every tree was made available for them to taste and encounter with all their five senses.

There was however a boundary to their experience of this wonderful life. The one exception they were expressly forbidden to eat from was called the tree of life, and the knowledge of good and evil. Right here we see that unlike other life forms humankind had the capacity for choice, therefore a moral capacity.

Morality is not just about choices to do with our bodies; it is about decisions that can and do ultimately affect the quality of life within us and around us.

Whether we are aware of it or not this morality has a profound causal life and death connection as to how life will be experienced in the future. Knowing good and evil is not simply a cognitive process.

Different ways of knowing truth: Life wisdom or death

Right here we see that for us humans there are different ways of knowing truth and also the distortions that are inclined to deceive us. The Bible calls some of them, *"the lust of the flesh, the lust of the eyes and the pride of life."* In this temptation all 3 are to be found.

In the moral vignette that is played out before us in Gen.3:1-7 we see the temptation to accept a lie, one that appeals to the ego - the pride of life: *"You will be like God."* (Gen.3:4)

This is profound for their primary attachment if God is truth.

The integrity of God's word is being impugned, in this next question : The lie : Gen 3:4-5 : *"You will not surely die... and then you will know good and evil by your own experience."*

Here we see the old lie; that you have to experience some thing before you can truly know it. A chemist can tell me that cyanide will kill me and precisely how it will or I can take a spoonful of it and experience the death it will bring. However this latter form of knowing will not be useful 3 minutes after I imbibe it.

All this of course reveals the different kinds of ways of knowing and understanding.

God's kind of truth was life-giving, which meant humankind could be awakened to discern the profound truth that life and death have moral boundaries.

God's truth mattered: it aligned one with all that is life giving.

We see a whole new order of being and life coming into existence, one that reflects the very moral nature of the one who created it, God! Just as theologians have reminded us, as in the original in-breathing of the divine nature the great human spiritual distinctives that reflect both God's nature and our own highest selves are seen.

The meaning of the key descriptors is both disclosed and put in place

So we are told God is love, God is truth, God is Creator and God is ruler. Of course the clear inference is that we too are by nature (when we are reflecting our original humanity) distinctive in the created order in our sensitivity to love, truth, creativity and control.

We know that life is rich when we are alive in these human expressions, on the other hand they are the source of our unique human distress when they are absent or inverted.

They are a source of our joy or angst

When we are spiritually alive and coming from the part of us that is loving, truthful and creative and expressing what is called field independence, we are showing spiritual intelligence. From this place we as human beings are able to bring wisdom, life, and peace to all the networks we are part of. We are given a number of metaphors in the Bible that illustrate this profound human experience.

The dancing skeleton in Ezekiel

After Israel has lost her essential life through disconnection and even rebellion against the Divine Being, the people experience spiritual death.

The result is the nation finds herself in the lifeless desert again. We are given the metaphor of a desert valley filled with dry lifeless bones. (Not this time a beautiful garden as in Eden, but a dry and lifeless desert caused by their own recalcitrance.)

That is until the divine breath brings them to life again

Time and again we see this spiritual life and death pattern manifest itself throughout human history, often when the pride of life (nationalism), the lust of the flesh (decadence) and or the lust of the eyes (envy and greed) have distorted moral vision. One is reminded of the poem by T.S. Eliot, *"The Wastelands"*, thought to be possibly the most important poem of the 20th century. *"The Wastelands"* is a long poem presenting a bleak picture of the landscape of the contemporary world and its history. How close do you think we are right now to the wastelands?

Jesus in the upper room: He breathes on them. John 20:19-22

Another metaphor but I believe this one to be the revolutionary passage of the whole Bible. This short story sums up the underpinning of the whole human spiritual narrative.

Despite what was lost in the garden this special breathing incident reveals the good news that we have a second chance - a chance at redemption. We note that this breathing incident is post resurrection which means a spiritual revolution is indicated.

What was lost in the Garden of Eden is being returned

When Jesus breathes on the disciples the metaphor is profound. This is not simply a picture of God breathing again on uncompleted man as was the story in the garden, but this is Jesus, a divine being who has become one of us, and been through our hell yet transcended it. He not only came out the other side but we now see him breathing onto the dejected and incomplete disciples (who are a metaphor of us) his divine mix of human and transcendent life.

The vacuous disciples are a metaphor for us

The text shows how his disciples (apprentices) became apostles (sent ones). Through Jesus' ordeal and execution he had beaten the human inclination for sin and evil and was now on the other side of the worst that human power structures could do. These power structures had shown time and again their capacity to block the highest human yearning for a spiritual journey to completion.

The breath that gives life also gives spiritual intelligence

Jesus had said, *"I have finished the work you have given me to do."* He had been exhibit A of how one lives above external political games and internal inclinations to seek comfort and avoid suffering. In doing this he demonstrated how to rise above self-absorption and how spiritual intelligence works.

He stands before them not a theory or some kind of abstraction

Here he was standing in front of them in their moment of defeat, revealing the path to victory. He was fully alive, having beaten not only the fear of men and the fear of death but was showing that whatever others might try to hold over him he had the kind of life that could rise above it. He had beaten not only our greatest source of fear but also the emotional and physical implications of it as well.

He was demonstrating that a dramatic and historic revolution had taken place

He is symbolically breathing into those who are willing to receive it the very same kind of life that was first breathed into mankind in the Garden of Eden with its natural inclination to be loving, truthful, creative and to enjoy responsible freedom. This is why in the Bible he is called the second Adam.

The implications are profound for all forms of work with human kind

So the good news is for those who want to be free of their fallen humanity Grace has now come.

He has returned this time through the fire of temptation, torture, rejection and physical and spiritual death, to make His kind of life available to the *"humble willing."*

The genius of all this is that in doing so he potentially restored all the broken life networks that were shattered when the human ego and self-centeredness usurped the throne removing the very source of life from his rightful place. Of course in doing this destroying the innate harmony in the cosmos that only God himself could sustain.

With the removal of the divine will and wisdom from the centre of the universe, also gone was the source of harmony with its joy of peace, hence the world as we see it today.

The possibility of a great return

And here is the crunch: In this act of breathing on them, the second Adam is reminding us all of the possibility of a return of the unique and remarkable distinctives that characterise a healthy transcendent human spirit and its place in the universe.

This was demonstrated by Elihu

This can be summarised as bringing love, truth, creativity, responsibility and life-giving harmony, all of which when integrated and expressed reveal spiritual intelligence.

It is interesting to note the words of computer entrepreneur Michael Dell: *"To impact for good you don't need to be a genius or a visionary or even a college graduate for that matter: You just need a framework and a dream."*

The book of Genesis was not meant to give us all the answers but it has given us a framework and a dream.

In the next chapter we survey how the ego and its machinery throw us off our game.

Chapter 18

OUR UNOBSERVED MIND AND HOW IT FUNCTIONS

"One may understand the cosmos but never the ego; that understanding of the self is more distant than any star."

G.K. Chesterton (1874-1936) London England: His diverse output included journalism, poetry, biography, Christian apologetics, fantasy and detective fiction.

Reality or shadow?

I was recently mesmerised by a video of a 2 year old girl who had become totally engrossed when she discovered her shadow for the first time. She seemed to be alone in the afternoon as the sun began to set. Stepping forward she then tried to spin round all the time watching her shadow over her own shoulder. It could be said that this is the task of a healthy ego - to help us sort out the reality from the shadow.

The task of a healthy ego

The Australian rock band Skyhooks reassured us in the seventies that *"ego is not a dirty word."* Very few of us have a clear view of ego and how it works and how it affects the functioning of our spirit. When we use the word ego we usually use it to infer some form of self-centredness.

If our ego is not functioning well we are in emotional trouble

Sigmund Freud (1856 – 1939) Austrian neurologist and founder of psycho-analysis, used the word ego in a technical sense to describe one of the most powerful influences on our patterns of thinking. To grasp what he was driving at we need to unpack what he believed were the three most powerful sources of influence at work in our thinking and feeling world.

One he called the id which is short for what he believed were our instinctual drives where such things as hunger, anger and sexual energy emanate from. In Freud's view however the id is not very bright or discerning. If these instinctive drives are hungry or sexually aroused their main aim is to gratify the instinctual appetite immediately if not sooner.

Our instinctual drives, he suggested, had no values or impulse control of themselves. It would seem then that it takes a highly disciplined and integrated person not to be held to ransom by them.

It is too easy to be captured and held to ransom by these instinctual drives

As well as the id we also have what he called the super ego - a bit like an accusing voice in our mind. It's rather like a replay of controlling parent messages in our head and is largely the source of our inhibitions and guilty feelings. In contrast to our instinctual drives and super ego there is what he called the function of the ego.

According to Freud a healthy ego helps us engage with our current reality

This is where we need the ego to come into play if we are not going to be paralysed or controlled by our base inclinations or imprisoned by archaic parent messages. It is meant, according to Freud, to help us be integrated and autonomous and to take over the effective administration of our own live. As we will show though, as useful as his framework work was in helping us acknowledge the subconscious and unconscious forces at work in our thinking, there is still more to become aware of.

It is said that most adolescents have a large ID but a weak ego

This is why Freud believed the ego had the task of putting off the insistent impulses of the ID and the stifling inhibitions of the parent tapes.

Canadian born psychiatrist Eric Byrne (1910 – 1970) who created the theory of transactional analysis as a way of explaining human behaviour based on Freud's ideas but distinctly different, used parent tapes to be similar to what Freud called the superego. Byrne was interested in freeing what he called the natural child - our authentic nature

I also believe it is the source of what I call the human spirit which, when inspired is free to lift us from the concerns of the ego and illuminate our human conversation with life.

Too often though, the shadows we chase or run from, set our agenda

In Freud's paradigm it is the ego that sorts out the impediments that limit our capacity to see reality clearly. This is why he called the ego *"the reality principle."* But what if the ego is itself distorted or contaminated? How can this spirit made in the likeness of God himself not be itself distorted?

This is why early philosophers and theologians talked about both the *"incurvitas"* of the human soul and the need to be born-again spiritually.

While we are made as a unique creation designed to engage with life and reality in a special way, we have a shadow that follows and haunts us. This obsessive inclination to curve in on ourselves negates our spirit's capacity to free our mind to naturally think lovingly and creatively.

Our "incurvitas" inevitably undermines our objectivity.

This inclination also distorts what Freud hoped would be the very function of the ego, the integration of our inner and outer worlds that was meant to keep us sane.

It is however, the compulsion of our ego to think well of itself and hold itself together at all costs that becomes our very undoing. According to Freud, if the ego is healthy and working well it will enable us to decontaminate what we are seeing and feeling in the moment, thus letting us effectively engage with the demands and responsibilities of the exciting real world.

Much more though has been uncovered about the human soul than Freud could have ever imagined. In his own time brilliant as he was – having given us the notion of sub-conscious and unconscious dynamics, sadly there was so much more he was to miss. For example, as well as the whole world of neuroplasticity he also managed to leave the whole dimension of the spirit out of his model.

As we will show there are yet other forces at work in our soul.

(See the diagram at the end of the next chapter that shows the self-concept or ego in action and the powerful forces that are inclined to contaminate it).

As we will show, so much feeds into our feelings about ourselves as we attempt to engage with the real world. No wonder huge corporations are placing a premium on spiritual intelligence. And no wonder our respect for those of the political class wanes so significantly as we see clear evidence of their contaminated egos distorting their judgement.

Making the "unobserved mind" a fitting title

When it comes to sorting out reality, objectivity is very rare and there is in fact no such thing as an unbiased or uncontaminated opinion. As we probe all the subjective factors we have come to terms with it is no wonder we often find we ourselves in a bit of an anxious and indecisive fog. In the words of Charlie Brown, *"How can you be so wrong when you're so sincere."*

We need to learn how to switch on and switch off

We need a deep inner sorting out process if we are to retain some semblance of integration and sanity. This means the more emotionally significant the situation is the more we have to learn how to do what is called *"soul work"* ie sorting out what the truth really is rather than either what we fear it is or what we desperately want it to be.

Our best bet in doing that will be to learn how to transcend our ego. That of course is nigh on impossible unless we learn the inner discipline to gain the capacity to tune into the perspective that comes from the inner prompting of the spirit. We are too prone to slide into our favourite subconscious self-talk with its emotional madness.

What do we mean by sane and insane?

A good question if we are to sort ourselves out, according to American psychiatrist Albert Ellis (1913 – 2007) who developed Rational Emotive Therapy in 1955.

It is also essential if ever we are going to be helpful to others as well as avoid the trap of sliding unwittingly into the trap of emotionally based dramas. How does it work?

Dr. Ellis put it this way, *"It is essential that we must always be alert in the therapeutic process, for what I call sane and insane messages that are inevitable in a troubled person's communication - or any interpersonal interaction for that matter."*

He explained, *"A person may say, 'I have failed my exams today' which may or may not be a statement of fact. If however they go on to say, 'I am such a stupid twit I will never be able to get myself together'"* this according to Dr Ellis is a clear illustration of what he would call insane self- talk.

Archaic material replaying itself and clouding perception

If any person is to be a healer of souls they need to be able to hear the sane and insane messages of the client who in my view needs to be helped to become alive and aware in their spirit, furthermore to be helped discern the various voices at work. Then of course to learn the inner strategies and spiritual disciplines that might help them work at the business of tuning out the madness.

Then to actively work at including the spirit's illumination in our dialogue with life

In the next chapter there are yet more dynamics at play, all of which operate like an unobserved mind. It will become clear that spiritual intelligence has the innate awareness and capacity to see beyond the fog. Let's assume a good and healthy ego informed by the spirit's perspective cannot only help us keep in touch with the real world, but also have the faith imagination to see one's way to a preferred future. If the ego is working well it may help us to be functional but while it may be able to tell us how we can do something, it will not tell us if we should.

Why not? The ego is devoid of a moral framework

Freud may have seen the ego as the source of our sanity yet because he seemed to have little or no awareness of the human spirit's capacity to illuminate, unlike Viktor Frankl he was not able to activate its contribution to the therapeutic process. It could also be said that Freud over-reacted to the more legalistic and narrow mindset of the day.

As a result he tended to put spirituality and religious experience into the same bag labelling them all simply as the functioning of an overactive expression the super-ego: and too often he was right. Freud then became reductionist joining the *"it's only crowd"* not able to see beyond their own labels and missing the spirit's vital contribution to our human nature.

The spirit is significant to the process of the healing of the soul

Many therapies like that of Freud's psycho analysis were inclined to miss the essential healing function of the spirit; that is the essential factor in the healing of a human personality.

Many left brained psychological practitioners have like Freud, been too inclined to become blinded by their own categories and reductionist thinking.

Of course Freud was right when he believed that what he called the ego or sense of self was in fact a significant part of what we bring to the part of us that attempts to engage with the external world. He in fact believed that we as human beings make valiant attempts to organise our complex inner worlds around this thing he called ego, while in fact it is having a courageous yet fragile attempt at being and remaining sane.

Whatever it is called it is the operation of our unique soul attempting to cope

All psycho therapeutic models posit a fundamental sense of this soul, ego or self that we try to integrate around. For the Portuguese born American Neuroscientist, Antonio Damasio it is called our sense of self, for those who use the *"Rogerian"* approach to therapy it is called the self-concept, for Eric Berne it is what he called ego states with the executive ego state being what he called the rational adult. All of these concepts of the human operation are more similar than different. Paradoxically though whatever you call it, a person with a healthy sense of self will not tend to be self-centred.

A person with a strong and healthy ego is not so inclined to be self-centred

In fact Freud believed that our mental health was contingent on our ego functioning well. In Freud's system, and most would agree with this aspect of his thinking, the assumption is that it takes energy to put off the demands of our internal machinery so as to keep engaged functionally with external reality. We now know however that what he called the ego can often be messed up and misshapen by the impact of trauma, substance abuse or early parental abuse. In these cases this unrecognised and invisible mind, Freud's ego, itself often becomes misshapen and contaminated with the resulting effect of choking off the spirit's illuminating influence. This brings with it instability with profound therapeutic challenges.

We could call this contaminated ego an unobserved mind

We now know much more about what Freud called the ego. Along with the theoretical systems, what is posited is very much like an unobserved mind which often operates like a distorted voice in our head that tells us, it is the real us and everything is going to end badly.

Unfortunately if we are not attuned to the spirit its influence is all pervasive, colouring the very way we experience life. Yes you heard right! The very way we think and feel is usually determined by our misshapen ego hence its challenge to our mental health.

It is also our unobserved emotions. Our body's unconscious feeling reactions are triggered by what this inaudible voice in our head is saying.

It is continually distorting the way we think about ourselves in the world.

It is under all we think and feel as we encounter the unpredictability of life. When it was clearly dysfunctional in the past it was called a neurosis, we now call it a maladaptation. And it is almost always found to be in opposition to the gentle promptings of our inspired human spirit.

To get beyond the self-orientated machinery of the ego there are particular spiritual exercises in which one has engage in order to bring the spirit alive in our awareness.

A mind deeply rooted in old emotions and our struggle for esteem

This subliminal ego voice engages in the kind of thinking that most of the time, leads us away from our latent real self that is, our spirit. This causes us ultimately to be out of sync with the intuition and the moral sensitivities of our highest self. When we lose our moral compass we increasingly lose our capacity for objectivity.

The result is we become increasingly like a boat without a rudder

Viktor Frankl said, *"If we no longer know what we ought to do we will no longer know what we want to do and we will find ourselves in an existential vacuum."* He believed the clearest evidence of this is boredom - the curse of a whole generation that hungers continually for external stimulation.

This also led Frankl to believe the condition had become the mental health plague of the Western world in the late 20th century. He called it a noogenic neurosis which it could be said happens because we have lost connection with our spirit and its sense of higher meaning.

This Frankl believes, sets up an inner disquiet and depressive sense of bewilderment

A bewilderment that is actually heightened, not assuaged by greater education and intelligence. And our headlong rush into materialism may provide a brief tranquilizer, but in the long run only serves to heighten ones sense of angst, because at least if you're poor you can still believe a winning lottery ticket might solve your emotional problems.

We have become a culture without a rudder and it has consequences

Regardless of any rational content in our cognitive processes these contaminated and uninspired thoughts of our ego cannot help but lead us away from our spirit with its sensitivity to truth. Ultimately of course it cannot help but rob us of our inspired will that yearns to be at the centre of our life's direction and action. This will of the spirit yearns to transcend the crippling instinctive inhibitions of the ego's anxieties.

Of course the spirit senses its own unique pathway to validation when it is freed to manifest the authentic attributes of its essential nature (as focused in the previous chapter and free of ego contamination the spirit's discernment inevitably produces trust). The spirit doesn't waste time and energy trying to look good and convincing itself and others that it is right. That energy and discernment is then available to see the moment in terms of its long range perspective.

This is the spiritual intelligence corporations are looking

Darryn L. Johnson, American author, expert motivator and inspirational presenter who, having worked with companies such as Nissan, General Motors and Hughes Aircraft, focuses on identifying and overcoming the neurotic barriers that prevent personal and professional growth. He says, *"Anytime there is a struggle between what is actually right and what seems right then your ego is inevitably interfering in your decision."*

As we have said before, the ego or self-concept, will never transcend itself by focusing on itself yet it will always be caught in a vast web and driver that is an eternal quest to think well of itself.

We don't have to go too far back to see what happens when the contaminated ego distorts moral judgment in the quest to be a bigger version of themselves. (Bring to mind the key players who helped trigger the global financial crisis.)

Some people can read a negative message into a cook book!

We can be so blinded by the ego's contamination that our capacity for discernment becomes blindsided by certain events that are capable of affecting and challenging our esteem. How do we remain integrated?

Chapter 19

GETTING YOURSELF TOGETHER

"A human person is meant to be a being with the power of self-awareness, however we are generally so poorly integrated that we tend to experience ourselves as an assembly of many personalities each saying 'I'."

E.F.Schumacher (1911-1977) German -British statistician and economist. His book Small is Beautiful was ranked by Times Literary Supplement as one of the 100 most influential books since World War II. Also wrote A Guide for the Perplexed, a critique of materialist scientism.

How do we get ourselves together? It's our personal dilemma

It is possible then, to tune into the voice of our spirit and in so doing avoid disaster. Simply knowing our own mind is however, often challenging enough.

How do we sort out what is of our spirit and what is of the Spirit?

If we are honest with ourselves our situation is too often best expressed as by the apostle Paul centuries ago who said, *"My own behaviour baffles me, for I find myself not doing what I really want to do but doing what I really loathe. Yet surely if I do things that I really don't want to do it cannot be said that I am doing them at all."* Romans 7:15 (J. B. Phillips translation).

The ego's contaminated and dysfunctional thinking and motivation emanate from its distorted emotional base. When the Apostle Paul warned us about what he called the flesh many thought he was talking about our sexuality but no, he was talking about all that prevents our being attuned to the Divine Spirit by the human spirit within us. The patterns laid down both by our emotional history and our natural ego defences form a formidable diversion from the normal responses of our human spirit.

These emotions operate without any reference to a moral compass

All this is precisely what our uninspired central nervous system reacts to. How? It does this by blindly responding to life from archaic emotion which has us live emotionally in another older reality, hence our dysfunction. It is as if we are driving a car by looking only in the rear vision mirror.

We are blind and deaf to the promptings of the spirit

We can't help but respond like this when our archaic and dysfunctional drivers have replaced the gentle promptings of the spirit. The spirit would normally delight in revealing to us wise insight and right and functional action but too often we find the uninspired soul has many other more disturbing promptings.

It is interesting that Jesus said, *"Don't be anxious about anything."* (Matt.6:2). Why did he say this? It almost seems destructive to tell a *"worry wart"* to stop worrying.

The impulses designed for ego survival invariably lead us astray

This is profound because it is the supreme test of how attuned we are to our spirit as more often than not our spirit is gently saying things to us like, *"It's ok,"* *"Be patient here"*, or possibly, *"Be cautious now."*

This other disturbing voice in our psyche that we call the unobserved mind initially tells as its starting point a story that the body and mind uncritically believe. Thus triggered the unobserved mind will react emotionally, replaying its anxious past. This is why it appears to have a mind of its own.

Inspired will

By contrast the human will, when inspired by the spirit is inclined to have what is called field independence. It is not so readily overwhelmed or determined by the emotions triggered by its current environment or situation. Thus the spirit remains outside the emotional chemistry of pathological relationships or threatening situations and can remain truly free. When the spirit is exercising its positive influence the contaminated will is not even invited into the crazy drama.

In contrast, when the archaic emotions are being hooked by all parties in an emotional dispute people will often do and say things that on reflection they are likely to regret.

When in the grip of old feelings we can look like quite another person

This explains why many people seem to be what the Bible calls double minded. When not connecting with our spiritual compass we can seem to be in in a bit of a fog, unable to make clear and appropriate decisions. On the one hand, we may be unable to be appropriately assertive, while on the other hand we may react too quickly, often jumping to emotionally based conclusions. Spiritual intelligence is the moral clarity to see what is right.

The sad genesis of our soul's distortions and complexities

A child who receives constant negative feedback or is not given necessary space to develop skills that build healthy ego-strength may react to each new situation with extreme self-doubt and feelings of nervousness, even fear. A person brought up in a family quick to respond with anger-based dramas may be almost programmed to live off a similar set of responses. A person who is inclined to trust their own perception more than that of any other member in the family pecking order may develop a pseudo confidence not always based on reality.

Much of what we believe and have pseudo-confidence in, is coloured

This is why I don't go along with people who say it doesn't matter what you believe so long as you're sincere. People who are paranoid are sincere but that doesn't make them right. Because of its emotional history the ego can be braced against scary shadows and intimations of disaster that are never likely to happen, or it can cheerfully beckon us to opportunities and ego-enhancing fantasies that will often turn into nightmares: They won't pass the first test they are put to in the cool clear air of reality.

We never see things as they are; we see them as we are

We may live emotionally in the shadowy and distorted reality of our archaic belief systems. These emotionally derived beliefs are like tinted spectacles that will put us on a slippery slope, inclining us emotionally to fragmentation and alienation. The alternative is an inclination to hear our spirit and let it take us home to the very place we are designed to inhabit.

What does home look like? What does it feel like?

It is where our spirit has learned to be comfortably attached to and inspired by, the Divine Spirit. Home is where we will naturally be inclined to be loving, truthful, creative and field independent, all of which will lead to personal integration, clarity and peace.

At the crossroads of personal existence

Here are the amazing crossroads the Bible calls the spirit or the flesh. The flesh is not simply about sexual pleasure but about all the survival machinery of body and soul. Without the spirit's engagement body and soul are worse than mindless. (It is spelt out in Galatians 5:16-26).

This is the path of life Elihu's key opens the door to

Right here we see not simply how to have right theological ideas but more importantly we are given the secret of how to have a rich and rewarding human life, one we were made for; our telos or purpose. We are in fact shown how to escape what can be called our primary circuit, the set of controlling archaic belief systems few of us are even aware of.

Our primary circuit though mindless, will determine our thoughts and feelings

The intention of this chapter is to use other language to reveal the primary circuit in all its subconscious power and function, so if what I am saying seems not to make a lot of sense at the moment give it time, and perhaps re-visit it later. We all have neurotic dynamics at work in us that are committed to an unhealthy and predetermined equilibrium so the attitude is 'Don't confuse me with facts because no matter how unhappy I feel, my mind is comfortably made up.' This is why a challenge to growth and reflection is usually disturbing.

A profound consciousness shift is likely when the spirit is welcomed into the discussion with life

Spiritual liberation and transformation will be the most normal outcome if the spirit is invited into these archaic and limited belief systems. This transformation of identity is best described by the Greek word metanoia. Though some try to tell us it means to turn around (quite another word) it is about changing the way we see ourselves in the world. This is what the Bible means when it uses the word repent though it is almost impossible to do this through sheer will power. It is in fact an outcome of inviting God's Spirit into our heart and soul to illuminate and activate our human spirit. When this happens it also has the effect of sensitizing us and tuning us into the promptings of the Divine Spirit.

This will in turn shed light on and give wisdom to all we reflect on

Right here we will be given the prophetic light to see the source of internal and external disharmony. We will also find we are drawn to home, the human soul and spirit's rightful place in creation; it is an agent of shalom – (peace, harmony, wholeness, or completeness). We are told, *"Blessed are the peace makers, for they will rightfully be called the children of God."* Matt 5:9

Alienation from our spirit produces inner chaos.

Cognitive emotive therapy is the name of the therapeutic psychological process that attempts to help people confront and rise above their false beliefs and can be helpful in the company of a skilled therapist, however it is difficult to do or to sustain without the illumination of one's divinely inspired spirit. We all have archaic and subconscious systems that inevitably hook and trigger the unhelpful emotions that distort our capacity to see and function productively.

It is one thing, with skilled help, to recognise the emotional soup that is setting off disharmony between our body, soul and spirit, but the therapeutic challenge is always to find a way to permanently habituate a healthy change.

The key that unlocks the confusion is the spirit and also leads to shalom

The disconnect between the spirit, soul and body is usually the source of our dysfunctional belief systems. These disordered archaic emotions are those we are calling our unobserved mind. Here is the source of the emotions that sabotage the mature and valid attempts we make to fulfil our deeply held dreams and visions. They are the self-defeating reaction formations that drown out our spirit's promptings, inevitably trapping us. They usually have a history that shapes them.

This is how it becomes our actively operating uninspired pseudo mind

Without the inspiration of the illuminated intuition that comes from the spirit our very sense of self or identity is largely derived from these archaic emotions. Usually these emotions have themselves been shaped and subconsciously triggered by what often feels like a large and fearful world in the face of which this uninspired mind - our ill formed ego and all that sits under it - is courageously trying to hold itself together.

Remember the words of Spanish poet Antonio Machado, *"Under all that we think, lives all we believe, like the ultimate veil of our spirits."* Of course this is where we find our hidden drivers.

We do this by trying ever so hard to look good and always to appear to be right

Hidden from our conscious view is the plethora of subconscious and unconscious dynamics we now know to be at work. Of course these are happily going about the business of interfering with our capacity to think straight.

Among these drivers are our deficits and bruises (Diagram at the end of this Chapter) Too often they have come to form the maladaptive characteristics other people call us. Usually we have unwittingly let these reaction formations settle in our personalities.

Our character is made up of the characteristic behaviour others call us

Too often we have called these inflexibilities that become characteristic of us, our nature. Our real nature is ready and yearning to be expressed by our spirit. However, because our old coping behaviours are not derived from our spirit they become impediments to satisfying and intimate relationships. When these behaviours are permitted to become settled into our coping mechanisms without challenge they come to form an unhealthy and often destructive internal psychological equilibrium.

This of course, is our problematic and driven neurotic self. No wonder Socrates said, *"The unexamined life is not worth living."*

The role of deficits and bruises in creating a neurotic vicious circle

These complex neurotic emotions in turn feed energy back to the thoughts that created the emotion in the first place. This becomes the source of the emotional state we usually call unhappiness. It is the seductive circle that takes place between our unexamined thoughts and emotions. Here we see the unrecognised process that gives rise to the emotion-based thinking and irrational story-making that divides families and good friends. This disturbing process can create havoc in otherwise intelligent people and their relationships.

Irrational story-making when believed, creates havoc in families and societies

I know of a person who as a child, only felt loved when some kind of disaster made her the centre of attention. She was often likely to create dramas. I've seen a 14 year old, raised in a home in which there was a disabled sibling, use crutches for the slightest bump on her ankle. Even more often I've heard heartbroken fathers tell of their daughter's so-called memories of being abused by them, which never actually happened. Families were divided depending on whom they believed.

Where do bruises and deficits come from? How do they work?

Let me illustrate from a case history:

She had been a trusting Christian wife in what she thought was a happy marriage. She had raised two children now aged 13 and 10. He had been a wealthy business man. Then she found out that her husband had had a relationship with another woman since before their first child was born. The shock to her belief system was profound. What could she now believe about all the loving comments and gifts he had given her? Just imagining him being intimate with this other woman turned the many years they had lived together into a lie.

An emotional bruise will echo throughout the psyche

She had seen him speak in church and present himself to friends and family as a fine Christian. How could the children process this without becoming bitter? Divorce was against everything she valued and stood for but how could she deal with so many memories – their romantic holiday breaks, without the children, and the gifts and flowers he had bought her over the years? These memories now left a bitter taste where a warm glow used to be.

She would have felt trapped and depressed

He wanted a divorce. This forced her to face her worst nightmare; that the whole marriage relationship had been a sham. She resented herself for being so trusting and naive, something she vowed she would never do again. Most haunting was the numbing sense that life as she had known it was over. She was totally powerless in it all; able to do nothing to repair her world.

The emotional nightmare had subtly but powerfully changed her feelings about men

She felt she was caught like a fly in a spider's web. A hollow and empty feeling now lived in her stomach where her sense of happiness used to live. She became withdrawn and depressed. Understandably, her view of men became negative and any warmth from a man produced a defensive response. She made the effort to go to church, but would leave soon after every service to avoid the torture and embarrassment of having to answer the probing question, *"How are you going?"* and the searching look that came along with it.

She had been badly bruised spiritually and emotionally

During the same period there was the salt-of-the-earth builder who went to the same church, had been keen on her for years, but being the gentleman he was had never let on. Now he wondered, would there be a chance?

As bruises do, this one had generalized for her and built a neurotic aversion to all men. Every time the builder made an approach he received rebuff after painful rebuff.

It all looked hopeless until 18 months later when she needed the help of the builder for a leaking window frame. On being called he turned up and fixed it without fuss, with warm but non-invasive cordiality. When he had finished the job she offered him lunch and a cup of tea for his efforts.

For the first time she was able to believe not all men were like her husband

Eventually she was able to see something of his authentic nature and generous spirit as he went about his work and relationships. She could not help but note the difference in attitude to that of her former husband; it struck her deeply. After a while she began to warm to him.

They are now happily married and she says her new marriage has had a most surprising and healing effect on her personality.

Her beautiful spirit could transcend the psychological bruises caused by her betrayal. Her ongoing relationship with God could strengthen her own spirit's influence enabling her to swim against the tide of her own psychological machinery.

Lady Diana's story a double whammy

To see the double whammy of both a deficit and a bruise one only has to remember the late Lady Diana's story. As a little girl her parents' separation created a deficit for which she compensated by developing the romantic fantasy of the fairy-tale wedding. When Charles turned up and proposed it was like a fairy tale come true.

Sometimes sensitive souls would rather have physical pain; at least it can be known

Imagine how Diana felt when she discovered his ongoing sexual attachment to Parker Bowles. An explosive combination of bruises and deficits would have rattled her young mind. No wonder she looked as though she had gone mad. No wonder she threw herself down the stairs. At least real pain can divert from the more searing pain of excruciating ongoing emotional torture. One wonders what kind of psychological damage might have been passed on to her much loved boys had she not been encouraged to turn her visibility and pain into a God-given mission at the mentoring of Mother Theresa. Fortunately the boys seem after some rough water to have identified more with the ongoing humanity of the mission rather than the pain.

We need the nurturing of the spirit if we are to overcome the flesh

Emotional bruises can contaminate and distort attitudes for life. The impact of emotional bruises on our underlying attitudes can be profound which is why we call this dynamic force that is at work, along with bruises and deficits, an 'unrecognised mind'.

Because the ego obsessively tries to *look good and be right*, it is almost always going to use its intelligence not to seek for truth, but to distance itself from - to avoid - the very truth that could set it free. This explains why neurotic people can be both intelligent and at the same time destructive. The greatest fear of the neurosis – the underlying mal-adaptations - is their own annihilation.

The neurosis gets control by activating old emotionally based beliefs

The neurosis doesn't want truth; that is too frightening for it. It is however, only the truth that can set one free from the shadows that control. The function of the left hemisphere in our brain is to form both speech and our self-concept, our sense of self.

Why are we so often morally blind?

You can be in search for truth or ego-comfort, but not both at the same time. The self-concept or ego, is the part of us that is continually chattering away when our identity is at risk. No wonder it triggers our anxiety and self- doubt, and we often can't get to sleep.

IQ that is not inspired by the spirit can have a narrow horizon

In the past, because we have been inclined to worship at the altar of IQ we have unwittingly been inclined to celebrate the features and functioning of the brain's left hemisphere, where we now believe our sense of self is shaped and our self-talk and inner chatter are inclined to emanate from. Yes! It is the source of the process designed to validate, project and protect our persona - not so much to work hard at the business of separating the worthless from the precious or engage in the search for truth.

It is perfectly clear then why, without the illumination of the spirit, the left brain's functioning in a high status person can not only leave a person morally blind, but also very destructive.

Too often we have been held to ransom by the unobserved mind

In this following diagram we come to the framework that will I hope, help in understanding the main message of this book. It also reveals where Elihu was coming from.

Let's look at the diagram at the end of this chapter

Here we see that it begins to symbolize our experience of life. In the five-sided box we see the profound working of the self-concept (or ego). It has the task and function of attempting to give us an integrating place in our attempt to cope with life. The free-form shape is meant to represent the current real us, with its archaic attitudes, sexual energy and history of deficits and bruises along with the state of our central nervous system and current health challenges. We all have days we find it difficult to hang it all together.

It takes energy for the ego or self-concept to hold it all together

The whole of this book is an attempt to show how our amazing human spirit is present and is in fact a distinctive aspect of who we are as human beings. Whether we are aware of our spirit or not, the intention of this book is to give a first glimpse of all the human machinery with its unfinished business that is at work in our being and continually clamouring for our attention.

The mystery of the spirit and what moves and engages us

While the spirit is always present it is usually sub-conscious and tends to take us by surprise when it surfaces. There are also other dynamics at work within us which are what the Apostle Paul called the flesh - the operation of all the other archaic factors which is why Paul typified the flesh as warring against the spirit. It is as if we have two big dogs within, one black and one white, fighting each other. The one that wins is the one we feed the most.

Let's look at the sub-conscious dynamics of the emotional shadows

In the following diagram we will attempt to glimpse all that our spirit has to contend with if it's to register on our awareness. (This will be developed more extensively in the next chapter in which we attempt to separate the spirit from the body and soul.)

Note the five-sided box: This represents who we think we are - My sense of me. You will note it sits in as part of the larger grey mass we call *"the real and potential me"* meaning there is so much more to us than we can be aware of.

This represents who we currently happen to be

It is presented this way because every significant emotional experience modifies us, though does not change our essential nature which resides in our spirit.

You will note this larger *"real-self"* has what we call deficits and bruises, which though sub-conscious and unconscious tend to set our emotional agenda. They will often however develop some behaviours that others will call us and when habituated they will become characteristic of us. It is this behaviour and its source that therapists try to help us with.

You will note two things:

1 Part of the box is outside the grey area which shows we often tend to have illusions about ourselves.
2 Just below the 5-sided box is a round shape which symbolizes the presence of our human spirit.

It is there whether we are aware of it or not. Theologians have called it the divine spark or the 'spiritus divinitatus.'

We can only see what is symbolized as being inside the five-sided box

That which is just outside the box is what we call the subconscious, but that which is much further away – eg bruises and deficits, we could call unconscious. The task of personal growth through a healthy therapeutic process is to facilitate the expansion and growth of the sense of self so as to integrate more of what is unknown.

Since we can only decide about what we can see and know, the therapeutic task is raise our awareness so that one's will is then more able to take productive choices over what was previously subconscious. This has the effect of freeing what had been unconscious so it becomes at least subconscious and in time will be more available to awareness and thus available to choice.

This is the nature of personal growth

As you can see in the diagram there is so much more to us than most of us can normally see and the good news is that it's not all bad. Currently locked up in our soul lies aptitudes and personal gifts that we are not even aware of.

You will also note that the human spirit is represented as just below and outside the box. In our secular culture this means that the spirit is largely neglected and subconscious. For the many people who, in a particular moment become aware of it and say yes to its influence, this becomes a transformative moment. Many even call it being born again.

The Apostle Paul talked about the eyes of one's heart being opened

A remarkable phenomenon is that as we become more aware of God and his Spirit, the promptings of our own spirit become more discernible and obvious to us (Note Chapter15 on promptings, and the source of wisdom James 1:2-8).

Our real and potential self is found in the spirit

This is also the way we can become more in touch with our essential sense of real self with its potential.

In your imagination visualise the five-sided box expanding so that it is able to integrate more of the spirit into its awareness. It will then healthily make us more aware of both the spirit and that which is subconscious in ourselves.

Leading us to the path of shalom

The result of this is that more of the potential and real self now illuminated by the spirit can be released into one's authentic identity. The rest of the diagram shows what we could call the un-inspired real self.

The shaded part outside the box shows what we are blind to. The deficits and bruises still impact our feelings and behaviour no matter how unaware of them we might be. As represented by the diagram, just below the sense of self or our self-concept is our spirit. Unless we have developed awareness of it or been born-again, we are usually barely aware of it.

My next chapter is an exploration of its significance. And how we can actually become more attuned to its promptings.

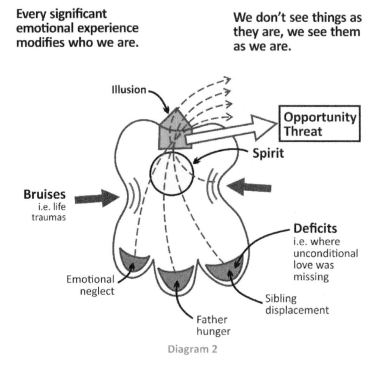

Every significant emotional experience modifies who we are.

We don't see things as they are, we see them as we are.

Illusion

Opportunity Threat

Spirit

Bruises
i.e. life traumas

Deficits
i.e. where unconditional love was missing

Emotional neglect

Sibling displacement

Father hunger

Diagram 2

We will eventually show in the next chapter and beyond, how we can know the peace that naturally comes when we are focused by our spirit beyond our self-concept or ego. And its attempt to feel valid.

On what will be found to be the purposes of the Divine being.

Chapter 20

THE SELF-CONCEPT AND SPIRITUAL INTELLIGENCE

"Half the harm that is done in this world is due to people who want to feel important. They did not mean to do harm. They are however, absorbed into the endless struggle to think well of themselves."

T.S. Eliot (1888 – 1965) American poet, essayist, publisher

The me I am? The me others think I am.

Neuroscience can tell us how the brain functions to enable us to fill out our humanness but it cannot as most religions attempt to, explain how we can escape captivity by our ego. We have at least two selves. First, there is the me I tell myself I am, my ego. The late great social scientist, Hayakawa called it the self- concept.

Second, there is the self that others think I am. Then there is the me that comes from somewhere else; it is where I know things that I didn't learn. It is where my heart or spirit rises up to knock at the door of my consciousness; it is the source of my up-cry's and my *"ah-ha"* moments. It is where my spiritual intelligence is to be found.

What holds these selves together and expresses our human personality?

Descartes is recognised as one of the leading lights of the Enlightenment, and his name has been given to what we call the Cartesian Split - that phase of history where mind, emotion, thought and feeling, were seen to be quite separate. He was joined by Newton, Galileo and others in establishing the Enlightenment. Most of them had a deep and personal belief in God, some even assuming that their faith would be established in the minds of others by reason.

This didn't stop their introducing as an unintended consequence the assumption that the universe was mechanical, like a big clock. They assumed reason would help them become the clock makers of this discoverable universe.

We now know they were coming from their brain's rational left hemisphere which they maintained, given time, could work everything out. They were brilliant men and one can't deny the mathematical genius of the likes of Newton but they were children of their own time and were validly trying to free science from the ignorance and superstition of the dark ages.

Trying to free science from ignorance had unintended consequences

Descartes thought he was challenging the superstition and the prevailing Aristotelian scholasticism that hung like a dark cloud over the medieval world and the Southern European Church. He and many who joined him thought they were bringing the church and society into a more enlightened phase of its history.

Descartes believed he was going back to the first principles of reason when he said *"I think therefore I am."* in other words, as I can sense myself thinking, I know for sure that at least I'm existing.

He thought he was laying down foundations that would eventually prove the existence of God and the immortality of the soul: unfortunately he was also laying a foundation that had the unintended consequence of creating rationalism that had many surrender their thinking to their brain's left hemisphere. Of course at that stage Descartes probably didn't even know he had a left hemisphere.

What we now know about neuroscience that he could not know

As scientific as Descartes thought he was being when he declared, *"I think therefore I am,"* he was missing some profound realities that had to do with his neural, psychological and spiritual nature. He was not just processing pure thoughts: they were being processed through his sense of self.

In his book *"Self Comes to Mind,"* one of the best known students of the neuro-biology of the human mind Antonio Damasio said, *"The key to understanding humanity, is to grasp that we do have a self which is the integrating factor in our neurology."*

The central thing Descartes did not know was that the *"I"* he was referring to in his equation was his ego - the Greek word for I is ego. His ego - also called the self-concept, was both holding his consciousness together and limiting what he thought was his objectivity.

While his contribution to philosophy was profound it was also limited by his lack of awareness of currently available data.

We are all children of our own age

How could Descartes possibly have grasped what we now know was happening inside of him neurologically, let alone psychologically and spiritually? I will attempt to share this remarkable integration of body, soul and spirit.

Let's look at what neurologists would now tell Descartes about the biological source of his consciousness:

- Without his ARF, (Ascending Reticular Formation) Descartes would not have been awake and therefore could not have reached his so-called historic conclusion that, *"I think therefore I am."*

- The neurons in his brainstem bathed the neurons in the cerebral cortex with activating neurotransmitters and he didn't have a clue about it.

- Without those neurotransmitters Descartes could not have begun to integrate his internal experience into the I he was calling himself.

- Without his invisible hippocampus on each side of his brain Descartes would not have been able to remember and would therefore not have been able to maintain the continuity he needed even to formulate his concept of an I.

- Without his normally functioning frontal and prefrontal areas, Descartes could not have gained the necessary perspective to experience himself as a separate I. He would have been submerged in a continual barrage of internal and external events stimulating his neurons, from the total reality that made up his experience of his so-called real world.

- If his anterior cingulate was not working he would not have been able to focus his attention long enough to come to his historic conclusion.

Yet Descartes was more than his neuronal machinery

Beyond the physical aspects of Descartes' brain that enabled him to make his historic statement, *"I think therefore I am,"* there was the remarkable person who was aware of himself and whose spirit was trying to help him make sense of his existence.

Beyond the details of the neuronal functioning of the brain is a person

Yes, we are fearfully and wonderfully made and the whole is much more than the sum of its parts. The words of Damasio again: *"Had the subjectivity of consciousness not made its radical appearance, there could have been no knowing and no one to take notice, and consequently there would have been no history of what creatures did through the ages. No culture at all."*

The whole of who we are is much more than the sum of its parts

Samuel Hayakawa (1906-1992) was a Canadian-born American academic and politician – a professor of English and then a U.S. Senator from California. He sought to understand the sense of self Descartes referred to, coming to the conclusion that, *"We spend all of our waking moments maintaining, protecting and enhancing our self-concept."* This self-concept is of course, the *"I"* that Descartes spoke of. Our preoccupation intrudes on our capacity to read and manage reality functionally. It is why we never see things as they are but rather, see them as we are or more accurately, as we feel ourselves to be at the time.

Our feelings of *I can* or *I can't* often limit our field of vision and these inner sensitivities settle to become our life position. If we don't have a timeless vision beyond ourselves eventually these *"I"* sensitivities become the permanent belief system we have about ourselves : *"I'm shy," "I'm not at all creative," "I just can't pass exams."* This means that all our remarkable neurology remains at the service of our thwarted identity.

Without a spiritual life our neuronal system will serve its own equilibrium

If a person sees themselves as a failure it will be written on their circuits. As they start becoming a success, rather than be freed from the sense of worthlessness woven into their brain paths stress will begin to rise in the psyche. Self-doubt will make them so conscious of failure that the slightest mistake will tend to get an overreaction of self-blame because it is reconfirms the past.

The parent voice from the past that helped shape their self-doubt will kick in, and the self-talk will be, *"You idiot you've gone and done it again; that's why you will never make it."* This of course, is the self-concept regrouping around its old life position in the left hemisphere of the brain.

We relive the past until our spirit is freed to help us understand i

The neurotic part of us always wants equilibrium even if it's negative and we will therefore relive the past until we understand it: Hence the collective intake of breath as concerned friends watch one failed relationship after another or a perennially struggling student gains top grades one term and is back to bottom of the class the next. Many of us have an excited thrill when we realize we are winning, only to begin immediately to lose. Why?

At the very edge of potential success we have an inclination to sabotage ourselves. The very possibility of success produces stress in our identity so that the neurosis triggers so much self-doubt as to sabotage our moment of victory. We fatalistically go along with it as though it was inevitable.

The more flawed we are the more we need a mentor who knows the game

The neurosis' subconscious gravitation to equilibrium means our emerging success, rather than produce liberation, produces anxiety that will bring us down unless we have the support of a trusted inspired mentor or coach who is able to read the game that is underway. Our capacity to read our moment and be discerning in it will always be flawed unless the spirit is freed to join the conversation. If though, the spirit is active and we are alert to it, remarkable things can happen.

The insights of the spirit waiting for us to become free of our past

The most sensitive of us live in the midst of an inner battle between a psychologically lazy part that just wants to drift with the old equilibrium, and the other part - who we really are, the source of our spiritual intelligence. If we are living life even half effectively - without being conscious of it and mostly intuitively, we rely on other sources of wisdom and insight to live our lives.

We unwittingly make use of our spiritual intelligence

Professor Gillian Stamp was from 1981 until 2005 the Director of the Brunel Institute of Organisation and Social Studies (BIOSS) a self-financing research institute founded at Brunel University Uxbridge, 40 years ago. The focus of BIOSS is on people at work and the conditions that help both to thrive. Professor Stamp did a 20 year study on how people make decisions when there is not enough information. She asked people, *"How do you make decisions when you don't know, and cannot know what to do?"*

The initial responses were surprisingly consistent. In developed economies the question evoked in people a sucking in of breath through their teeth and the exclamation, *"There are more and more of them about these days."* However in developing economies where people are more spiritually inclined, there would be a glance of surprise and a comment like, *"Is there any other kind of decision?"*

The mysterious source of decisions when there is insufficient data

Professor Stamp reports that the people interviewed lived in different cultures and economies, with some from a mix of multinationals like Rio Tinto and I.C.I., others from cooperatives in South Africa through to utilities, insurance companies, right down to a company that makes computer games and products for the internet. They included men and women of many different ethnic backgrounds who'd had a large range of educational opportunities ranging from leaving school at age 10 or 12, to having three Ph.D.s.

The mystery of implicit knowledge

Not only did these people wonder at the mystery of the decision- making process when insufficient information was available, but also when there was enough information. They asked questions about how we know when we've got it right and when we've got it wrong.

The response is typified by a manager who said, *"It's as if something inside me simply knows what to do. The analysis may point another way but maybe something, my experience I suppose, often says, 'No not that way, go this way!'"*

Professor Stamp says, *"People are reporting that they know that they know something; they simply do not know what it is or where it comes from. They know that they can use this knowledge and usually trust it. And strangely at times it even seems to use itself."* She believes this intuition, or this implicit knowledge as she calls it, is robust, resilient, rich and complex.

The moral base to everyday wisdom and common sense

She concluded that the two main characteristics of this source of insight are:

1 That it is somehow obtained without any conscious intention to learn.
2 What is received always exceeds what can be easily expressed to others.

Truth and insight that is recognised as having its source in spiritual intelligence always seem to be more organic than propositional. In other words, if we have the spirit of truth it will lead us to more truth. If therefore we can transcend the neurotic motives and distortions of the ego and stay attuned to the source of spiritual intelligence we will inevitably grow in wisdom. True wisdom can almost always recognise more wisdom.

Uncovering the moral and organic nature of truth

This implicit knowledge always proceeds from a moral basis and provides a sense of what is right and what is wrong - a sense of the appropriate or inappropriate response in a given set of circumstances. Being attuned to one's conscience or moral compass is pivotal in being able to trust the outcomes of the decision-making process.

Good decisions tend to come from good people who have learned to transcend the distortions of their ego.

Spiritual intelligence and its importance in the workplace

Studies of human judgment from way back in the 70's indicate that issues of rationality and logic were largely independent of good executive decision-making. It was found that the best people often did not seem to know what or how they knew.

Back then it received its name *"implicit learning,"* and research showed it provided a sense of direction and knowledge in complex and intricate situations. It was believed that implicit learning is gathered as a person attends patiently to the tiny signs and the regular irregularities in events resisting the temptation to come to a conclusion too soon. As they remain open and sustained in an Elihu posture, *"that which I see not teach thou me"*, the experience itself would teach, producing yet more discernment.

Implicit learning discernment and spiritual intelligence

Professor Stamp's research uncovered what the various spiritual traditions had called discernment. She believes it to be the outcome of *"patience with uncertainty."* As one remains open to the truth something rises from one's spirit that switches a light on. She quotes a top international banker who describes this process as *"that most valuable human skill for making decisions in factual obscurity."* She described it as *"the ability to see what might not be there yet,"* and likened it to *"Moving softly through the forest tracking that beautiful beast reality, and discovering signs of its passage, the metaphorical broken twigs and flowers."*

The Bible calls it faith. It is a different kind of knowing- one that produces the distinctive and beautiful experience of spiritual intelligence.

"Tracking that beautiful creature reality"

Professor Stamp quotes Professor G.L.S. Shackle, acclaimed author and Professor of Economic Science from Liverpool University until his retirement in 1969. He said, *"It's as if one has discerned some of the threads of that shawl of loosely inter-knotted strands which waves in the wind of other human influences, political contention, technological intervention, and explosion of population."* It's as if a person who has remained open to life and permitted their spirit to teach them eventually emerges as a Level 4 thinker with the joy of the God-given gift of spiritual intelligence.

Inspired imagination and the human spirit

It seems this fascinating process of having to make decisions without sufficient data not only leaves room for inspired imagination but brings with it the hope of actually uncovering new knowledge. This is where spiritual self-regulation is necessary because our unbounded imagination could become a self-indulgence leading only to fantasy. Professor Shackle who was fascinated by this phenomenon explained that it has the effect of creating a life strategy from one's imagination. It not only changes and develops what one deems to be possible, but it leads to acceptance of the need to discipline the ego, the necessary first step in becoming wise.

Poet T.S. Eliot asked the question of our age when he said, "Where is the knowledge we have lost in information?"

The Buddha described our life as being suffused with anxiety and uncertainty. Anxiety rises from our ego: It hates uncertainty and is anxiety prone because life by its very nature is insecure and uncertain. Uncertainty brings stress and suffering because we crave security and we unwittingly seek to escape insecurity in materialism and sensual pleasure. Some of us try to deal with our anxiety by dominating others, while others in yielding become dependent. Still others opt out of the responsibility of life by choosing one or more of the many ways of simply giving up.

Some avoid the responsibility of life and the need for wisdom by giving up

G. Claxton author of the book *"Hare Brain, Tortoise Mind and The Fourth Estate,"* described wisdom as *"Good judgment in hard cases."*

In the words of the French psychologist E.Jaques, *"What makes people wise is not expert technical knowledge but knowledge of the issues that are a part of the human condition. Wisdom is one's ability to see with penetration into those structures that relate to our common humanity."*

The twin sources of our thinking - the ego's self-indulgence or the spirit

This is why the ego's intrusion into our perceptions will always rob us of wisdom and discernment. When reason alone has nothing to offer we see the role of the spirit in bringing its way of knowing to a variety of life situations. This is the source of what we are calling in this book spiritual intelligence. Can you bring to mind the words of Elihu that I believe are the key? *"It is the breath of God in a man, the spirit in a man that gives understanding."* As we move further into the 21st century we will find this understanding increasingly pivotal.

What is it and how does it work?

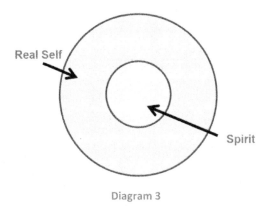

Real Self

Spirit

Diagram 3

Time and time again we hear of CEOs having to make what they say is a judgment call. The term is most often used in those situations in which explicit knowledge is either not to be had, or is insufficient for the intricacies and complexities of what is having to be decided. Speaking of this John Locke, English philosopher and leader of the Enlightenment age said, *"The faculty which God has given man to supply the want of clear and certain knowledge in cases where it can't be had, is called judgment."*

It seems that good judgment depends on experience and experience depends on having the humility to learn from bad judgment. In fact it is probably as T.H. Huxley 19th century biologist, anthropologist and philosopher said, *"There is the greatest practical benefit in life of making a few failures early in life."* Huxley might be interested to know that in the Bible it is called the wisdom of the farmer. Found in Isaiah 28:23-29 it is the same kind of knowing that infants have before the sense of self has begun to bring uncertainty into their perceptions. (The following diagrams will show we have a sense of self that has been impacted by the slings and arrows of outrageous fortune.

Events that influence our feelings and perceptions

In Diagram 4 our real self is drawn this way to show how we are impacted by every significant emotional event: Deficits of unconditional love caused by an absent father, a preoccupied mother or sibling, displacement created by the arrival of and affection for another child - or maybe bruises caused by life events beyond anyone's control. All evoke feelings that impact on how we see our spirit's capacity to bring its intuition to our sense of discernment.

Good judgment depends on our capacity to learn from our bad judgment.

It is now clear that academic training without growth in self- awareness and spiritual discipline does not of itself provide discernment, imagination, judgment or wisdom.

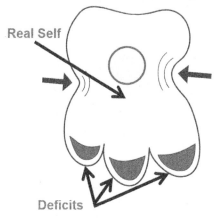

Real Self

Deficits

Diagram 4

It is salutary to recall that Ken Lay the head of the spectacularly failed company Enron, had a Ph.D. in economics. His second in charge Geoff Skilling, had credentials from Harvard Business School. It seems Skilling was more inspired by Darwin's idea of the survival of the fittest and by Richard Dawkins, author of the book *"The Selfish Gene,"* than by any of the great moral or spiritual teachers.

If Lay and Skilling had been more spiritually aware it could have ended differently

Apparently they were more interested in looking successful than being humble. Ken Lay was a church-goer but this did not give him the inner discipline needed to think past his ego. His behaviour showed he felt he was beyond the need to learn from Jesus' Sermon on the Mount.

They and others who took the world to the edge in the global financial crisis did not recognise the need for spiritual intelligence. They were not open to the disciplines that lead us to transcend our need for significance and the ego's need to look good and be right, thus missing the path that leads to discernment, judgment and wisdom.

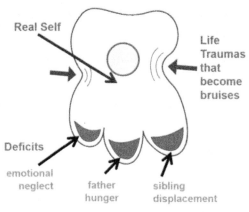

Diagram 5

Inevitably, in times of uncertainty there will be stress for our ego

We experience stress every time a life reality demands more of us than we feel we have the resources to cope with. It is at this point we find ourselves at a crossroads. We may be spiritually lazy, letting our ego defences and mechanisms take charge, and distorting the reality that brings stress. We may on the other hand have the inner discipline to reach for the spiritual intelligence that keeps us integrated.

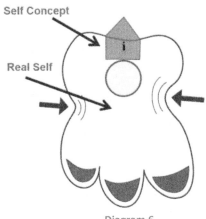

Diagram 6

What does spiritual intelligence – or ultimate intelligence - look like?

Danah Zohar, an American-born physicist and philosopher, teaches at Oxford Brookes University in England and lectures throughout the world and her husband Ian Marshall is a psychiatrist with a very strong background in physics and mathematics from Oxford. They are co-authors of the book *"The Ultimate Intelligence"* in which they listed the qualities and special indicators that they believe are evidence of spiritual intelligence in operation.

Self-awareness: I know what deeply motivates me, what I really believe in and what I value.

Spontaneity: living fully and being responsive in the moment.

Vision and Value-led: Acting from principles and deep beliefs and living accordingly.

Holism: Seeing larger patterns, relationships and connections; having a sense of belonging.

Compassion: Having the quality of feeling 'with' somebody, (deeply and with real empathy).

Enjoying diversity: Valuing other people for their differences, not in spite of their differences. Inclusiveness is a significant feature of what theologians call Trinitarian and higher level thinking.

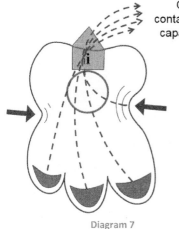

Our past contaminates our capacity to see clearly

Diagram 7

Field independence: Standing against the crowd and living deeply one's own convictions.

Humility: Having the sense of being a player in a larger drama; having a sense of one's true place in the world.

Tendency to ask fundamental questions: *"Why"* and *"What if"* questions: Needing to understand things and get to the bottom of them.

The Ability to Reframe: Standing back from the situation or problem and seeing the bigger picture; the ability to see problems in a wider context.

Positive use of adversity: Learning and growing from mistakes, setbacks, and significant suffering.

A profound sense of vocation: Feeling called to serve and to give something, so as to make a difference.

Zohar and Marshall claim that spiritual intelligence is the ultimate intelligence. It is the intelligence with which we can place our actions and our lives in a wider, richer, meaning-giving context. It is the intelligence with which we can assess the course of action of all our life paths. Of course the question remains; if this is true why don't we do it?

What is this intelligence, and how do we get it?

American developmental psychologist Howard Gardner was the originator of the theory of multiple intelligences. He chose not to include spiritual intelligence among his intelligences because of the challenge he had of trying to codify quantifiable

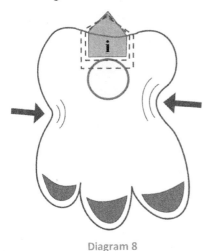

scientific criteria; he did however recognise that there is something important to this dimension of human experience. He chose to call it the "existential intelligence." He believes it is a unique capacity that enables a person to be aware of and comprehend the nature of our being.

Many peers have responded to him with research that charts existential thinking as being fundamental to spirituality. Their conclusion? That it should necessarily be seen in that framework.

Diagram 8

We admire most those who transcended their ego for the higher good

Regardless of how you label it those we admire most and hold up as icons are those who have managed to transcend the limitations of their self-absorption.

Becoming free of the unobserved self that limits spiritual intelligence

A major thrust in the thinking of all religions is about getting beyond oneself. Clearly the more self-absorbed, the less spiritually intelligent we are. Christianity talks about dying to oneself.

What self do you think we have to die to?

It is the self-concept or ego, and this can feel excruciating particularly when it seems it is the only integrating self we have a handle on. In what way? The process of dying to one's ego can involve for the sake of a higher purpose acceptance of disapproval, enmity or negativity; of being without the trappings of success like money smart clothes, nice house, car, success in business, acceptable credentials, influential friends and accompanying lack of respect. In the Biblical account of Jesus' life, the lawyers, teachers and leaders had the biggest egos and were not open to teachings of the spirit. It was the ordinary people – often the beggars or people in despised groupings like the Samaritans, who were open to truth.

Whether I can or I can't is usually felt through our limited sense of self

The reason it is so difficult to die to this self is that it is informed by our unobserved self which for years has had its hands on the steering wheel. From the time we were toddlers trying to attract approval and attention and receiving certain responses in return, our unobserved self has fed our sense of self with *"I can. I can't"* messages.

Only when we become sufficiently aware of it through our spirit can we begin see the negative and limiting impact of our unobserved self and so begin to trust our spirit to free us from the blind spots it produced and become aware of a transcendent reality. This leads us to an awareness of God and his view of our reality.

The Greek word metanoia literally means getting a new way of seeing oneself.

Koine was the language spoke in Mediterranean countries between 4 and 6 BC and

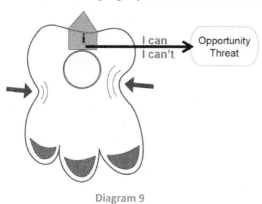

Diagram 9

the Koine word metanoia - the word we translate repent literally means the transforming of the way I see me; to change the way you orientate to the world inside and outside of yourself. The self-concept or ego is the main source of orientation for all human beings until our spirit becomes alive to us. It is then written on our neurons.

Diagram 9 shows how, before this transforming experience, the self- concept is held to ransom by our unrecognised self which in turn is contaminated by our past deficits and bruises. Every time this sense of self is threatened, our defences are triggered and our ego - or self - concept's survival machinery - automatically goes into action, filtering reality. We become inflexible and unable to listen. This explains why it's often difficult for us to accept the very thing that might open the way to change, growth and wholeness. In contrast, as we transcend our ego by our spirit becoming open to God's vision of reality, this expands our sense of self and our mission in the world. This is the *"Elihu"* orientation through which we escape the power of the ego.

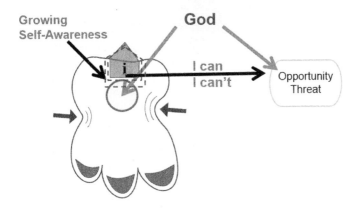

Diagram 10

In diagram 10 above we see that the more the self-concept can expand, the more the spirit dawns on our awareness, heightening our awareness of God and drawing us into the joy of being a Level 4 thinker - thus opening us up to the source wisdom. Ibn

Chapter 21

"OH WHAT PEACE WE OFTEN FORFEIT"

"If wrinkles must be written upon the brow let them not be written upon the heart. The spirit should never grow old."

James A Garfield (1831-1881) 20th president of the United States killed by assassination 6 and a half months after his election.

The real life journey

Oscar winning actress Anne Hathaway said of Aussie actor Hugh Jackman, *"He is so likeable sometimes we overlook that he is among the finest and most committed actors of his generation. And I have personally discovered him to be genuine, truly, deeply egoless. For me, it's been like loving chocolate or puppies or rainbows; effortless."*

Yet Hugh Jackman himself said, *"I am often reminded, the real-life journey we have to take is within."*

The necessary inner journey to human wholeness

Many intelligent people can be quite neurotic. Past disturbing experiences can and will leave bruises and deficits that can setup what are called mal-adaptions, another name for neurosis. These in turn are inclined to be so emotionally loud that they swamp the gentle promptings of the spirit.

It's as if our machinery has a mind of its own which is why we are told in the Bible, *"A double-minded man is unstable in all his ways."* (James 1:4-8) This is why the best way to deal with the condition is purify our hearts: in other words to face the archaic material that impinges on our desires and emotions. It is about recognising and facing with the spirit's help, every inclination that would contaminate our heart which is the source of our inner division and the contaminator of our healthy will.

The source of a pure heart is an uncontaminated spirit and pure literally means no mixed motives; no intrusion of ego needs or any other appetites. This is also why we are told, *"The wisdom that comes from above is pure, peaceable and open to reason...".* (James 3:17-18)

Why are we often unstable and lack inner peace?

This is because the neurosis as it seeks false comfort will ultimately divert us from the integrating and peacemaking inclinations of our authentic heart or spirit. Right here the battlelines are drawn between what is called the spirit and the flesh. This is why our uninspired mind left to its own devices will run around in circles, in the words of Solomon, *"Chasing after the wind."* (Ecclesiastes 2:26)

Our heart, or spirit, tends to express itself from the right hemisphere of our brain where our intuition is also to be found. This is not to say that the heart is simply and only about the brain's appropriate functioning.

Peace comes when our soul is resting on the focus the spirit gives

Regardless of how we think currently, the construction of our sense of self and our chaotic self-talk are both inclined to come from the left hemisphere.

When the 5 sided shape that represents the self- concept is in focus the sense of inner chatter that keeps us awake at night will inevitably keep us from the peace that resting our focus on the spirit alone can give.

It is about another way of knowing: or Elihu's way of knowing

It is also the unconscious and unrecognised archaic feelings mentioned in the previous chapter, the bruises and deficits along with our ego's attempt to use the left hemisphere of our brain to rewrite our narrative, that fundamentally distort our way of knowing.

This is how it intrudes on our reason and its capacity for clear thinking

Who hasn't had some kind of disquiet stir up disturbing self-doubt? Yet when given time for space and meditation, who hasn't been saved from some terrible mistake by the self -same inner doubt well processed? Here we catch a glimpse of how spiritual intelligence works.

Spiritual intelligence shows how giving the time to the deep connection with the spirit - the source of wisdom, the noisy clamour can settle. One can then learn to step back in a relaxed way from the neurotic buzz saw. What a relief no longer to always need to be right, or always suspect and fear you're wrong.

"Oh what peace we often forfeit, Oh what needless pain we bear."

Both of these previous positions show that the ego and its frailties are intruding on our capacity to see clearly.

There is, as Hugh Jackman indicated, a need for all of us to do some inner work so as to decontaminate our perception from our neurotic processes, which too easily and normally spring from our toxic sense of self, thus becoming the unobserved mind of the previous chapter: Unless transformed this will set the course of our lives.

This is why we are also warned not to be conformed to the forces that shape and mould us from this world, but we are told to be transformed by the renewing of our mind. (Romans 12:2)

Sadly, negative thinking breeds when mirror neurons get engaged

Unfortunately the stakes are very high. Why? Because our remarkable mirror neurons almost compulsively tune into the fear and other negative emotional components of whatever is floating around in the social atmosphere, so the ego's neurotic dysfunction will be disruptive unless there are one or more spiritually intelligent people around at the time.

No wonder people with spiritual intelligence are needed in times of crisis

If spiritually intelligent people are missing I have seen years of positive and productive culture unravel. I have also seen quite dramatic collapses of inspired movements; it is part of my original motivation to write this book.

These irrational ways of seeing and feeling will result in emotional dramas and a dark emotionally-based mood being transmitted from person to person. It explains how negative thinking is so incredibly contagious even amongst so-called rational intelligent people.

Negative thinking breeds

This is so often the source of collective emotional dramas that can take place, particularly amongst groups of un-individuated people. I, among many other leaders, have from time to time been on the receiving end of such hysterical and irrational collective responses.

I have often seen sincere and well-meaning Level 2 thinking people sincerely slide into this kind of emotionally based quagmire, consequently dividing many faith communities. They seem to be prone to it because their very identity and sense of safety are often tied up in ideology that they think is belief.

It is confronting to see that so much of unintelligent religion is far from being spiritual. This is never more observable than when it is unwittingly operating in the service of the uninspired ego and its defences. However, one must never quickly judge those caught in its insidious web.

The speed of emotional reactions and why they distort reality

Subconscious thoughts that spread an emotional response in the body may sometimes come so fast that they are in operation long before the conscious mind has become aware of them. It takes more disciplined reflection to become aware that it is these irrational emotions that are their source. Small wonder there is real difficulty in being able to voice them.

The body is already responding to the emotion with a rush of feeling and neuronal activity before there is any awareness, hence the destructive power of dramas. The emotion will itself have already turned into a precognitive behavioural reaction. Perhaps this is why Gestalt Therapists say, *"All talking is lying; only the body tells the truth."*

The pre-verbal reaction that powers the distorted ego

These subconscious thoughts that exist at a pre-verbal stage are in fact unspoken, unconscious assumptions. They are likely to have their origin in the deficits and bruises of a person's past conditioning, usually from early childhood.

Eric Byrne believed these unconscious assumptions tend to operate as subconscious *"life scripts."* They are shaped by a person's primordial relationships -those primary ones with parents or siblings.

If these relationships were damaging, not supportive and did not inspire trust, the unconscious assumption absorbed and believed by the ego is likely to shape deep beliefs like, *"People cannot be trusted."* Here are a few more common unconscious assumptions: *"Nobody respects and appreciates me." "I need to fight to survive." "There is never going to be enough money." "Life always lets you down." "I don't deserve abundance." "I don't deserve love."*

Why the pre-verbal assumptions of the ego block our spirit's voice

Unconscious assumptions create emotions in the body which in turn generate mind activity and/or instant behavioural reactions. In this way they create a personal reality that excludes the spirit's gentle protesting voice of sanity, hence the name life script. It is like an unexamined script from which we act out our life, fully believing it to be true. A child given no space to speak because of overly verbal siblings is likely to conclude they have nothing to contribute unless they find their voice in a setting other than that of family. A child whose parents have no ability in mathematics is likely to fail no matter what their potential skill, simply because of the family script.

The voice of the ego continuously disrupts the body's natural state of harmony

We were made to settle gently on the foundations of our spirit which is the internal and the normal way of seeing truth: *"It is the spirit in a man, the breath of God in a man that gives understanding."* Through the ego though a false belief system has intruded on our consciousness so our spirit with its hope orientation is increasingly excluded.

Coping with what is usually the source of anxiety

Jesus gave an explicit command, *"Don't be anxious about anything,"* which almost seems a bit cruel for those poor souls who are prone to anxiety. Anxiety is a natural state all who are operating from their ego will experience. The body of those without a genuinely spiritual orientation is under a great deal of identity strain and stress, not because they are threatened by some external factor, but because life gets shot at us from point blank range and few of us feel fully prepared for what it throws up at us.

The emotional bruises and deficits tend to take on a defensive life of their own

As well as the challenges life throws at us we have archaic emotionally loaded shadows that have been created by bruises and deficits. The ego projects a persona - a facade of phony but positive reactions in an attempt to compensate for the negative feelings it has about itself. This is one of its main strategies for managing the challenges and threats to its esteem. The shadows, because we're not conscious of them, tend to dictate what is necessary for us to do if we are to be acceptable.

The psychic shadows drive us toward neurotic mal-adaptations

A younger brother may do weight-lifting for hours to counteract the ego pain of having an older brother who draws validation because he is very strong, while young women go to unhealthy and self-destructive lengths to lose weight in an attempt to look acceptable and to attract male gaze.

A small child needs loving and focused attention as a fundamental part of its emotional nourishment and if it goes missing a shadow is left that could well become a permanent existential exquisite ache, one that becomes a subconscious driver of behaviour.

The need to attract focused loving attention begins at birth and lasts a lifetime

It is seen when an infant or toddler loudly attempts to hold attention that is being diverted to a computer, or to a new baby brother or sister or to anything that threatens to break the sense of attachment. There is much in a mum's busy program that is bound to stretch the emotional umbilical cord. As a result we often find ourselves wrestling with underlying self- doubt and fear thrown up by the shadows cast by our hidden driver. A perfectly normal experience, it will tend to make us a mystery to ourselves and others.

Answering the question, *"Who am I?"* becomes something of a complex task if the spirit is missing from the inner discussion. Not surprising then that the ego with its unending task of working at the business of looking good and being right brings to one's sense of identity a constant state of stress and anxiety.

When Jesus said, "Don't be anxious," it was a test of the reality we are living from

Our body carries within it an ego which is just like another mind. It feels like us: it is a mind that is hyper-sensitive to anything that will challenge its esteem and disturb its equilibrium. Of all the feedback we receive it's amazing how deeply sensitive we are to anything that feels like a discount.

It seems the body can't help but respond to all the dysfunctional thought patterns that make up the equilibrium of its contrived and frail sense of self. Because It is a left brain construct it is often the reason we can't sleep and our head spins. If we are not anchored in the spirit we are often held to ransom by these disordered emotions. A stream of negative emotions regularly accompanies this flow of incessant and compulsive thoughts.

It is how we miss out on some of the most significant moments of our lives

Our worries live our life for and through us and blind us to the experience and richness of the life we have been given to live in every moment. Have you ever been to an event or gone on a holiday but found you were too stressed to enjoy it? Looking back at old photographs you may be surprised to see how special the experience was, how privileged you really were, and how much of your life you have missed out on.

The path to peace is also a path that is willing to confront negative emotion

A negative emotion is toxic to the body and interferes with its balance and harmonious functioning. Fear, anxiety, anger, bearing a grudge, sadness, hatred or intense dislike and jealousy, all interrupt the normal integration and life energy flow through the body. These emotions affect the heart, the limbic system, digestion and production of hormones. Once again I encourage you to read Galatians 5:16-26.

Mainstream medicine is beginning to recognise the connection between negative emotional states and physical diseases although it knows very little about how the ego operates or how the spirit is meant to be the natural resting place of our soul.

The harm caused by negativity contaminates the environment we exist in

An emotion that does harm to the body also affects the people we come into contact with. Indirectly, through those people a chain reaction can take place, capable of contaminating countless others we will never meet. We are a life-giving factor in all of our social systems or a life- taking factor. Energy and hope are either building in our relationships or entropy is taking place - the winding down of life and hope-giving collective energy.

There is a generic term for all negative emotions – unhappiness

I have seen whole corporate cultures become destabilized, unhappy and therefore unproductive when infected by negative and destructive emotions. Because the ego is driven by a need to look good and be right these situations are difficult to turn around without significant attitudes of humility in key opinion formers. If this doesn't happen because of the inflexibilities of people with frail and sensitive egos the prognosis won't look good. Those driven by frail egos with hyper-sensitivity to their own esteem will tend to blame everything except their own frailty and blindness for the situation. If they have the courage to look, they will soon discover that scapegoating will never bring resolution and peace.

But what of positive emotions?

Do positive emotions have the opposite effect on the physical body? They do indeed but there is a difference between short-term positive emotions that are ego-centred and ego-generated and the deeper emotions that emanate from our natural state of connectedness with our spirit.

The ego is always looking for happiness in all the wrong places. Happiness for the ego comes when happenings are going the way the ego wants them to go. In contrast our spirit always wants to lead us to joy. Joy comes through our spirit harmonising with and finding its place in, the divine narrative that is continually unfolding. It is an experience with a unique quality.

Why ego happiness is always anxiety prone and contaminated

What appears to be positive emotion generated by the ego already contains its opposite which it can too often quickly become - what the ego calls love is often possessiveness and an addictive clinging that can turn into hate within seconds. Anticipation about an upcoming event that looks like hope is really the ego's infantile overvaluation of the future. It easily turns into its opposite - feelings of anger or of being let down if the event doesn't fulfil the ego's expectations which in turn becomes bitter disappointment.

Whichever way you see it, the ego's happiness is always conditional. Praise and recognition may have you feeling alive and happy one day while being criticised or ignored can have you dejected and unhappy the next. The attention paid to you by a member of the opposite sex might send you to cloud nine but the removal of that attention can let you down badly

The ego's pleasures are always vulnerable to a change of circumstances

The pleasure of a wild party can quickly turn into the bleakness of a hangover the next morning. The ego's so-called happiness is transient because it stems from the mind's ego-centred identification with external factors. These external concerns are all unstable, being tied to circumstances that are liable to change at any moment.

Joy and peace are unconditional spiritual states of inner being

What we call these deeper emotions are inner conditions that are not really emotions at all but spiritual states of being. These are the states of being Jesus taught his followers and tried to lead them into.

Jesus, along with all the most significant spiritual teachers, taught the need to escape ego

The first lessons he attempted to teach his new followers were in the Beatitudes found in the gospel of Matthew chapter 5:1-12. In the Greek from which they are translated they are a remarkable psychological paradigm. It's a shame Freud didn't take the time to study and learn from the master teacher. There is nothing in the Beatitudes that will, if integrated, inflate the ego: just the opposite. They are all about living a life detached from the powerful demands of the ego.

Happiness is when happenings are going the way our ego wants them to go

While the emotions the ego pursues as pseudo-happiness all exist within the realm of opposites, there is sharp distinction from the spiritual states of being which have no opposites because they emanate naturally from deep within the wellsprings of our own spirit. Joy is not dependant on circumstances.

The fruit of living in the spiritual state

From within the spiritual state of being comes its fruit - love, joy, hope, peace, patience, and endurance. They can be found in the book of Galatians 5:22-23. These are all expressions of an ego free of the need to look good and be right because the spirit that transcends the ego knows it is in fact ok and doesn't have to work hard at proving it.

Here we see a profile of the life lived by Jesus

Integration and authenticity without a driven-ness to be something else, are clear hallmarks of being one with one's spirit and Gods Spirit.

Christian spirituality and how it functions

With all of these forces at work within us how can we operate without getting confused?

In the next chapter we discover the amazing process whereby we become our best selves.

Chapter 22

TRANSCENDING BY IDENTIFYING

"The pendulum of the mind oscillates between sense and nonsense, not between right and wrong."

Carl G. Jung (1875 – 1961) Psychiatrist and psychoanalyst who founded analytical psychology.

Getting it together

How do you order your chaotic interior world in the light of what you are learning? How do you put your sense of self together in a healthy way that attunes to the spirit and transcends the ego?

Have you ever watched the tv show *"Who do you think you are?"* in which a person is helped to trace their family tree? Have you seen the person who is the subject of the episode become overwhelmed and sometimes moved to tears by the changing fortunes of a family member of an earlier generation, one they've just heard of for the first time.

It was for me!

That emotional resonance is called identification and it is part of our recognising and integrating those parts of ourselves that have yet to be incorporated into our sense of self - our self- concept. This is why the late great Anglican theologian John Stott would say, *"No proclamation without identification and no identification without proclamation."* The power of the Christian story is in fact that Christians really believed that their faith was not simply about Jesus dying on a cross centuries ago but that he was doing it for them. It was as they identified with him their internal world (spirit) would identify with the external event making it transforming and personal.

How do you order your chaotic interior world in the light of what you're learning? How do you put your sense of self together in a healthy way that attunes to the spirit and transcends the ego?

An inner and outer engagement with life and the shaping of identity

Author Mauro Pesce was Professor of the History of Christianity at Bologna University from 1987 and also President of the specialist degree course of Cultural Anthropology and Ethnology. He has extensive credentials from Universities in Italy, America and Israel and along with Adriana Destro has spent considerable time examining the dynamic of the transforming psychology implicit in early Christianity.

They made a study of the Apostles John and Paul who took the narrative and thinking of Jesus and translated it into the non-Jewish world. These two key New Testament figures were not only itinerant teachers but today we have a considerable amount of their writing.

Destro and Pesce have thoroughly examined the issues of self and identity as they turn up in John's gospel and Paul's letters. They have come to a fascinating conclusion, one they believe goes a long way to explaining the power of the consciousness change that takes place in both individuals and groups, and they believe this change has impacted the thinking of the whole Roman world and eventually the whole of Western Civilization.

The inner and outer and the above and below of personal transformation

Their study led them to conclude that St Paul's emphasis is on the *inner* and *outer* experience the transforming person enters into, while in the case of John it is a *above and below* experience. What does this mean?

The nature of personal transformation of the early Christians

At first glimpse it looks like some kind of duality but they say it does in fact set up a dialectic - a kind of conversation between the different elements of who we are.

John writes about the *"new birth,"* while Paul thinks in terms of *"a new creation."* They both refer to a profound transformation of identity brought about by God's Spirit engaging with a responsive and willing human spirit.

The integrating understanding

Destro and Pesce introduce helpful insight into the discussion of an inner and outer reality in which they assert that an integrating understanding implicit in the early Christian writers was that, *"The spirit when in contact with God's Spirit not only influences the mind, but through the mind influences the body, finally influencing the entire person."* Noting the power of mirror neurons it becomes clear that this spirit if welcomed, will lift the culture of the whole network.

The mystical source of the beautiful life

This produced what the early Christians became famous for and what the apostle Paul called *"the fruit of the spirit"* - love, joy, peace, patience, etc.. Destro and Pesce deny there is any radical dualism in early Christianity as some have asserted ie that the soul is more important than the body. They see a remarkable building of shalom - or peace - between body soul and spirit.

The journey to transcendence through loving identification

Destro and Pesce go further, bringing to the surface issues to do with the permanent transformation of personal identity. They do this by showing that John and Paul are known to be reflecting on their own personal transformational spiritual experience. Their view is that Paul and John are asserting that the self is on a journey from a previous self-identity to a new identity and that this arises out of God's Spirit working in and through our human spirit.

The focus is on what is happening on the inside and the expression of a new spiritual self that is manifesting itself on the outside producing what every human being yearns for - inner and outer integration and harmony. This they believe is the key.

The spiritual power of identification

The operational key to the understanding of this transformational journey is the power of identification. Jesus said, *"Follow me,"* the apostle Paul said, *"Follow me as I follow Jesus."*

Fritz Perles the father of Gestalt therapy pointed out that what we deeply admire in another we admire because it is latent in our real selves, so we see the secret Jesus used in the spiritual formation of his followers picked up by Paul and John and the other writers of the New Testament.

When we are spiritually sensitive and alive we look around for somebody more spiritually integrated to identify with: in doing so we enable our spirit which is alive in our subconscious and unconscious to become integrated and formed into our sense of self.

When our spirit or the highest self in us is inspired, it typically yearns to become completed and fulfilled by transcending its ego or old sense of self.

Losing yourself to gain yourself or losing your ego to gain your best self

It is interesting to note how Jesus said it: *"If anyone will come after me he must do three things: 1 deny himself, 2 take up his cross and 3 follow me."*

In other words, we must have an awareness of our own self orientation and be willing for our ego to be crucified. We do this by acknowledging that Jesus gave his life for me therefore I now choose to exchange my life for his: To which our spirit, now freed of the ego cries out, *"Free at last; praise God almighty I am free at last!"*

We are then invited to live continually from the best of who we are by identifying with Christ - by walking in his footsteps! The good news is that is exactly what the best part of us wants to do. This is the starting place for spiritual formation or more accurately, transformation. In the writings of Paul we note that it is as we invite God's Spirit to come into our spirit we then experience the life Jesus lived.

Even though Jesus is God he chose, we are told, to live with our human limitations yet by his spirit Jesus was continually at one with the Holy Spirit thereby revealing the way we broken humans can find our way back.

This engagement with God's Spirit by our spirit produces a unique and transformed core to the personality, one that enables the person to bear what the Apostle Paul called "spiritual *fruit."*

The fruit is the outcome of being freed from a naturally self-indulgent nature and having Jesus' life in our life, and of course this life can be summarised as love, joy, peace, long suffering, patience, perseverance etc.

How a life becomes spiritually fruitful

In his letter to the Galatians Paul's picture of those who are filled with this spirit is in sharp contrast to those who are still controlled by the ego and fallen yearnings (Gal.5:16-25). He cites a considerable list to describe both naming the fruits of the spirit as love, joy, peace, patience, kindness, goodness, faithfulness, gentleness, and self- control.

Interestingly these are in fact a typical profile of Jesus himself. He said, *"Love one another as I have loved you. My joy I give you; not as the world gives."* He was called the Prince of Peace. Patience, long-suffering, self-control, are all expressions of how he lived his life.

The fruit of the spirit or the works of the lower nature

The outworking of the ego with its archaic yearnings or what Paul called the *"flesh"* or old life, is typified by the words hatred, discord, jealousy, bursts of rage, selfish ambition, slander, dissension, factions and envy.

Right there is the choice: To choose to invite God's Spirit into our spirit and have our choices informed by the indwelling Spirit and for those choices to become habituated in our personalities thus transforming our character. (Or transforming the characteristic behaviour others observe from us.) This is how we are transformed.

It is then the spirit or the flesh. We are told we might even fool ourselves, *"but God is not mocked..."* (Galatians 6:7-9).

Where do remarkable souls like Mother Theresa and Francis of Assisi come from?

Destro and Pesce have given us the key that opens the door to an understanding of the remarkable phenomenon theologians call *"incarnating the life of Christ."* This is giving expression in one's own personality to the unique spiritual nature that was and is, in Christ. This can then express itself through us and can eventually become characteristic of us. For those who've taken this choice this character eventually becomes written on our brain cells, and a remarkably transformed human mind becomes normal.

So then, St Paul beckons us, *"Not to be conformed to this world but to be transformed by the renewing of the mind."* (Romans 12 :1-2)

We begin to see the source of Job's dilemma and Elihu's insight

Elihu said, *"It is the breath of God in a man, the spirit in a man that gives understanding."* Job's left hemisphere was never going to grasp the way things were because we're told in the back story evil was at work - something we need spiritual insight to grasp. He was fearfully and wonderfully made but he needed to come to terms with the unique functioning of the human spirit. It is the spirit alone that is able to grasp the unifying and spiritual understanding that gives life its transcendent form and purpose.

Self-shaping power of attunement, co-regulation and self-regulation

You may remember an earlier reference to the stroking patterns: The ways in which mothers attach and attune to their children means they create the complex chemistry that gives permission for a child's essential spirit or nature to surface in their consciousness. This is how a sense of self emerges in the child. For good or ill the most powerful part of this becomes a continual inner dialogue, one that will be repeated over and over again.

It is how the child's sense of themselves develops inside of them. They have feelings like: *"I'm a star," "Whenever I'm in need people come to help," "Life is an adventure,"* or *"I'm invisible and worthless," "People are a source of pain," "Life is suffering; how can I get out of this suffering?"*

The self-concept that emerges becomes a subconscious script we act out throughout our lives without even knowing it. The saddest part of all this is that this sense of self will readily dictate to us our beliefs about our potential. Eric Berne believes our life position is established by age three which is why we all need somebody outside of ourselves who sees and is fascinated by our spirit thus giving us permission to locate and express that part of ourselves. We all need somebody outside of us who can see and become attuned to our real potential self.

Our potential self is waiting to be recognised and realised.

You may recall the earlier diagrams. In diagram 2 at the core of the self, below the self-concept lies our spirit that animates our essential nature. This is our potential self, waiting to become actualised and integrated into the self-concept. If our mother was spiritually attuned to us and could sense the contours of our uniqueness and celebrate it, this permitted us to know and live the real *us* from deep down within ourselves. Whether we know it or not the deepest yearnings at the core of our being well up from our spirit. It is this remarkable part that has the intention to rise and integrate into our identity.

Rising to our highest self

This shaping of the self-concept is the sense of self we call the psyche. It is this sense of self or psyche that naturally locates from a purpose outside of the self: it can then rise beyond the limitations of its self-interested ego to become what it is capable of becoming. Karl Jaspers the philosopher said of this external purpose, *"We become who we are by the cause we have made our own."*

We have already alluded to the Latin word *"incurvitas"* and a phrase that puts it in context, *"incurvitas in se"* which means *"curved inward on oneself."* It is believed that Augustine of Hippo first coined the phrase and Martin Luther expounded on it in his lectures on the book of Romans. In so doing they pinpointed the fatal flaw we humans have.

The fatal flaw that prevents us from flying

We have a fatal flaw that explains our unhappiness. It is as though we have an exquisite ache and the more we turn in on ourselves to try to deal with it, the worse it becomes. It is something like an itch in our soul and the more we scratch the worse the itch becomes. It is the crazy paradox of human existence. The more we focus on trying to satisfy ourselves the less satisfied we become.

Show me a self-centred person and I will show you a miserable person

It is a double whammy for us because we have a sense of our existence and yet we don't know what to do so that it becomes a fulfilled existence : one only has to think of the celebrities who are viewed as models of success - Marilyn Monroe, Elvis

Presley, Michael Jackson, to name but a few. You can name so many of them. Fame lifts them up, puts them in the spotlight and then destroys them when they stumble.

The late financial guru René Rivkin, a loud atheist obsessed with money said in an interview just before he committed suicide, *"I could never imagine a world without me."* Toward the end of his life this sad man spent his days in a darkened room crying, not leaving his bed.

Just below the level of consciousness lies the zoo clamouring with unmet needs

Our self-concept (ego) that gives us our sense of self also has the task of holding this sense of self together. It has the anxiety-producing job of being a kind of ringmaster to all the clamouring demands of the emotional deficits and bruises that linger just below the level of consciousness. This unfinished business in our psyche sets the agenda of the whole of our unsatisfied inner existence.

The voice that will lead us to the completion of our story

Another possibility is for us to find a narrative which will mirror back to us our own higher story, a transcendent narrative residing in our spirit waiting to be written. This is the story that will lead us on to our telos - our completion of our reason for being. Our spirit usually lies below our awareness until some event narrative or inspirational communication elevates it to our consciousness.

When this happens it will often take us by surprise.

We are likely to be surprised by what British academic C.S. Lewis called joy. We are also likely on occasions to mysteriously and unexpectedly have our eyes fill with tears.

If we have the humility to welcome the divine moment and what it is saying to us, the moment can be the beginning of personal transformation. We are then likely to discover an awareness of what we already knew deep down; it has simply been made conscious to us.

In 1: Corinthians 6:17 Paul writes, *"He who unites himself with the Lord is one with him in Spirit."* This verse strangely comes in the context of people uniting themselves in an inappropriate way but it makes clear how identification leads us to transformation.

This encounter will introduce us to that special joy and integrating experience we call the up-cry.

EPILOGUE

"A 'good book' leaves you wanting to re-read the book. A 'great book' compels you to re-read your own soul."

Richard Flanagan (1961 -) An Australian novelist considered by many to be the finest of his generation.

I certainly hope you will want to reread this book or maybe dip into it from time to time. It was designed to give you a way of re-reading your own soul from the perspective of the human spirit.

Beyond this however, a supreme motivation for me was to leave something of a legacy for the emerging generation – my grand-children's generation, whom I believe to have been largely betrayed.

They are part of the generation that adolescent psychologist Michael Carr-Greg said was *"spiritually anorexic."* I agree with film producer George Lucas who revealed his main motivation behind the Star Wars franchise was to give a new generation a story that explored the great human questions to do with good and evil. It is the never-ending battle all humans need to engage with in order to find within the spiritual resources to rise beyond themselves.

I am reminded of the words of Viktor Frankl, *"If we no longer know what we ought to do we will know what we want to do and we will find ourselves in a personal vacuum."*

As I reflected on what had given my own life inspiration and purpose I felt compelled to share at least some of the values and insights that had informed my own spirit and helped me to make sense of it all. This is when I came across Elihu.

I agree with Corrie Ten Boom, who said, *"In order to realize the worth of the anchor we need to feel the stress of the storm."* Currently our whole world has been experiencing the stress of the storm. Maybe it is time to examine again our anchoring values and their source.

As American German psychologist Erik Erikson theorised, all honest souls when they reach the last phase of their lives have to come to terms with the spiritual dimension of their existence if they are to finish well.

My personal journey with its challenges and opportunities has fuelled in me a deep sense of reflection, one that has inspired a desire to share my deep sense of gratitude to God for the grace that has led me to this gift of spiritual awareness and personal discovery. It is why I have felt compelled to make these insights available to any who might be interested, if for no other reason than to leave something of a legacy that might serve my beautiful grand-children and their generation. So to you Maddie, Josh, Dan, Sophie and Simeon, Anya, Joe and Bridie and Zoe and Olly and Lily: This is for you!

The greatest and the most important gift I can leave you is that because of Jesus you too can acquire this God-given capacity to attune your soul to the voice of the Divine Being, God - through the Spirit.

ACKNOWLEDGEMENTS:

I would like to acknowledge the following people who I wittingly or unwittingly borrowed from. I found them to be companions who seemed to wrestle with some of the same questions that I struggled to find illumination for. I have seen them as valued fellow travellers *"on the road to find out."*

The writings of Dr. Jill Bolte Taylor: the neuro-anatomist who had a massive stroke when a blood vessel exploded on the left side of her brain. She lived through an experience she had been brilliantly trained to deal with academically, coming back from the harrowing experience to share a unique insight into our brain's functioning (More in Book 2).

I once had the privilege of interviewing on air Danah Zohar who co-wrote with her psychiatrist husband the book *"Spiritual Capital"*, the definitive work on spiritual intelligence.

I also want to acknowledge the many stimulating interviews with author and academic from Latrobe University David Tacey who was something of a thought leader particularly on our need for what he called, *"Spiritual Re-enchantment"* (His latest book *"Post Secular"* is worth a read).

I enjoyed interviewing and reading columns by the regular Herald Sun columnist Bryan Patterson (who is now working as a journalist for World Vision).

You will find Viktor Frankl quoted throughout the book. For many years I led seminars on his work in my Youth Work Training Course.

And I enjoyed interviewing a number of times, brilliant ABC journalist and broadcaster Carolyn Jones who discovered the importance of the spiritual dimension in her later years.

The late Tony Morphet, one of Australia's leading movie and television script writers was another companion *"on the road to find out."* He was a regular interviewee.

Dr. David Williams, President of Taylor College Canada – a thoughtful man who was able to share with me an understanding of my approach to spiritual formation.

There are so many people to thank: My wife Jennifer Mary, who not only typed the first drafts over many months but also read aloud these first drafts to help me make sure I was comprehensible.

Ronnene Anderson, a professional editor who made some suggestions after working on some of the first edits and good friend Deirdre Smith and my daughter Elizabeth who waded through my first attempts helping me to bring clarity to my communication. Dan Evenhuis who did a major job in polishing, editing and laying the text out for publishing, Jennifer Newton for her eye for detail in proofing and last but not least, Jocelyn and the Fusion Canada team who carried the responsibility for seeing it published.

THE FOUR LEVELS OF CONSCIOUSNESS

"All conditions and all circumstances in our lives are the result of a certain level of thinking. When you want to change the conditions and circumstances, we have to change the level of thinking that is responsible for it."

Albert Einstein (1879 – 1955) German born theoretical physicist who developed the theory of relativity, one of the two pillars of modern physics. Also known for his influence on the philosophy of science.

What and how we see

Look up quantum physics on YouTube and you will see a professor beginning a lecture on quantum physics. He bravely tries to prepare his students by saying, *"If you have a golf ball size awareness you will have a golf ball size experience of what I am about to say. Similarly if you read a book and have a small level of consciousness you will only get a thin experience of what is being represented in the book. If however you have a large awareness, you will experience the book in deeper and broader ways than most other readers."*

Now to attempt to show how various levels of consciousness affect what and how we see:

We never see with our eyes but with the open heart and mind behind our eyeballs.

To some extent we have all experienced this. A friend gives us a book and says, *"You must read this."* We try to read it but it completely misses the mark. Months later we pick up the same book and are totally captivated by it. It's hardly likely our I.Q. has changed. More often than not, the frontiers of what is important to us have changed. This says nothing about our intelligence or the marks we left high school with but probably has everything to do with our changed conversation with life itself.

The salutary story of the Norwegian tragedy

A few years ago we saw the traumatising of Norway by an intelligent young man who felt his nation was moving away from its cultural anchoring point. This young man called himself a Christian and believed he was on some kind of crusade to prevent his nation from sliding in to a multicultural abyss that made it prone to Islamization.

Let's save the whales by blowing up the government!

It's a crazy proposition but it is the kind of thinking un-individuated people are inclined to. It can seem logical inside the head of somebody who feels they have to rescue something they believe to be valuable.

Not only has one to read the document produced by the young Norwegian to realise he was quite intelligent but inflexible in his ability to see the world through other eyes. He had a world view that he felt was under threat. The prayer of Elihu, *"That which I see not teach thou me,"* would have been alien to him.

Thinking you are right does not make you right: It makes you a Level 2 thinker

There are times when otherwise delightful religious people lack the broader consciousness we call spiritual intelligence. This is intelligence of a different order. As we open ourselves to the illumination of the book of Job through the journey of the main characters we see three levels of consciousness. There is the thinking of Job's wrongheaded comforters, Eliphaz the Temanite, Bildad the Shuhite and Zophar the Naamathite, all of whom are clearly seen to have what we call a Level 2 type consciousness.

Then there is Job who all his life has been a righteous soul and therefore assumes his goodness will keep him in a place of safety and blessing. After the shock of losing everything he held dear he has become a grieved and bewildered soul.

Job's belief system shattered

Like many good people before him to whom bad things have happened Job increasingly looks and sounds like an angry victim. He looks toward the heavens and virtually shakes his fist at God, asking, *"Whose side are you on?"* He is showing all the reactions of a person with what we will call a Level 3 consciousness. Finding his assumptions about life haven't worked the way he expected he is inclined to look around for someone to blame. He is passing through a severe time of questioning that is leading him to a Level 3 type consciousness.

Once one grasps how the various levels of consciousness work, what lies behind apparent inconsistencies and even hypocrisies will become clearer. I will try to explain what lies behind these anomalies: At first glance a level 3 person may appear counter dependant but they probably think they are fighting for their integrity.

The Level 3 consciousness is inclined to doubt. Trust is an issue.

Job is the central figure of the book. Caught in an all too normal web of hopeless personal disaster he becomes a metaphor for all who presume our good fortune will never run out. As they say, *"It's easy to be an angel until someone ruffles your feathers."*

Finally, we come to our hero of this book, Elihu who has observed the others and remained silent because of his youth, but he is frustrated both by Job and his three friends. He is the inspiration for this book because he is a model of the level of consciousness I would like to direct you to.

Elihu's integration indicates a Level 4 consciousness.

For those who can recognize it the things Elihu says reveal a Level 4 consciousness. To understand it more fully I rely on the research of academics who have gone before me, particularly on the insights of the late Scott Peck who also borrowed heavily from them.

A development of the four levels of consciousness referred to by Scott Peck in his book "A Different Drum."

Scott Peck writes, *"There is a pattern of progression through identifiable stages in human spiritual life and social awareness. Let me list my own understanding of these stages and the names I have chosen to give them:"*

1.   Chaotic- antisocial
2.   Formal- institutional
3.   *Sceptic- individual*
4.   *Mystic -communal*

I will use Scott Peck's framework enhanced by the work of Steve McIntosh, and others, and my guess is you will recognise people you are familiar with who will fit the various profiles. You may even glimpse aspects of yourself in these frameworks. What do they mean?

Level 1 - Chaotic, anti-social:

"Most young children and perhaps one in five adults of the more dis-regulated and narcissistic kind fall into this category." Scott Peck

Level 1 people are at a stage of self-absorption with either a non-existent or undeveloped spirituality. There is no cohering centre to their personality. They are not able to honour contracts, be consistent, or carry out responsibility. They may be vivacious, intelligent even quite gifted in some ways. They will usually lean on somebody else to carry the burden of responsibility for their lives, and many will have addictive personalities.

After a crisis, some occasionally convert to an authentic spiritual faith and move to become a Level 2 personality. Scott Peck said, *"Such conversions are usually sudden and dramatic and I believe are God-given."* If, however, these people are to go on growing spiritually they will need pastoral care that is fair, firm and friendly. Why? Because it is just possible, that without a mentor to help with their self-regulation, their spiritual narrative may not go on much beyond their conversion.

Their spiritual growth will be dependent on their establishing a sense of authentic spiritual agency and autonomy - the daily disciplines of prayer, meditation and studying the sacred texts in the company of those for whom these disciplines are a normal part of life. These disciplines will produce the kind of self-regulation and maturity that develops via worked-through values. It produces an ethical infrastructure based on an inner values-based discipline.

Level 2 consciousness: formal, institutional:

"Why can't the status quo be the way forward?" These are the words uttered in the general synod of the Church of England and quoted by Charles Handy in his book *"The Age of Reason."* The topic being debated was the then controversial proposition that women be admitted to the priesthood. Handy quotes a speaker from the floor of the chamber who was speaking with passion: *"In this matter, there is so much else that is good in our great country, why cannot the status quo be the way forward?"*

According to Handy it was a heartfelt plea. Not only is this the mindset of traditionalists within the church it has also been the mindset of most of those in power throughout the ages. This man illustrated almost perfectly what Scott Peck called the Level 2 traditional thinker.

Why can't the status quo be the way forward?

This is the stage of the majority of religious people, churchgoers and conventional believers. Scott Peck believes some are so attached to the canons, the liturgy, even the familiar furniture - *the form of things* - that they become very upset if changes are made to anything.

Why are they upset? Their faith has probably performed an important task for them in an uncertain world. It has given them equilibrium and this is what gets upset by rapid change of any kind. The order of service particularly the music, or the words used to describe their faith experience, the very culture of the gathering - all give a feeling of continuity and should be respected. Steve McIntosh who wrote the book *"Integral Consciousness"* calls these people traditional thinkers.

Most of them are solid citizens, the salt of the earth and worthy of respect

The structure of institutions is important to Level 2 thinkers. They usually make solid citizens and more often than not are the backbone of society, giving it stability through difficult times. This is where we believe people like Job's friends start out. The very structures that supported them will often contain them and their inflexible way of seeing the world. Because they are so emotionally and spiritually defined by their current world view and its structures they are also sub-consciously totally committed to it.

Their moral compass is shaped by the past so that they're fearful of the future

They can be generous and sacrificial until their paradigm is threatened, then they often feel they have to go on some kind of crusade to protect what is important. This hypersensitivity to what *is*, limits their capacity to see what *might be*, so they run the risk of becoming stuck in a certain level of consciousness. They tend to present as being sensible and are more inclined to protect what they have, than have the flair of the spiritual entrepreneur inspired by faith imagination. They are not so likely to continue in the adventure of personal and spiritual growth. At this stage, whether they are aware of it or not, happiness and a sense of equilibrium seem to be conjoined.

Not only are Level 2 thinkers stuck, but so are those who are unable to grasp real spirituality in both media and politics

Because they seem predictable, lazy thinking media presenters and journalists find it easy to caricature Level 2 folk as unintelligent and blinkered, stuck in the cultural past. They are dispensed with, without any serious consideration and the baby of authentic spiritual experience is blindly thrown out with the bathwater.

This easily ridiculed human experience is put in the same pigeonhole as that of all other eccentrics. These ideologically focussed Level 2 thinkers have had profound experiences but their subculture gave them old language that only the initiated could make sense of.

This is tragic for two reasons: it assumes there is nothing at all in the experience of these people that is of value, yet there are profound human experiences that have given shape and meaning to their lives. It is often their culturally contained language that limits their capacity to give expression to what is in fact ineffable. As in many schools and community institutions of the past, the Australian state of Victoria has just used an inappropriate expression of special religious education as leverage to remove this frail but historic introduction to spirituality from all its schools. To a generation that's rightly been called spiritually anorexic this is a tragedy.

We may not want a divisive form of religion but how do we supersede it? If we lack an integrated spiritual life we will in fact lack a rich human life and unwittingly, will be the source of a dehumanising and negative dynamic in all we do.

How can we discover an authentic journey from what in the past we have called religion, to life-enriching spirituality?

I was once asked how one moves from this fraught Level 2 position to a Level 4 consciousness. Everything in our psyche conspires to keep us in our uninspired vacuum, which at least seems to give shape and form to our lives. That is until we are hit by some unimaginable tragedy.

We are brought back to Elihu, our inspiration from the book of Job. His is Level 4 thinking spiritual intelligence. What is the secret? In religion it is too easy for the ego to be still in play despite the profound teachings of Christ and other spiritual leaders.

How did this play out in the experience of Job and his so-called comforters, who in fact became his torturers? Originally Job had great status which could have been the reason his so-called friends wanted to know him. But what happens when circumstances rather than enhance your ego, leave you destitute and emotionally tortured?

Here is the shift! On being hit by a crisis many find as did Job, that the ego loses its grip long enough for the pain of reality to dawn. For Job there is little in his situation left for the ego and the painful situation has also become a real test of friendship.

The ego-suffering of this time is not worthy to be compared with the spiritual reality likely to dawn on us

Remember? Happiness is usually when happenings are going the way our ego wants them to go. When the ego's tyranny is destroyed it is usually both liberating and psychologically painful, and is often brought about by some dark night of the soul in which a person feels they have lost control.

This is profound: a person can feel shattered

One should care for a person in this situation with empathy and a commitment to facilitate their experience of faith while being sensitive to what is called suicidal ideation (possible suicidal thoughts). As their own spirit's voice is recognised it will inevitably create the platform for a shift from the old internal machinery to a new autonomy. They will need dedicated support in the early stages but with encouragement this could lead to a new and special spiritual intelligence with its experience of faith and freedom.

A permanent solution to a temporary problem

However it may appear, suicide is clearly a permanent solution to what is usually a temporary problem. Paradoxically a temporary crisis lived through so that the spirit is acknowledged in the process, may have all the appearance of a tragic breakdown yet with the right support can become a spiritual breakthrough. The process can shake loose the ego's grip on the soul, freeing the spirit to make itself known at a conscious level.

Right here we catch a glimpse of Job's situation. He has lost all that defined him, that in the past has given him a sense of validity. This has produced in him an identity crisis with a significant spiritual and emotional component.

Here we see Job's real and existential crisis

Perhaps many people identify with Job because they too are in profound transition. In fact the whole of civilization is going through something of an identity crisis.

The take-home message of the book of Job is that when you are going through such a crisis don't turn it into an emotional drama. Level 2 people who react without referencing their spirit - which most are likely to do - can make things worse by resorting to blame or scapegoating.

Grace can go missing and be replaced by legalism and judgmental attitudes

If it is true as Greek philosopher Socrates said, *"The unexamined life is not worth living"*, Level 2 people are in danger of missing out on a life worth living. Why? If they are not inclined to use an external source like the Bible to help them to *"separate the worthless from the precious,"* or as it says in Hebrews 4:12, to *"divide between the soul (ego) and the spirit,"* it may instead be used to build an ideology from which they feel free to look down their nose at others and judge them.

The lack of values will never give them a life worth living

Those not skilled at understanding the source of their own behaviour find it difficult to empathise with others, let alone understand them. Without a sense of empathy and with a lack of patience, personal discipline and social skill, it is easier for them to express their emotional and spiritual laziness by falsely interpreting and judging those they accuse and blame.

Religious people are among those most inclined to judge

Despite what Jesus the founder of our faith said about not judging and forgiveness, it has often been a bewilderment to me a Christian, that Christian fundamentalists find it so easy to actively hate Level 3 and Level 4 people. How will they change?

While I would not wish it on anybody, nothing will bring about change quite like a soul-shaking crisis in which one's whole sense of identity has to shift from the easy answers of a Level 2 awareness to journey towards the complexities of a Level 3 and 4 awareness.

Level 2 people are often shattered by a life crisis

The superficial certainty of Level 2 people is often shattered by a profound life crisis that confronts the ego's equilibrium loosening its grasp and control. Why is this? It is because they tend to believe that their virtuous life should insulate them from what Shakespeare called the *"slings and arrows of outrageous fortune."* This is not only Job's dilemma, but also the frame-work that his so-called comforters come from, hence their question, "Who sinned?"

What have you done wrong to deserve this?

I have met many fine people who indulge in a kind of self-torture when things go badly wrong: *"Why did I do this?"* or *"What did I do to deserve that?"* Emotionally their response makes everything worse, but as they go about their business of self-flagellation it sometimes has a strange sense of integrity about it. Why? It is in fact the parent tapes beating up on the inner child, or the inner primary circuit replaying an old familiar pattern of self-torture that has at its base, an archaic belief.

If only this person had the presence of mind to be aware of this or the services of an aware mentor to help them. Few realise they are simply indulging their old inner sense of reality shaped by their parent tapes.

Blame and self-torture indulge the past but do not help anyone arrive at the future with awareness and wisdom. This is why politicians hopping on board a drama cycle over the most recent crisis ignore any data that seems not to back up their position, making loud accusations about anyone who holds a position different from their own, and just as loud assertions about their own wisdom and compassion. Some would say they are not going to let the facts get in the way of a good story. They tend to be blind to their ego's place in the whole cycle and would be absolutely indignant to think anyone might not see them as looking good and being right!

With someone in the Stage 3 drama cycle there is no opening for rational discussion and sharing of wisdom.

We will replay the past until we can become aware of it and understand it

How do we get awareness, and where do we get wisdom from?

The answer is that one can always pick the chosen. They bear the scars and wounds that come from memories of difficult and character-shaping battles, however we don't learn from experience, but by honestly reflecting on our experience. Most importantly the chosen hang on until they have faced their fears and shadows and made it through by transcending them.

The heroes of our culture have transcended their difficulties

One only has to read the lives of those who have made a difference in the world including those mentioned in the Bible, to know that universally, life is not easy. From Abraham through to Joseph, Moses, Daniel, the Apostle Paul and even for Jesus himself, goodness was no guarantee of a comfortable life.

These people had in common a consciousness of a God-given life purpose and an unfolding story they believed to be more important than life itself. In spite of their difficulties and crises they remained committed to completion of their purpose which in turn gave them a sense of direction and an inner spiritual compass.

There are no real spiritual victories at bargain prices

Those who go through an intense time of doubt and severe suffering, of necessity examine the foundations of their world view and their faith. It is often experienced as a dark night of the soul. Many in the midst of what seems like mindless torture, have been known like Elihu, to cry out in anguish, *"That which I see not teach thou me."*

This is the authentic nature of humility – the rug of certainty finally being pulled out from under the ego's confident pride. In this process of doubting themselves and God for a time, they move to a new way of seeing.

The experience has disrupted the ego's invisible and distorted control. The emotional crisis far from destroying their spirit, will simply shift them from the glib easy answers of opinion masquerading as insight. A by-product of these experiences for all of us is that we are likely to become a little more restrained in our inclination to make quick and glib judgments about situations and people in difficulty.

Wisdom from above: the source of spiritual intelligence

The wisdom from above as the Bible calls it, is anchored. It has a divine confidence that has been tried and tested and has stood the test of time. It is not moved by the sensitivities of a frail ego working hard to validate itself. In contrast the foundation of the spirit – the source of wisdom, is buttressed by eternal verities. It is as if the spirit's own foundations have no need of validation since all who are aware of their spirit's promptings have long endured and out lived the passing parade of popular sentiment, despots and dictators and natural catastrophes.

This form of knowing is not tainted by greed or moved by fear. There is nothing in this temporary world that can prevent it from holding its head high as it stares down any challenge from the bloody face of history.

The wisdom from above stares down the worst that can be thrown at it

Spiritual intelligence is conceived within the human spirit and born as a consequence of the labour pains that come along with our having the kind of intense wrestling matches between ourselves and God that we see Job having.

In the words of the British Academic C.S. Lewis, *"Pain insists upon being attended to. God whispers to us in our pleasures, speaks to us in our conscience but shouts in our pain. It is his megaphone to rouse a deaf and self-serving world."*

Those most likely to experience a shift of consciousness after the storm are those who welcome the dawning of a Level 4 consciousness. They will have an inner sense of the truth that matters. They will know and recognise phony and glib religion. Because of their personal anchoring point they will treasure the real thing and become very impatient with anything counterfeit.

While Level 2 thinkers want to cling to the certainties of law, Level 4 thinkers actually enjoy the work of discerning the truth of a situation as it helps them sharpen the focus of their moral compass. In a crisis a Level 4 person will enjoy processing what is happening and attempt to penetrate beyond superficial appearances. If not exhausted they will enjoy the challenge of asking the question, *"What is really going on here?"* Whatever the ambiguities, they will try to get a handle on it, and enjoy the spiritual exercise of *"separating the worthless from the precious."*

If it is personal, rather than ask *"why me?"* they will probably ask, *"What am I meant to understand here?"* If it is a broader social issue they will probably want to ask their spirit to show them, *"What is the nature of justice here: Is mercy likely to go missing, and what does compassion require of me?"* They will love the adventure of bringing heart and mind together to wrestle with any moral ambiguity, until the clear moral light dawns in their spirit

They will have spiritual discernment: wise eyes in their heads

A Level 2 person will subconsciously reference the past to find the answer to current dilemmas which often prevents their seeing the unique dimensions of the present. Like Job's Level 2 thinking comforters they are unwittingly likely to make things worse, doing violence to the present.

If they can't find the way out of the fog by reacting to it as they have been programmed to think about it in the past, they will inevitably fall back on clichés for arguments. If they are religious they are likely to use quotes from the Bible often taken out of context, or they might appeal to some parent-like authority figure, or a book of rules.

They do this because they don't have the spiritually integrated values that might help them transcend their unrecognised anxieties that are threatening the power and esteem of their vulnerable ego.

They need an external moral system because they haven't yet developed an internal one.

In Scott Peck's book The Road Less Travelled, he writes about Level 2 thinkers: *"I used to tell people somewhat facetiously that the Catholic Church provided me with my living as a psychiatrist. I could equally have said the Baptist Church, the Lutheran church the Presbyterian Church or any other."*

Why? The feature that marks people as Level 2 thinkers most clearly is their inclination toward blame, guilt and excuse-making. This keeps them trapped in their primary circuit reliving a subconscious past and projecting it blindly onto others.

All this keeps them from taking the existential leap that would let them open up to the next level of authentic spiritual discernment and wisdom. In failing to trust themselves to that leap of faith, they miss out on welcoming the kind of responsibility that would give them the dignity and confidence to guide them to the next chapter of their unfolding God-inspired narrative. What a shame!

What about Level 3 consciousness?

Level 3 – Sceptic, individual

Many of these people went to a traditional church-based school or grew up in a religious family. It is amazing how many grew up in a parsonage.

They began to say to themselves, *"I am an individual. I no longer need the control of this non-scientific medieval way of thinking; this stuffy old church with its silly superstitions."* They may have come across inconsistency in church leaders or have had some profound and tragic crisis befall them, such as some form of abuse as a child, that shattered a Level 2 trust.

Some trust-shattering event may well have undermined their faith in the intuition of their own spirit. Or it may be the simple push back process that comes along with the business of becoming individuated: for example a female psychiatrist who is also a person of colour may be inclined to define herself as Afro-American at a predominately white male conference of psychiatrists, but the same woman in a conference of mostly coloured social workers might be more inclined to define herself as a female psychiatrist.

It is how we all are inclined to self-definition

At this point unless they are remarkably self-aware other dominant factors will play into the process. Without being aware of it they are probably only able to receive input from their brain's left hemisphere: ie the place where the ego is shaped.

This in turn is likely to lead them to come from what Eric Berne, creator of transactional analysis and author of *"Games People Play"*, called *"The I'm OK you're not OK position."* This I'm ok you're not ok position will unwittingly contaminate all of their relationships: they will be inclined to look stiff and proud.

Trust and control issues will normally begin to surface

Their characteristic behaviours will give them an orientation of a need for control, thus compounding their difficulties in trusting themselves to others.

They will also be inclined as level 3 are likely to do, to define themselves against any shared prevailing world view, inclining them to become contrary much to the hurt and despair of other family members.

While convincing themselves they are more intelligent and logical than most others they of all people will be vulnerable to becoming *"useful idiots"* in contrarian causes.

They not only slide into becoming Level 3 - sceptic, individual thinkers, but having amputated the influence of their spirit with its intuitive sense of truth, they are now vulnerable to serious untruths.

If they don't move on they can become stuck as loud and cynical atheists

This is sad because below the persona lies a beautiful spirit that will miss out on the intimacy their spirit hungers for and the intuitive echoes that produce real innovation.

They are the vulnerable unbelievers, many but not all, with high IQs but little deep self-reflection: they are inclined to repeat old arguments over and over with little new insight.

Level three thinkers are inclined to know the price of everything and the value of nothing

Scott Peck wrote, *"Anyone who has known a died-in-the-wool atheist will know that such an individual can be as dogmatic about unbelief as any believer can be about belief. It raises the question, is it a belief in God we need to get rid of, or is it dogmatism?"*

The surprise that awaits honest level 3 thinkers.

However many honest and doubting people in Level 3 are on an important spiritual journey. They will find their human spirit will not be denied forever and the gentle promptings of another reality will continue to knock at the door of their consciousness. We can put together a significant list of so-called atheists who in their maturity had spiritual encounters that were profoundly disturbing.

If these people move on from a Level 3 consciousness, in the words of Scott Peck: *"They generally can become more honestly reflective and spiritually developed in their sensitivity to the values of truth, justice and mercy, than sadly many Christian believers. Many of whom are content to remain with the comfortable certainties of their Level 2 thinking."*

As it turns out many of the more sensitive Level 3 thinkers who are also truth seekers and care about integrity will themselves become embarrassed by loud unthinking atheists.

The eventual encounter with the ultimate reality

Advanced and sensitive Level 3 men and women thinkers whose spirit is prompting them are likely to become active truth seekers. However intelligent Level 3 thinkers will often find that they are in for a surprise.

Don't tell them, but the truth and the integrity their spirit yearns for will lead them on, until it eventually dawns on them that the love they have for those nearest to them has its own truth! While this can't be proved intellectually it can be known profoundly. Acknowledgement of this truth can eventually lead them by grace to a humbling encounter with the kind of ultimate truth that only the heart can grasp.

The essential truth that leads to wisdom and awareness can only be welcomed by the heart.

Carl Jung believes that in fact, *"No human being will become well-adjusted in middle age until they have eventually come to terms with the spiritual dimension of their existence."* The very spirit that leads them on the honest quest through doubt to non-belief, will now lead them through honest doubt about their doubt to a fresh encounter with their authentic spiritual selves.

Honest doubt about their doubt, will take them to the next stage of their spiritual development.

This new level of awareness will bring with it a new level of clarity – a level of awareness called mystic, communal.

Level 4 – Mystic, Communal:

Karl Rahner, 20th century German Jesuit priest and theologian said, *"The Christian of the future will be a mystic or he or she will not exist at all."*

Level 4 people are mystical in that their whole sense of self, not just the cognitive left hemisphere part of the brain, is open to sense the truth.

They may be and often are, conventionally intelligent. They will also bring a compassionate heart and a touch of inspiration to all they are involved with.

There is something charismatic about people with a Level 4 awareness

Their capacity for unconditional love and moral clarity will be particularly enhanced, coming as it does from their transparent relationship with their own spirit which in turn connects them with the source of wisdom and discernment namely the Divine Being. These new points of reference free Level 4 people like Elihu from the inevitable distortions of the ego. Assuming the disciplines that keep the ego in check are sustained they will often come at life from their spontaneous core, thus becoming social attractors.

They are instinctively communal and appreciate people, so become social attractors.

They are communal in that their spiritual awareness and intuition informs their social and emotional awareness and as a result they often seem to sense and see things long before others do. If they are not the first to see something they will quickly recognise the truth inherent in a situation.

Because they are focused on the good that might be, they will resonate to any healthy vision when they hear it. As a result of their sensitivity to any issues to do with justice, mercy or compassion, they will always be committed to helping bring to birth a better world, and their enthusiasm for it will be contagious.

It has been said that those who can see the invisible can seem to do the impossible.

Those who have the heart to join with others to see a better world brought to birth often become the architects of it. This is why it has been said that those who see the invisible seem to do the impossible. Level 4 thinkers often emerge as what are called prophet myth-makers. The apostle Paul was one of these thinkers. (2 Corinthians 4:18.)

This is why Level 4 consciousness is called the mystic-intuitive communal stage of spiritual development. These people have the capacity to be prophet–mythmakers. Their morally focused faith-imagination with its innate sense of hope can not only sense the better future, but they will also feel a calling to participate in the shaping and sharing it. Being more ego free than most, they naturally build alliances.

They will also enjoy listening deeply to others and thus naturally facilitate a vision-based community. These people will surprise themselves as they become natural leaders. Not being focused by the ego's need to look good and be right they eventually attract more trust than they are looking for.

They enjoy the mystery of the not yet.

Unlike Level 2 thinkers who love things to be black and white some Level 4 thinkers acknowledge and are fascinated by, the mystery of the *not-yet*. They love the opportunity to bring in a better world. The unknown is not feared but welcomed with fascination as some kind of sport enabling them to make a difference.

This is what marks Elihu as a Level 4 thinker. He says in Job 34:32 *"That which I see not teach thou me."* Of course this is a taxing position to hold if your ego is frail and you are short on hope. People in Level 4 love mystery and awe in dramatic contrast to those in Level 2 who have anxiety about it. Level 2 thinkers need things to be simple black and white clear-cut, so are less inclined to grow in spiritual intelligence no matter how high their I.Q.. They are more likely to use their intelligence to construct plausible reasons why Level 4 people are dangerous.

The enormity of the unknown fascinates.

The enormity of the unknown stimulates the spirit of the Level 4 person. Rather than be frightened they seek to penetrate it with growing understanding, going ever deeper. They are not bewildered or disturbed by paradox. They actually enjoy holding opposing points of view in tension. They intuitively grasp what the philosopher Santayana showed – *"out of apparent contradiction when authentic harmony is found between the opposing points of view, the new will be discovered."*

Level 4 people love to open themselves with enthusiasm to their faith-imagination. They love the sense of vocation they have when they feel they are in the right place with the right team. They enjoy the anticipation of and participation in, the shaping of a hope-filled better tomorrow.

There is a deep yearning to work with others to shape shalom

There is a yearning in their spirit for unity within themselves, with others and the cosmos. They tend to be thought of as romantics because they yearn for the grand and harmonious shalom where all things come together with a serendipitous sense of celebration.

They enjoy doing the internal soul work by honestly reflecting on their own interior world and facing any unfinished business; they also see themselves and others in a process of becoming. They feel privileged as they recognise the whole of civilisation is in a state of becoming which leads them to grow in emotional intelligence.

Their yearning for harmony between people leads them towards growth in social intelligence, and their enjoyment and sense of responsibility for creation gives them a sense of their place in the organic wholeness of things.

They know the whole is more than the sum of the parts

Among human beings, they are the ones most aware that the world is meant to be an organic whole and civilization an interconnected community. They also realize that what divides us into warring camps is a lack of spiritual awareness and intelligence in which the ego's quest for power and validation reigns supreme. Level 4 people are revealed by their deep desire to see people both in terms of their personal potential and their positive contribution to the whole redemptive story.

Level 4 people, because they can see both persons and the big story, inevitably become producers of the next chapter of the unfolding history of goodness. That is, if their internal negative and neurotic script doesn't cloud their capacity to see and respond to the glory of the beckoning, divine narrative.

Still to come:

In book two I will seek to spell out (among other things)

- How to hear the voice of God's Spirit through our spirit.

- What we can know about life after death.

- How to start a global movement.

- How to discover one's own personal vocation and calling.

Printed in Great Britain
by Amazon